Gertrude Stein Advanced

Also by Richard Kostelanetz

Gertrude Stein Advanced

An Anthology of Criticism

Edited by
Richard Kostelanetz

McFarland & Company, Inc., Publishers
Jefferson, North Carolina, and London

British Library Cataloguing-in-Publication data are available

Library of Congress Cataloguing-in-Publication Data

Gertrude Stein advanced : an anthology of criticism / [edited] by
  Richard Kostelanetz.
      p.   cm.
    Consists of previously published articles.
    Includes bibliographical references (p. 219). ∞
    ISBN 0-89950-433-7 (lib. bdg. : 50# alk. paper)
    1. Stein, Gertrude, 1874–1946 – Criticism and interpretation.
  I. Kostelanetz, Richard.
  PS3537.T323Z6145   1990
  818'.5209 – dc20   90-52506
                                                                CIP

Manufactured in the United States of America

McFarland & Company, Inc., Publishers
  Box 611, Jefferson, North Carolina 28640

To Susan and David Barron

Table of Contents

Preface

The traditional canonical view of Gertrude Stein held that she wrote two charming books—*Three Lives* and *The Autobiography of Alice B. Toklas*—and a lot of "incomprehensible junk." Until recently most selections from her work, and most critical writing about it, have sustained this myth. Beginning with articles published in 1974, I tried to suggest that the putatively more difficult books are comparatively richer in innovation and literary quality. My argument has been that if claims for Stein are based upon *Three Lives* and *Alice B. Toklas*, she is a minor modernist; but if our sense of her reputation is founded upon *Geography and Plays*, *Making of Americans*, "Stanzas in Meditation" and other works in that vein, then Stein becomes the greatest experimental writer in American literature, an inventor whose achievements are, indicatively, scarcely understood, even today, more than four decades after her death. (Compare the collective paucity of Stein criticism with writing devoted to, say, Faulkner and Hemingway.)

My initial criterion in selecting essays for this book is, simply, those that expanded my own critical understanding of the more consequential Stein, illuminating what is otherwise murky. Then the selections proceed from the general to the more specific, roughly through Stein's fiction, poetry, drama and experimental prose, before returning to broader considerations. In emphasizing literary analysis, I have necessarily left out some interesting recent examinations of her life and her relationship to Toklas. Beyond that I favored essays that are not readily available elsewhere. I would have included my own extended critical essay, initially from *The Hollins Critic* (1974) and then from the introduction to *The Yale Gertrude Stein* (1980), had it not already appeared recently in another book of mine from this same publisher (*The Old Fictions and the New*, 1987). As it is scarcely my intention to terminate critical discussion about this other Stein, this book closes with a bibliography of other criticism I have found illuminating.

I am grateful to McFarland for commissioning *Gertrude Stein Advanced*, to Edward Burns for bibliographic advice, to Sara Gleason for practical assistance, and to the contributors for granting me permission to reprint their essays. Every effort has been made to verify the spelling of all proper names and to trace the ownership of all copyrighted material, in addition to making full acknowledgment of the latter's use. If any error or omission has occurred, it will be corrected in subsequent editions, providing that appropriate notification is submitted in writing to the editor.

Richard Kostelanetz

By forcing the reader to pay attention to the word, Stein makes the word seem new again. But by presenting each word in an unusual context, she directs attention not only toward its sound but also toward its sense, as the reader is forced to grapple with each word one at a time. The reader must confront the word and language itself with a sense of bewilderment, wonder, and discovery.
— Randa K. Dubnick, *The Structure of Obscurity* (1984).

This will be to explain as much as I understand of what Gertrude Stein did in writing.
— Donald Sutherland, *Gertrude Stein: A Biography of Her Work* (1951).

And not even the unintelligible writing should be considered incomprehensible. I have done what I can in this essay to tell in what that incomprehensibility consists.
— Wendell Wilcox, "La Véritable Stein" (1938).

The Work of Gertrude Stein

Sherwood Anderson

One evening in the winter, some years ago, my brother came to my rooms in the city of Chicago bringing with him a book by Gertrude Stein. The book was called *Tender Buttons* and, just at that time, there was a good deal of fuss and fun being made over it in American newspapers. I had already read a book of Miss Stein's called *Three Lives* and had thought it contained some of the best writing ever done by an American. I was curious about this new book.

My brother had been at some sort of a gathering of literary people on the evening before and someone had read aloud from Miss Stein's new book. The party had been a success. After a few lines the reader stopped and was greeted by loud shouts of laughter. It was generally agreed that the author had done a thing we Americans call "putting something across"—the meaning being that she had, by a strange freakish performance, managed to attract attention to herself, get herself discussed in the newspapers, become for a time a figure in our hurried, harried lives.

My brother, as it turned out, had not been satisfied with the explanation of Miss Stein's work then current in America, and so he bought *Tender Buttons* and brought it to me, and we sat for a time reading the strange sentences. "It gives words an oddly new intimate flavor and at the same time makes familiar words seem almost like strangers, doesn't it," he said. What my brother did, you see, was to set my mind going on the book, and then, leaving it on the table, he went away.

And now, after these years, and having sat with Miss Stein by her own fire in the rue de Fleurus in Paris I am asked to write something by way of an introduction to a new book she is about to issue.

As there is in America an impression of Miss Stein's personality, not at all true and rather foolishly romantic, I would like first of all to brush that aside. I had myself heard stories of a long dark room with a languid woman lying on a couch, smoking cigarettes, sipping absinthes perhaps and looking out upon the world with tired, disdainful eyes. Now and then she rolled her head slowly

Reprinted from his preface to her *Geography and Plays* (1922).

to one side and uttered a few words, taken down by a secretary who approached the couch with trembling eagerness to catch the falling pearls.

You will perhaps understand something of my own surprise and delight when, after having been fed up on such tales and rather Tom Sawyerishly hoping they might be true, I was taken to her to find instead of this languid impossibility a woman of striking vigor, a subtle and powerful mind, a discrimination in the arts such as I have found in no other American born man or woman, and a charmingly brilliant conversationalist.

"Surprise and delight" did I say? Well, you see, my feeling is something like this. Since Miss Stein's work was first brought to my attention I have been thinking of it as the most important pioneer work done in the field of letters in my time. The loud guffaws of the general that must inevitably follow the bringing forward of more of her work do not irritate me but I would like it if writers, and particularly young writers, would come to understand a little what she is trying to do and what she is in my opinion doing.

My thought in the matter is something like this—that every artist working with words as his medium, must at times be profoundly irritated by what seems the limitations of his medium. What things does he not wish to create with words! There is the mind of the reader before him and he would like to create in that reader's mind a whole new world of sensations, or rather one might better say he would like to call back into life all of the dead and sleeping senses.

There is a thing one might call "the extension of the province of his art" one wants to achieve. One works with words and one would like words that have a taste on the lips, that have a perfume to the nostrils, rattling words one can throw into a box and shake, making a sharp, jingling sound, words that, when seen on the printed page, have a distinct arresting effect upon the eye, words that when they jump out from under the pen one may feel with the fingers as one might caress the cheeks of his beloved.

And what I think is that these books of Gertrude Stein's do in a very real sense recreate life in words.

We writers are, you see, all in such a hurry. There are such grand things we must do. For one thing the Great American Novel must be written and there is the American or English Stage that must be uplifted by our very important contributions, to say nothing of the epic poems, sonnets to my lady's eyes, and what not. We are all busy getting these grand and important thoughts and emotions into the pages of printed books.

And in the meantime the little words, that are the soldiers with which we great generals must make our conquests, are neglected.

There is a city of English and American words and it has been a neglected city. Strong broad shouldered words, that should be marching across open fields under the blue sky, are clerking in little dusty dry goods stores, young virgin words are being allowed to consort with whores, learned words have been put to the ditch digger's trade. Only yesterday I saw a word that once called a whole nation to arms serving in the mean capacity of advertising laundry soap.

For me the work of Gertrude Stein consists in a rebuilding, an entire new recasting of life, in the city of words. Here is one artist who has been able to accept ridicule, who has even forgone the privilege of writing the great American novel, uplifting our English speaking stage, and wearing the bays of the great poets, to go live among the little housekeeping words, the swaggering bullying street-corner words, the honest working, money saving words, and all the other forgotten and neglected citizens of the sacred and half forgotten city.

Would it not be a lovely and charmingly ironic gesture of the gods if, in the end, the work of this artist were to prove the most lasting and important of all the word slingers of our generation!

Gertrude Stein and
the Twentieth Century

Donald Sutherland

Gertrude Stein is said to have said once that there have been only three originative Jews—namely, Christ, Spinoza, and Gertrude Stein. Her companion, Alice Toklas, did not believe she really made that remark, but I still think she very well may have, because of the rather peculiar inclusion of Spinoza in the triad. Why, for so intensively and consciously contemporary a mind as Gertrude Stein's, should Spinoza, of all people, crowd out such figures as, say, Freud and Proust and Einstein? I asked Miss Toklas if Gertrude Stein had really had so high an opinion of Spinoza, and she replied, "Not so high as to read him." Well, the answer to that is that Spinoza is pretty thoroughly unreadable unless you are deeply interested in technical theology, but this does not prevent anyone's knowing that some of his major ideas or intuitions are quite relevant to Gertrude Stein and to much of the twentieth century.

One idea in particular I should like to consider in relation to Gertrude Stein's writing and her view of the world, as well as to the arts of the twentieth century and even to politics. Spinoza argues very simply that since God is a single infinite substance, all things are in God. That is to say that since God is infinite He stops nowhere, not even at matter and evil, and nothing can be excluded from Him. One may refuse the proposition as rank pantheism or as too trivial a turn of logic to swing the realities of experience, but it implies both an ontology and a vision of the world which are of the utmost importance to us. If all things, literally all things, large and small, good and bad, if all things are in God, then they all share equally and directly in final Being, or if you like they are all equally sacred and equally important, all equally and indiscriminately divine presences. I do not feel this way about everything, and most probably you do not either, and it does take a special gift or a special mentality to sustain such a feeling more or less constantly, but such a mentality can be found, not only in Spinoza but in certain Christian saints, remarkably in two of them who were favorites of Gertrude Stein's—Teresa of Avila and Francis of Assisi. It is told of Saint Teresa that when her nuns objected to

Reprinted from *A Primer for the Understanding of Gertrude Stein* (Black Sparrow, 1973).

kitchen duty as beneath their calling she rebuked them, saying "God moves among the casseroles." Or words to that effect. And as it was said of Spinoza that he was drunk with God, it could be said of Saint Francis that he was drunk with fraternal affection for all of God's creatures and creations, not excluding even bodily death, which he called our sister. Gertrude Stein had a good share of this kind of feeling or vision. Let me tell two anecdotes to that effect.

In the summer of 1939, when war was impending, we were sitting in the garden of Daniel Rops, Gertrude Stein's neighbor near Belley, and we were, most of us, getting very depressed over the possibilities of the war, and how in the world, if the world was at all fit for human habitation, could such atrocities as we imagined be possible. And Gertrude Stein said, "Oh yes, I know all that, but to me the world is very beautiful." In strength of conviction and love of the world, this is not unlike Saint Francis's praise of bodily death.

One more anecdote, which has meant a great deal to me, but the point of which is not easy to convey. When Gertrude Stein came to lecture at Princeton thirty years ago, I was a student there and was invited to a reception for her in a professor's house along with a good many other students. Naturally she sat and talked while we hovered and milled about her, most of us in an agitated and awkward adolescent way. Suddenly she made a little sweeping gesture out in front of her, and said, "How is one to describe all this?" All this was disconcerting, because there was nothing in front of her but a casual bunch of Princeton boys, who, I thought, were scarcely worth describing, certainly not as we appeared just then. Perhaps we would have been worth describing separately, in single portraits, or doing something more significant or dramatic than just milling about, and perhaps our inner adolescent lives might have been worth describing, but all that was plainly not what she meant by "all this." What she meant was the immediate phenomenon before her, the actual group as it moved and composed itself and made noises before her, that for her was adequate subject matter, the phenomenon or thing which, like all other phenomena or things, was, so to say, in God. If God moves among the casseroles he may also move among a group of Princeton boys, unlikely as that may seem.

The association of Gertrude Stein with certain saints is real enough, though one can make too much of it. After all she was not a Catholic, not formally at least. Let me tell one anecdote about that, and I shall get back to ideas. In the Fall of 1957 Alice Toklas suddenly announced that she had become a Catholic convert, or rather returned to the Catholicism of her girlhood after an absence of many years. This made things difficult, since I am an atheist, and it did not make things easier when Alice Toklas claimed I was largely responsible for her conversion, because in the summer when we were vacationing about I had taken her to a very beautiful and very ancient Byzantine or Carolingian little church, Germigny-les-Prés, and the grace of conversion had reached her through the beauty of the building. But one gets used to one's

friends being converted and one tries to be nice about it, and when I saw Alice
Toklas again I rather egregiously tried to assure her that there was no great incoherence between her belief in Catholicism and her belief in Gertrude Stein,
since the Catholic ontology based on Being was not unlike the doctrine of
Being and essences implied and explicit in the work of Gertrude Stein. I was
rather tiresome about it. I expatiated. She finally stopped me by saying that
she had had to announce her conversion to Picasso, too, with some trepida-
tion, because as a Communist he ought to be a dogmatic atheist and not
patient with Catholic converts. But he was very nice about it, and when she
asked him what Gertrude would think of her return to the Church, he said,
"Oh, she was there long before you." In some ways this is true, and very like
Picasso to say so in so round and short a way. But there are other traditions
besides religion which brought Gertrude Stein to her sense of the equal value
of all phenomena. Poetic fervor of a kind can replace religious fervor in sustain-
ing such a sense—you find it very evidently in Walt Whitman—and even the
scientific attitude can sustain it, since for science all phenomena are equally
in existence, all equally fact.

The most decisive influence on Gertrude Stein in this direction—a mixture
of science, psychology, and philosophy—was certainly William James, her
favorite professor at Radcliffe. The extreme openness and hospitality to all
things which underlies the Pragmatism of James and even directs it articulately,
is plain enough, but it was a great pleasure to me to have this connection made
very definite by Dr. Haas's publication of the interview with Gertrude Stein,
in which she said that James had said to her that the minute you refuse
anything, that is the beginning of the end of you as an intellectual. Along with
James, or perhaps more *through* James, is the influence of Whitman, on whose
pantheism and ecstatic all-embracingness I need not elaborate.

I asked Alice Toklas what Gertrude Stein had thought about Whitman,
and she said, "Gertrude thought there was nothing wrong with him except that
he was over." Well, these days Whitman is far from over, but perhaps he was
over for Gertrude Stein, and in any case his literary influence on her, given
his very different sense of words, would have been slight, but his spaciousness
of mind, which contributed to that of James, may well count as an influence
on Gertrude Stein. And finally there is an influence which I cannot trace very
clearly but which may have been strong, that of Santayana, another professor
of hers at Radcliffe. As secretary of the Psychological Society at Radcliffe she
invited Santayana to speak to the group, but how far his ideas had come along
at that time, or how far they influenced Gertrude Stein, I don't know. But his
doctrine of Being and of Essences, though carefully schematized, includes practically all phenomena, as largely as James or Spinoza, and even his thought as
a young man may well have gone to reinforce the inclusiveness of James for
Gertrude Stein, and perhaps even induced a linear precision and Spanish
hardness into the rather high and nineteenth century eloquence of James.

But it is high time for me to illustrate by quotations how this mixed tradition — philosophical, scientific, poetic, religious — comes out in the work of Gertrude Stein. This is from *A Long Gay Book*, an early book of considerable interest though of incoherent form, as it makes the transition between the style of *The Making of Americans* and that of *Tender Buttons*. But you will recognize it as fairly typical Stein, and if you will also remember the traditions behind it which I have been describing, I think you will feel how exalted and passionate, as well as how precise, an expression it is.

> *Loving is something. Anything is something. Babies are something. Being a baby is something. Not being a baby is something.*
>
> *Coming to be anything is something. Not coming to be anything is something. Loving is something. Not loving is something. Loving is loving. Something is something. Anything is something.*
>
> *Anything is something. Not coming to anything is something. Loving is something. Needing coming to something is something. Not needing coming to something is something. Loving is something. Anything is something.*

And later in the same work:

> *Anyone being one is one. Anything put down is something. Anything being down is something and being that thing it is something and being something it is a thing and being a thing it is not anything and not being anything it is everything and being that thing it is a thing and being that thing it is that thing. Being that thing it is that thing and being that thing it is coming to be a thing having been that thing and coming to be a thing having been that thing it is a thing being a thing it is a thing being that thing.*

I asked you to notice in that passage, or those passages, the lyrical and caroling quality, the lyricism of ringing the changes on a single idea, as for example a litany would have it, and I do hope you got the hang or the ring of it; but now I want to treat in a very pedantic or scholastic way the fine distinctions that Gertrude Stein, as a student of philosophy and as a very committed intellectual, makes between *a* thing, and *anything*, or between *something* — as we would say in the vernacular, something that is really *something* — and *anything*, or as we would say in the vernacular, something which is just anything.

I don't know whether anybody but professors of philosophy can be interested, at this time of day, in Duns Scotus, a thirteenth century philosopher who was, oddly enough, the great inspiration not only of Leibnitz, who is in vogue again, but of Gerard Manley Hopkins, who has had a huge influence on the English poetry of the twentieth century, though not on Gertrude Stein. The importance of Duns Scotus to us, through Hopkins or not, is in his theory of the *species specialissima,* or the terminal entity of any immediate phenomenon, the peculiar character of which, in unique conditions of space and time, cannot be dissolved away into its component general forms, such as yellow, small, alive, animal, and so on, or its inclusion into a class, such as Bee. Scotus called, or presumably he did, this very individual character or specific quality of any concrete phenomenon, its *ecceitas* – or its there-it-is-ness – or again its *haecceitas,* its this-here-ness. This insistence on the immediate individual thing as a final reality, as final as general ideas, or even the featureless reality of Being Absolute or Being itself, is if you like a traditional problem, but I think it has never been so real in experience as in the twentieth century, when the individual has become as it were absolute, and at the same time the collectivity of individuals into a more or less coherent mass has become more imposing and practically imperative.

Let me give you an example of this problem in a passage from Gertrude Stein, not in full. There is a rather famous passage in a work called *Useful Knowledge* – and the word Useful is not altogether a joke – where she counts up to one hundred by ones. It goes, one and one and one and one and one and one and one and one and one and one and one, and so on mercilessly until the announcement that we have reached one hundred. I hope you see how crucial this is, that in the collectivity of one hundred, each of the things which are absolute ones to themselves, are perfectly respected and not lost in the accumulations of quantity, such as two or three or forty or seventy-five or whatever, until we get to the total. The equal insistence on the integrity of each component part is a very important twentieth century thing, obviously in politics, but even more evidently in the arts. I could easily remind you that Gertrude Stein grew up during the feminist movement, which proposed that women were equal to men, and Gertrude Stein finally decided that children too should have the vote, since they have equal stake in existence with adults, but the point is that the group or the family, especially the patriarchal family in which the individuals are severely subordinated to the group, is transcended for a view in which all the component individuals are absolute existents to themselves, and compose if at all a total of integers formed by all of mankind taken not as families, nations, classes or whatever, but as a sum of equal individuals. I shall not insist on this, but in spite of the formation in our century of elite or minority groups, in spite of the struggles in politics which exploit majorities and minorities, we do, deep in our hearts, have a strong feeling of the equal existence and of the right to an individual existence, of each and every one in the world. I don't think that this feeling has ever in history been so basic or strong as in the twentieth century, and indeed the counter-movements, Fascism and Communism, which respectively try to subordinate an unindividualized mass to an unindividualized minority or to subordinate all individuals and groups to a homogenized majority or totality, do nothing but try to change the more obvious twentieth century conviction that one and one and one and so on make one hundred, not cumulatively or in such proportions as twenty and eighty, but one by one by one by one.

Let me put it this way, very directly. If you say one and one are two, do you absorb the essential singularity of the ones into the group of two or do you not? In marriage, where one individual and another one individual are joined in a couple, do we any longer feel that the one or the other one is essentially a component of a couple or dyad instead of a single absolute unit, or do we not? I think that in people we now count by units instead of by groups, and that the family is no longer convincing. Nor larger groups, like the party, the class, or the nation itself.

So, one and one and one and one and one and so on. A Spanish poet once wrote that the angel of numbers goes from the one to the two, from the two to the three, and indeed it does take a supernatural power like an angel to sink one unit and another into a duality, and a duality with another unit into a triad.

Let me apply this to painting in the twentieth century. One of the major accomplishments of Cézanne was precisely the assertion of the equal existence of each inch or millimeter of his canvas with the existence of every other inch or millimeter. With Cézanne this is not a dramatic exaltation or subordination of certain parts of the picture over others, though they do, as we say, add up to a total. No doubt the origin of this in Cézanne was in part the impressionist movement, or the pointillist movement, in which every spot of color was an equally important and equally scientific optical or retinal event, but Cézanne made objects and shapes, not merely events, into an equally emphatic existence in equilibrium over his whole canvas. The Cubists took this up too, the equal diffusion of geometric shapes over a whole canvas, with no dramatic focus or culminating point. Parallel to this would be the care with which Rousseau painted each leaf of his trees, one by one, neglecting the collective bunches of foliage which say Corot had painted. And even now, with Mondrian or Mark Tobey or Pollock, we have gone on with his equal emphasis of visual events or shapes over a whole canvas, an equal tension if you like, though of course there are other theories and practices of composition.

What I mean may be clearer if I discuss something many of you may recently have read, *The Banquet Years*, by Roger Shattuck, which was recommended to you, and with reason, since it is a magnificent work and delightful to read as well. But Mr. Shattuck, though not unreasonably, takes issue with me on a distinction I made, in my book on Gertrude Stein, on the difference between a prolonged and a continuous present, and the difference is rather to the point I am now discussing. I did not make myself very clear, I am afraid, in the passage Mr. Shattuck quoted, but what I more or less meant was that a prolonged present asserts a theme and then proceeds to complicate and elaborate it, in the manner of say a fugal theme in Bach, so that the presence of the original theme, no matter how elaborately overlaid with variations, is maintained or prolonged as a going existence in each present passage or moment. It is as if one counted one two three four five six and so on, where the original unit of one is prolonged and present in the other figures in which it remains a component. But a continuous present, I think I meant, would be one in which each unit, even if identical or nearly with the previous one, is still, in its present, a completely self-contained thing, as when you say one and one, the second one is a completely present existence in itself, and does not depend, as two does or three does, on a preceding one or two. One and one and one and one. In this case, each one is a completely separate assertion of a complete entity and is not prolonged from the preceding unit or units, but comes as a new thing, and each one arrives in a continuous present, that is, the present is so continuous it does not allow any retrospect or expectation, as when you say, in such counting, two, you look backward to one and forward to three, or even more. You must also be aware of the most notorious sentence of Gertrude Stein: A rose is a rose is a rose is a rose. In this case, we have not a consecutive counting but a moment by moment insistence on the rose, and each moment of insistence is a heightened and refreshed recognition of the rose, not merely a prolongation of the rose, as could perfectly well be done in another era, as Goethe might have said to the rose, *Verweile doch, du bist so schoen,* even if the prolongation meant his damnation.

That is one way of feeling about things, and indeed the way I mostly feel, that things should if possible be prolonged to my present experience if I love them, but I think the twentieth century thing is certainly to take each present moment with its content as an independent and absolute event, even if the content has occurred before. One and one and one and one. Gertrude Stein came to thinking and saying that there was no such thing as repetition, since each time the thing or word recurred the insistence was different or new. And if one counts one and one and one and one, you might say that none of the ones is the same as any other, and if asserted as a complete thing in a continuous present, it does not look backward to a previous one or forward to another one to follow. Hence, in a modern composition of this kind, each part or moment or instant is complete in itself and does not proceed from anything else or look forward to anything else, and in the total they are as it were simultaneous, as when counting one and one and one and one and so on, the total of one hundred is simultaneously, not cumulatively or gradually, arrived at by all the units together. This may remind you of Leibnitz and his monads, which are mutually impenetrable units, absolute to themselves, but united in a preestablished harmony, like clocks set at the same hour and synchronous, under a total or arch-monad which is God.

Well, never mind Leibnitz. After all, philosophy does not justify anything in the arts, even if in a way it clarifies, and bringing in philosophy can be depressing. It should not be, but it usually is, so I shall stop it, and remind you instead of certain quite practical features of the twentieth century world which correspond to the sort of composition I am discussing. One evident feature is our extraordinary mass-production and series production, the assembly line and so on. It is still possible to have a custom-made car or a custom-made suit, but why bother—the normal thing is to have a car or a suit which is exactly like thousands of others from the same company. This worries some people, as if their individuality were at stake, but in fact if you have say a new Mustang it is your own Mustang, even if it is not fully paid for, and you go your own way in it and treat it as if it were unique. And even if there are thousands of suits exactly like the one you are wearing, it is still your suit, you are by yourself in it, and you make the particular creases in it all by yourself, the way it hangs on your posture is all yours. That thing is being that thing and not being just anything it is everything—that is, it is everything to you if you are fond of clothes and like the suit or dress you are wearing.

Another twentieth century thing which is getting progressively more insistent is the sky-scraper, all the stories of which are getting more purely identical, with less use of subordinate groupings or blockings in the facade. And apartment houses are much the same. They horrify some people, but they are more and more just that, one and one and one and one endlessly, and still, if you live in one and are living an intense private life inside it, this very identical apartment has to your experience a quality all of its own, it becomes independent and even quite disconnected from all the others like it. Subjectively and intensively speaking, that is, while objectively and extensively the units are progressively more uniform. Someone, I think it was Frank Lloyd Wright, called our huge apartment buildings and housing developments slums or tenements for the rich. Well, that is very interesting, that the rich and the middle class and the poor should all be living in much the same way. We still have zonings and brackets and Negro sections and Chinatowns, but really the distinctions are pretty well disappearing, with some violence and resistance, it is true, but disappearing all the same. You may or may not like it, but there it is.

The principle of this kind of composition is very aptly called by Mr. Shattuck juxtaposition—as against subordination or progression—what in grammar we call parataxis, eminently the dominant syntax in Gertrude Stein, not to mention Homer and the Bible, with which works she grouped her own. In this style things are associated, as she said, "so nextily." But there are, as Mr. Shattuck points out, two very distinct ways of composing in juxtaposition—first the juxtaposition of nearly identical though independent units, as in one and one and one and so on, and second, the juxtaposition of things that are very different in kind and quality. Gertrude Stein shifted from a style in which things were simply alike to a style in which things are simply different, so she put it, and she made the change in the course of *A Long Gay Book.* Let me read a passage from the later phase of that book, in which the juxtaposed elements are "simply different."

All the pudding has the same flow and the sauce is painful, the tunes are played, the crinkling paper is burning, the pot has a cover and the standard is excellence.

At least two important things can be said about this. One is that in any given immediate scene, no matter how commonplace, there is bound to be an association of disparate elements, which exist very vividly to a perception persuaded of the equal importance of all phenomena, even if they are largely irrelevant to the main gist of the scene. Instead of letting things go at "I had a good pudding with sauce piquante for supper" she gives an equable list of concomitant phenomena, some relevant, some not, to the main practical event, but all of them equally and simultaneously existing in perceptual fact. The written composition, made of the disparate elements abstracted, has certainly a strangeness, if you like a senselessness and lack of meaning, because it isolates or detaches from a perfectly commonplace or generic and generally recognizable event like having supper those elements which made it a special and unique event, which made it not *a* thing but *that* thing, those elements which make up its *species specialissima*. Here of course we run into difficulties, and the famous obscurity of most of Gertrude Stein's work after 1911 or 1912, since anything has meaning, that is, has a recognizability, by virtue of belonging to a general class of phenomena, such as having dinner, and here we have the subject presented, not exclusively but predominantly, by those elements which distinguish or separate it from its class. So you see what she must have meant at Princeton. She could have said, "I spent an evening with a bunch of Princeton boys," but that would not have described the unique immediacies of what she saw and heard before her.

Anyway, when she writes of unique immediacies and suppresses the generic element, one is always or nearly always tempted to puzzle it out, to induce or restore a generic element which will make the composition "comprehensible." But immediate experience in its real immediacy is not comprehensible, has no meaning, and when you do induce a meaning you falsify the essential immediacy. Gertrude Stein once remarked, "What is strange is this"—meaning that this thing as this thing is new and unfamiliar, as this thing it exceeds or comes loose from the class to which it belongs, from identification and identity so to say.

Now is this a twentieth century thing or not, a thing existing in its unique immediacy and not by its participation in a class of phenomena? I think it is. Let me give you a painful example, the assassination of Mr. Kennedy last year, followed by the murder of Mr. Oswald. Admittedly the whole weekend was both superb and intolerable; everyone, under the impact of those strange immediacies, surely lost several pounds of weight, as I did, and surely we all tried madly to explain what it was about, to get some sort of meaning into it. And one attempt was to classify it, we were reminded that presidents are assassinated, and we counted off Lincoln, Garfield, and McKinley, as if that more or less accounted for Mr. Kennedy.

And then there was the question of conspiracy, whether it was a Communist plot or a heavily disguised Fascist plot, or again just a result of the social and psychological forces at work in Mr. Oswald's case history. Well, one did try to escape from the tragic immediacy into classes of events and into causalities, but these escapes were surely much less interesting than the immediate events themselves, and by now, surely, nobody is much interested in how or why it happened. Some intellectuals, it is true, of the kind that insists on figuring everything out, are still disputing the matter, but I think the public at large simply treasures the event itself, the albums of photographs, so to say, rather than any possible explanation. Well, not that art in the twentieth century has the intensity of an assassination, even if the Surrealists tried to make it that way, but it can very well and usually does exist in disconnection from any reference or extrinsic meaning, by the beauty or intensity or character of its immediate properties. As one may say that the almost but not quite appropriate color of Mrs. Kennedy's dress is more intrinsic to the essence of the assassination than the political reasons for the event. Even if there are reasons, and of course there must be, the quality of most events in the twentieth century, whether in public or private life, whether in art or nature, is to be quite arbitrary and disconnected from everything else, to be, as it were, *something*. Our venture of getting to the moon, for example, has such very feeble reasons, such as the idle curiosity of Science, that Mr. Kennedy was quite right in saying simply and roundly, "We *choose* to go to the moon." And now it appears we are not stopping at the moon, but going straight on, for no explicit reason at all, to Mars.

What makes all this very different from the nineteenth century is that the nineteenth century was still interested in causes and purposes and explanations. It was dominated, if not by Evolution, under which everything, even if incomprehensibly, served some future purpose or other—contributed in some way to "some far-off divine event toward which the whole creation moves," at least by a sense of direction in History, whether Hegelian or Marxist or what not. In my younger and more Leftist days I used to think that the twentieth century sense of arrest in history, the suppression of the movement of time—as in the continuous present of Gertrude Stein or the substitution of relatively timeless forms like geometry by the Cubists for the temporal and optical events of the nineteenth century Impressionists—was a sort of bourgeois conspiracy to arrest the dialectic of history while the Bourgeoisie was more or less on top and in its element. One may perhaps still think that, and even think that the extraordinary domination of the scientific world by physics instead of biology—that is by an eventful but non-progressive science instead of one which was essentially a study of gradual growth upwards—has been a bourgeois conspiracy or at least a bourgeois intuition, but I do not in the least, at this time of day, take this kind of opinion seriously. Partly because politically it can reverse itself. The cause of the Negro, which in the nineteenth century could be thought of as committed to a gradual evolution, as slow as the development of new species in animals or plants, is now evidently advanced in the immediate manner of physics, as a sudden and constant movement, not a gradual one. The Negro has ceased to wait. And who does wait, now, for anything? And the reason we do not wait is simply that we no longer believe that things are progressing of themselves, and of course we have become quite habituated to the idea, under the bomb, that not only biology but human history itself can end at any moment. Thus we live, oddly enough, in a continuous present, in which nothing is felt to lead to anything else, because at any instant there may be nothing left for it to lead to.

After the first World War, which made it clear to the more sensitive members of civilization, that progress had been a delusion, and that individual existence was so expendable that it could not count on more than a span of a few days, and after the second World War, when the two nations of Europe which had a certain reputation for intense civilization, that is, Germany and Italy, showed themselves the most atrociously barbarous, with indeed the participation of certain elements in England, France, and America, and of course Spain, the whole question of history as something with a meaning, much less a value, came surely foremost.

In literature, and I shall mean mainly American literature, we have had a very interesting split, between those who still cling to history as a valid dimension for human habitation, and those who reject it. The school of T.S. Eliot and Ezra Pound is evidently of the twentieth century, but with their everlasting historicism, their infatuation with tradition, which they set against the going present for the most part, they are still not weaned from the superstitions of the nineteenth century. But any century includes, as part of its full character, an opposition to its major thesis, so one may say that the rear-guard action of historicist writing and art is still component to the essence of the century. Not only that, but now in 1964, when the present events are so demanding on the imagination, and hit the sensibilities with so violent a shock, it is natural that a great many people should try to find a ground of assurance or of perspective in the past.

The present, continuous or not, is a good deal too much, so that even the presumably most contemporary poets tend to take up Buddhism, a very ancient state of mind, or, as with Charles Olson, the oldest American history, or, as with innumerable young poets, descriptions of Renaissance Italian monuments. Henry James once called Europe the great American sedative, and indeed the European cultural past, and now the Asiatic cultural and religious past, have become the refuge of the nervous American against the arbitrary and miraculous violence of present events, when the recourse is not to actual intoxicants like peyote, marihuana, or alcohol.

Well, it is all very tempting. Gertrude Stein was determined, in her time, to stay with the twentieth century, come what might, but only in her art. For personal comfort she sat amongst Renaissance furniture, a devotion to the Republican Party, and fundamentally the moral views of a lady of 1902. We all need some sort of ballast for navigating the present, some distance from which to see it straight, some still point or continuity from which to measure or count off the chaotic events of the moment, but at least Gertrude Stein used her residual nineteenth century habits as a personal comfort, while as an artist she could risk taking on the twentieth century directly. She used to say that the twentieth century in the arts was created by America, meaning herself, and by Spain, meaning Picasso, but that it had to be created in Paris or rather in France, because France afforded a traditional and unchanging ground upon which or against which to erect the twentieth century compositions in writing and painting. That is the way she felt about it, and it may be more generally true, that France has not created much of the twentieth century, though she has been immensely present at it and exploited it well enough and refined it, in her painting at least, and her literature remains extraordinarily academic and traditional, even and most hilariously in Jean Genêt.

But to stay with American literature. As I said, there are the culture people, after Pound and Eliot, who not only use the past as a recourse against the raw violence and disconnections of the present, but prefer the past, and use it as a contrast and reproach to the present. Nevertheless, we have many writers committed to the present, without benefit of either a cultural heritage or so dubious an arrangement or prearrangement of values as is available at a price in the Catholic Church, or the Communist Party. But in a general way those writers and poets who do maintain the raw or unhistoric present do not get much beyond notation or documentation, that is, the bare recording of a passing impression or of how some group lives, whether urban hipsters or garden suburbanites or the oppressed. In short we are falling back on nineteenth century Naturalism; even if the writing is more violent, the content and the vision are strikingly those of the nineteenth century, of Naturalism, all over again. The innovations of form are very minor indeed, not much more than a bleaker or a more florid manner than usual.

For several years now it has been regularly said that the period of innovation in the twentieth century, so far as the arts are concerned, is over, and this may or not be a good thing. Good or bad, it may be natural and inevitable, not just as a reaction but as a maturation. Gertrude Stein used to compare the life of a century to any human life. In a century's youth it is naturally in revolt against the older century in order to establish a life of its own; it sows its wild oats and goes a little wild, but once it has won the struggle to lead its own life it calms down, becomes mature and civilized in its turn, enriching and refining the main attitudes of its youth and even affecting the mannerisms of its parent century.

Before she died Gertrude Stein came to feel that the twentieth century was unduly prolonging its youth, that it was time for it to slow down a little and behave itself, or simply enjoy itself. In a way one is tempted to agree; one would like a certain amount of tranquility in the Arts, just to offset the increasing violence of the real world. And such a comforting or consolatory art is indeed not alien to twentieth century art from the beginning.

You may have noticed in Mr. Shattuck's book the intention of Matisse to make paintings like armchairs, and of Satie and his group to make a music like furniture, as if it were an agreeable environment rather than an exciting series of auditory events. One may, especially from the French point of view, read the twentieth century that way, and one may even adopt the French point of view in the interests of civilization and pleasure; but I do think that from the American point of view and from what was once a Spanish point of view, one cannot go against the intrinsic energy of the century, its splendor, its violence, its savagery if you like. One may certainly try to transcend it, but one cannot, as a serious artist, or as a serious beholder of the Arts, content oneself with something which is not in on the essential realities and energies of one's time in the real world, or really enjoy something which is an evasion or a refusal. Interfused with the pleasure principle, as Freud called it, there is the reality principle, and though the two may conflict, I do think it is true that any assured and full and confident pleasure has to rest on some adequate satisfaction of the reality principle. So far so good, and it is easily said, but what is not so easy is our present difficulty, the incoherence between the violent or intensely realistic content of much contemporary writing and the fundamentally placid and unventuresome form in which it is expressed. And after all, in art the expression is everything, and the form is everything to the expression—at least I feel not only strongly but ferociously about this, being a professor of Greek and Latin, lo these twenty-five years.

Before getting to my point, let me make sure I am not misunderstood in connection with Greek and Latin. My classical training and profession, which you might think would exclude me from an interest in Gertrude Stein, commits me first of all to a very minute concern with words, an endless and almost pathological patience with their meanings, which is required for reading Gertrude Stein as it is for reading Homer; and second, and much more important, a quite fanatical belief in rhetoric, not in the least as a set of rules for correct writing, but as the indispensable source for adequate expression in words of the quality of the subject. The inventiveness of the Greeks and Romans as well in finding adequate formal tropes for the quality of anything they found themselves called upon to express is what has kept me at them all these years, and though many other things attach me to Gertrude Stein, what really holds me is her overwhelming rhetorical agility with the perfection of each syllable of her wording—perfection again not in the sense of being correct according to some high school standard of good writing, but in beauty of calligraphic poise and shape and a tight fullness of meaning, exactitude if you like. Perhaps I am still being pedantic, no doubt I am, but with the differences I have just described. Though Gertrude Stein announced often that she was a grammarian, I would go a little farther than grammar and say I value her also and most as a rhetorician. To a rhetorician, for example, there is no difficulty whatever in "A rose is a rose is a rose is a rose."

So now, to the point; her rhetorical resources were for the most part equal to expressing the quality and composition of the twentieth century reality as she intensely and devotedly experienced it, and that reality in her experience was conditioned not only by a hyperacute perceptivity but by an enormously broad and endlessly subtle intelligence, which took on the totality of the world — excluding nothing as I said at the beginning.

I cannot tell, just now, whether she is back in fashion again or out of fashion, as she recently has been except for a scattering of devotees, but I am quite persuaded, that if our present problem is to be solved, namely finding a rhetorical adequacy of expression for the essential realities of our time, the way things are and the way things go and the way things connect with each other or do not, Gertrude Stein will have been the great predecessor, the great teacher too in some degree. The literature I hope for will be sustained, as hers was, not on a literary or cultural tradition so much as on a minutely tuned and perfected verbal instrument, a radically philosophical intelligence applied to words and things alike in their most vivid aspects — and then, finally and most important of all, on a passion for the world. It can be a happy passion, or a tragically unhappy passion, but it has to be a quite unreasonable love for this disastrous and very beautiful world.

The Work of Gertrude Stein

William Carlos Williams

> "Would I had seen a white bear!
> (for how can I imagine it?)"
>
> *A Novelette and Other Prose, 1921–1931*

Let it be granted that whatever is new in literature the germ of it will be found somewhere in the writings of other times; only the modern emphasis gives work a present distinction.

The necessity for this modern focus and the meaning of the changes involved are, however, another matter, the everlasting stumbling block to criticism. Here is a theme worth development in the case of Gertrude Stein — yet signally neglected.

Why in fact have we not heard more generally from American scholars upon the writings of Miss Stein? Is it lack of heart or ability or just that theirs is an enthusiasm which fades rapidly of its own nature before the risks of today?

The verbs auxiliary we are concerned in here, continued my father, are am; was; have; had; do; did; could; owe; make; made; suffer; shall; should; will; would; can; ought; used; or is wont ... — or with these questions added to them; — Is it? Was it? Will it be? ... Or affirmatively ... — Or chronologically ... — Or hypothetically ... — If it was? If it was not? What would follow? — If the French beat the English? If the Sun should go out of the Zodiac?

Now, by the right use and application of these, continued my father, in which a child's memory should be exercised, there is no one idea can enter the brain how barren soever, but a magazine of conceptions and conclusions may be drawn forth from it. — Didst thou ever see a white bear? cried my father, turning his head round to Trim, who stood at the back of his chair. — No, an' please your honour, replied the corporal. — But thou couldst discourse about one, Trim, said my father, in case of need? — How is it possible, brother, quoth my Uncle Toby, if the corporal never saw one? — 'Tis the fact I want, replied my father, — and the possibility of it as follows.

Reprinted by permission of New Directions Publishing Corp.

> A white bear! Very well, Have I ever seen one? Might I ever have seen one? Am I ever to see one? Ought I ever to have seen one? Or can I see one?
> Would I had seen a white bear! (for how can I imagine it?)
> If I should see a white bear, what should I say? If I should never see a white bear, what then?
> If I never have, can, must, or shall see a white bear alive; have I ever seen the skin of one? Did I ever see one painted? – described? Have I never dreamed of one?

Note how the words *alive, skin, painted, described, dreamed* come into the design of these sentences. The feeling is of words themselves, a curious immediate quality quite apart from their meaning, much as in music different notes are dropped, so to speak, into repeated chords one at a time, one after another – for themselves alone. Compare this with the same effects common in all that Stein does. See *Geography and Plays*, "They were both gay there." To continue –

> Did my father, mother uncle, aunt, brothers or sisters, ever see a white bear? What would they give? . . . How would they behave? How would the white bear have behaved? Is he wild? Tame? Terrible? Rough? Smooth?

Note the play upon *rough* and *smooth* (though it is not certain that this was intended), *rough* seeming to apply to the bear's deportment, *smooth* to surface, presumably the bear's coat. In any case the effect is that of a comparison relating primarily not to any qualities of the bear himself but to the words rough and smooth. And so to finish –

> Is the white bear worth seeing?
> Is there any sin in it?
> Is it better than a black one?

In this manner ends Chapter 43 of *The Life and Opinions of Tristram Shandy*. The handling of the words and to some extent the imaginative quality of the sentence is a direct forerunner of that which Gertrude Stein has woven today into a synthesis of its own. It will be plain, in fact, on close attention, that Sterne exercises not only the play (or music) of sight, sense and sound contrast among the words themselves which Stein uses, but their grammatical play also – i.e. for, how, can I imagine it; did my . . ., what would, how would, compare Stein's "to have rivers; to halve rivers," etc. It would not be too much to say that Stein's development over a lifetime is anticipated completely with regard to subject matter, sense and grammar – in Sterne.

Starting from scratch we get, possibly, thatch; just as they have always done in poetry.

Then they would try to connect it up by something like—The mice scratch, beneath the thatch.

Miss Stein does away with all that. The free-versists on the contrary used nothing else. They saved—The mice, under the . . . ,

It is simply the skeleton, the "formal" parts of writing, those that make form, that she has to do with, apart from the "burden" which they carry. The skeleton, important to acknowledge where confusion of all knowledge of the "soft part" reigns as at the present day in all intellectual fields.

Stein's theme is writing. But in such a way as to be writing envisioned as the first concern of the moment, dragging behind it a dead weight of logical burdens, among them a dead criticism which broken through might be a gap by which endless other enterprises of the understanding should issue—for refreshment.

It is a revolution of some proportions that is contemplated, the exact nature of which may be no more than sketched here but whose basis is humanity in a relationship with literature hitherto little contemplated.

And at the same time it is a general attack on the scholastic viewpoint, that medieval remnant with whose effects from generation to generation literature has been infested to its lasting detriment. It is a break-away from that paralyzing vulgarity of logic for which the habits of science and philosophy coming over into literature (where they do not belong) are to blame.

It is this logicality as a basis for literary action which in Stein's case, for better or worse, has been wholly transcended.

She explains her own development in connection with *Tender Buttons* (1914). "It was my first conscious struggle with the problem of correlating sight, sound and sense, and eliminating rhythm;—now I am trying grammar and eliminating sight and sound" (*transition* No. 14, fall, 1928).

Having taken the words to her choice, to emphasize further what she has in mind she has completely unlinked them (in her most recent work) from their former relationships in the sentence. This was absolutely essential and unescapable. Each under the new arrangement has a quality of its own, but not conjoined to carry the burden science, philosophy and every higgledy-piggledy figment of law and order have been laying upon them in the past. They are like a crowd at Coney Island, let us say, seen from an airplane.

Whatever the value of Miss Stein's work may turn out finally to be, she has at least accomplished her purpose of getting down on paper this much that is decipherable. She has placed writing on a plane where it may deal unhampered with its own affairs, unburdened with scientific and philosophic lumber.

For after all, science and philosophy are today, in their effect upon the mind, little more than fetishes of unspeakable abhorrence. And it is through a subversion of the art of writing that their grip upon us has assumed its steel-like temper.

What are philosophers, scientists, religionists, they that have filled up literature with their pap? Writers, of a kind. Stein simply erases their stories, turns them off and does without them, their logic (founded merely on the limits of the perceptions) which is supposed to transcend the words, along with them. Stein denies it. The words, in writing, she discloses, transcend everything.

Movement (for which in a petty way logic is taken), the so-called search for truth and beauty, is for us the effect of a breakdown of the attention. But movement must not be confused with what we attach to it but, for the rescuing of the intelligence, must always be considered aimless, without progress.

This is the essence of all knowledge.

Bach might be an illustration of movement not suborned by a freight of purposed design, loaded upon it as in almost all later musical works; statement unmusical and unnecessary, Stein's "They lived very gay then" has much of the same quality of movement to be found in Bach—the composition of the words determining not the logic, not the "story," not the theme even, but the movement itself. As it happens, "They were both gay there" is as good as some of Bach's shorter figures.

Music could easily have a statement attached to each note in the manner of words, so that C natural might mean the sun, etc., and completely dull treatises be played—and even sciences finally expounded in tunes.

Either, we have been taught to think, the mind moves in a logical sequence to a definite end which is its goal, or it will embrace movement without goal other than movement itself for an end and hail "transition" only as supreme.

Take your choice, both resorts are an improper description of the mind in fullest play.

If the attention could envision the whole of writing, let us say, at one time, moving over it in swift and accurate pursuit of the modern imperative at the instant when it is most to the fore, something of what actually takes place under an optimum of intelligence could be observed. It is an alertness not to let go of a possibility of movement in our fearful bedazzlement with some concrete and fixed present. The goal is to keep a beleaguered line of understanding which has movement from breaking down and becoming a hole into which we sink decoratively to rest.

The goal has nothing to do with the silly function which logic, natural or otherwise, enforces. Yet it is a goal. It moves as the sense wearies, remains fresh, living. One is concerned with it as with anything pursued and not with the rush of air or the guts of the horse one is riding—save to a very minor degree.

Writing, like everything else, is much a question of refreshed interest. It is directed, not idly, but as most often happens (though not necessarily so) toward that point not to be predetermined where movement is blocked (by the end of logic perhaps). It is about these parts, if I am not mistaken, that Gertrude Stein will be found.

There remains to be explained the bewildering volume of what Miss Stein has written, the quantity of her work, its very apparent repetitiousness, its iteration, what I prefer to call its extension, the final clue to her meaning.

It is, of course, a progression (not a progress) beginning, conveniently, with "Melanctha" from *Three Lives*, and coming up to today.

How in a democracy, such as the United States, can writing which has to compete with excellence elsewhere and in other times remain in the field and be at once objective (true to fact), intellectually searching, subtle and instinctive with powerful additions to our lives? It is impossible, without invention of some sort, for the very good reason that observation about us engenders the very opposite of what we seek: triviality, crassness and intellectual bankruptcy. And yet what we do see can in no way be excluded. Satire and flight are two possibilities but Miss Stein has chosen otherwise.

But if one remain in a place and reject satire, what then? To be democratic, local (in the sense of being attached with integrity to actual experience) Stein, or any other artist, must for subtlety ascend to a plane of almost abstract design to keep alive. To writing, then, as an art in itself. Yet what actually impinges on the senses must be rendered as it appears, by use of which, only, and under which, untouched, the significance has to be disclosed. It is one of the major problems of the artist.

"Melanctha" is a thrilling clinical record of the life of a colored woman in the present-day United States, told with directness and truth. It is without question one of the best bits of characterization produced in America. It is universally admired. This is where Stein began. But for Stein to tell a story of that sort, even with the utmost genius, was not enough under the conditions in which we live, since by the very nature of its composition such a story does violence to the larger scene which would be portrayed.

True, a certain way of delineating the scene is to take an individual like Melanctha and draw her carefully. But this is what happens. The more carefully the drawing is made, the greater the genius involved and the greater the interest that attaches, therefore, to the character as an individual, the more exceptional that character becomes in the mind of the reader and the less typical of the scene.

It was no use for Stein to go on with *Three Lives*. There that phase of the work had to end. See *Useful Knowledge*, the parts on the U.S.A.

Stein's pages have become like the United States viewed from an airplane—the same senseless repetitions, the endless multiplications of toneless words, with these she had to work.

No use for Stein to fly to Paris and forget it. The thing, the United States, the unmitigated stupidity, the drab tediousness of the democracy, the overwhelming number of the offensively ignorant, the dull nerve—is there in the artist's mind and cannot be escaped by taking a ship. She must resolve it if she can, if she is to be.

That must be the artist's articulation with existence.

Truly, the world is full of emotion—more or less—but it is caught in bewilderment to a far more important degree. And the purpose of art, so far as it has any, is not at least to copy that, but lies in the resolution of difficulties to its own comprehensive organization of materials. And by so doing, in this case, rather than by copying, it takes its place as most human.

To deal with Melanctha, with characters of whomever it may be, the modern Dickens, is not therefore human. To write like that is not in the artist, to be human at all, since nothing is resolved, nothing is done to resolve the bewilderment which makes of emotion an inanity: That, is to overlook the gross instigation and with all subtlety to examine the object minutely for "the truth"—which if there is anything more commonly practiced or more stupid, I have yet to come upon it.

To be most useful to humanity, or to anything else for that matter, an art, writing, must stay art, not seeking to be science, philosophy, history, the humanities, or anything else it has been made to carry in the past. It is this enforcement which underlies Gertrude Stein's extension and progression to date.

The Revolutionary Power
of a Woman's Laughter

Jo-Anna Isaak

In the beginning was the gest he ᚛ jousstly
says, for the end is with woman, flesh-without-
word, while the man to be is in a worse case
after than before since sheon the supine
satisfies the verb to him! Toughtough,
tootoological. Thou the first person
shingeller. Art, an imperfect subjunctive.

—James Joyce

"When I use a word," Humpty Dumpty said
in rather a scornful tone, "it means exactly
what I choose it to mean—neither more nor less."
"The question is," said Alice, "whether you
can make words mean so many different things."
"The question is," said Humpty Dumpty, "which
is to be master—that's all."

—Lewis Carroll

For the most part Stein criticism has focused on Stein herself, not her work. There are more biographies of Stein than there are critical studies of her writing. This is indicative of the assumptions about her—that she was an interesting woman, who led an interesting life, and knew every interesting person at the time (one of these biographies is called *Everybody Who Was Anybody*). The assumption about her work is that it is boring, repetitious, childish nonsense. These are fairly accurate assessments. Her work is boring, repetitious, and childish. Consequently, it is not well received. This is one publisher's response to *The Making of Americans:*

> Dear Madam,
>   I am only one, only one, only one. Only one being, one at the same time. Not two, not three, only one. Only one life to life, only sixty minutes in one hour. Only one pair of eyes. Only one brain. Only one

Reprinted from the *Ruin of Representation in Modernist Art and Text* (UMI Research, 1986) by permission of the author and the publisher.

being. Being only one, having only one pair of eyes, having only one time, having only one life, I cannot read your M.S. three or four times. Not even one time. Only one look only one look is enough. Hardly one copy would sell here. Hardly one. Hardly one.

Many thanks. I am returning the M.S. by registered post. Only one M.S. by one post.

Sincerely yours,
A.C. Fifield

Inasmuch as Stein pushes the signifying practice of writing beyond its limits she is subject to the accusations of producing boring, repetitious, childish nonsense. It is precisely in those issues and the inversion of conventional attitudes towards them that the revolutionary aspect of Stein's aesthetic inheres. "If something is boring after two minutes," John Cage suggests, "try it for four. If still boring, try it for eight, sixteen, thirty-two and so on. Eventually one discovers that it is not boring at all but very interesting."[1] The point is that the interest does not inhere in the item heard or read or seen, but in the repeated reception of it: "Poetry is not the same as 'please pass the butter' which is simple imperative. But Gertrude Stein showed . . . that if you focus your attention on 'Please pass the butter' and put it through enough permutations and combinations, it begins to take on a kind of glow, the splendor of which is called 'aesthetic object.' This is a trick of the manipulation of attention."[2]

This manipulation of attention or focus, termed "foregrounding" (the accepted English translation of the Czech word *aktualisace*), is defined by Jan Mukařovský as "the aesthetically intentional distortion of linguistic components."[3] Foregrounding depends upon a "background" of conventional devices—that is, language used in customary and predictable ways so that it does not attract attention. Problems of intelligibility occur when the focus is not allowed to rest on the "background" of illusionistic literary conventions. "As soon as purely aesthetic elements predominate and the story of John and Mary grows elusive, most people feel out of their depth and are at a loss what to make of the scene, the book, or the painting. We have here a very simple optical problem," Ortega y Gasset observes:

> To see a thing we must adjust our visual apparatus in a certain way. If the adjustment is inadequate the thing is seen indistinctly or not at all. Take a garden seen through a window. Looking at the garden we adjust our eyes in such a way that the ray of vision travels through the pane without delay and rests on the shrubs and flowers. Since we are focusing on the garden and our ray of vision is directed toward it, we do not see the window but look clear through it. The purer the glass, the less we see it. But we can also deliberately disregard the garden and, withdrawing the ray of vision, detain it at the window. We then lose sight of the

garden what we still behold of it is a confused mass of color which appears pasted to the pane. Hence to see the garden and to see the window-
pane are two incompatible operations which exclude one another
because they require different adjustments.

But not many people are capable of adjusting their perceptive
apparatus to the pane and the transparency that is the work of art.
Instead they look right through it and revel in the human reality with
which the work deals. When they are invited to let go of this prey and
to direct their attention to the work of art itself they will say that they
cannot see such a thing, which indeed they cannot, because it is all
artistic transparency and without substance.[4]

The optical metaphor is appropriate, for reading is first and foremost an
exercise in vision. The child learns not to look *at* the printed words, but to
look *through* them as if they were transparent or invisible. But Stein's opaque
prose reverses this conditioning, it refuses to become a self-effacing medium,
it will not permit the reader's gaze to pass, like light itself, straight through it.
(A "surfeit of signifiers," Roland Barthes notes, "can keep the reader from
enjoying a 'rich,' 'profound,' 'secret,' in short, a signifying world."[5]) Instead, the
gaze is directed to the material object (or, more specifically, to the conditions
of its visibility), thus effecting what might be called a figure/ground reversal.
The movements of semantic and narrative construction are suspended or
reversed; the conventional ground, the transparent medium of language,
which we normally take for granted usurps the place of the solid narrative
figure. Stein describes her method of composition as having been derived from
an optical adjustment:

The only thing that is different from one time to another is what is seen
and what is seen depends upon how everybody is doing everything. This
makes the thing we are looking at very different and this makes what
those who describe it make of it, it makes composition, it confuses, it
shows, it is, it looks, it likes it as it is, and this makes what is seen as it
is seen. Nothing changes from generation to generation except the thing
seen and that makes composition.[6]

Stein's intention, however, is not just to reduce language to its surfaces,
but rather to conduct an epistemic investigation into the conditions of its
visibility. The focus from figure to ground is not just inverted, rather they are
in a continual dialectical interchange. Each convention of signification Stein
addresses she dismantles through an intensive scrutiny of what might be called
the "pathology of written meaning,"[7] enabling the conventionally suppressed
to come forward to the surface. She is not exploring subjective states of consciousness, but rather the structure of language which creates these states.[8]
Thus, each dismantling is experienced by the reader as an expansion of consciousness, an exposure to one of the otherwise partially concealed powers of
language.

The writing itself is the *instancing* of the continual discovery of ways to interrogate the generative nature and generative bounds of language, so that language itself shows the defining conditions of its constitution. This is not an attempt to master language *by* language, but rather to keep up a continual meta-language athwart the text, to play a joke, or make a pun that operates somewhat like the sentence, "This sentence has eight syllables." Stein provides a critique of her own practice in the only way available to her—in the guise of an amusement. The ontology of narrative art is not analyzable within the bounds of discursive language, it is not sayable in any serious possessive literal sense, but can dis-*play* through its own playful lapsus its ineliminable structural elements, its inviolable conventional limits, its immanent possibilities. It may be, as Walter Benjamin suggests, "that there is no better start for thinking than laughter. And, in particular, convulsion of the diaphragm usually provides better opportunities for thought than convulsion of the soul."[9] In this passage there are echos of Rabelais's theory of laughter as mis-rule, disrupting the authority of church and state, of Freud's *Jokes and Their Relations to the Unconscious* where the regalian power of language is disrupted by the witticism or "conceit" (pointe) by which the whole of its domination is annihilated in an instance by the challenge of non-sense. And, in the reference to the body, Benjamin comes provocatively close to Barthes and Kristeva's notion of laughter as libidinal license, the jouissance of the polymorphic, orgasmic body. Benjamin suggests that laughter may be a revolutionary strategy: "The class struggle, which is always present to a historian influenced by Marx, is a fight for the crude and the material things without which no refined and spiritual things could exist. Nevertheless, it is not in the form of the spoils which fall to the victor that the latter make their presence felt in the class struggle. They manifest themselves in this struggle as courage, humour, cunning, and fortitude."[10] In asking for the response of laughter Stein is engaging in a difficult operation; the reader must want, at least briefly, to emancipate himself from "normal" representation; he must recognize that he shares the same repressions in order to laugh. What is revealed by this revolutionary laughter is the "fictive" props of the social structure. What is asked for is a sensuous solidarity. Could the resistance to Stein's writing be evidence of an obsession with meaning, of an unfitness for anything but a privatized, depoliticized jouissance?

Sense and Non-sense

Stein's particular mode of foregrounding the materiality of language differs from that of her contemporaries whose experiments lead to the creation of neologisms. From the accusation of writing nonsense, even in the neutral meaning of the word, Stein should be exonerated. She did not use words in an intentionally referential way to say something "about" a particular subject, but they always retained the lexical meaning they carried in the English language. In spite of the 1929 "Proclamation" of *transition* (the issue in which *Four Saints* in *Three Acts* was first published) that every author "HAS THE RIGHT TO USE WORDS OF HIS OWN FASHIONING AND TO DISREGARD EXISTING GRAMMATICAL AND SYNTACTICAL LAWS." Stein's experiments did not lead to the creation of neologisms or to anything comparable to *zaum* or trans-rational language. As she explains her own methods in *The Autobiography of Alice B. Toklas*, her verbal revolution would erupt from within the English language: "She tried a bit inventing words but she soon gave that up. The english language was her medium and with the english language the task was to be achieved the problem solved. The use of fabricated words offended her, it was an escape into imitative emotionalism."[11] Freedom from meaning did not come so easily for Stein. "Of course you might say why not invent new names new languages," she writes in "Poetry and Grammar," as if to answer an imaginary interlocutor, "but that cannot be done. It takes a tremendous amount of inner necessity to invent even one word."[12]

Although Stein was interested in the presentational rather than the representational in language, she was not willing to take the short cut that neologisms provided. Conversely, her intensely immanent approach to language prevented her from attempting to break down the monological meaning system of language by overloading each signifier with multiple definitions as Joyce did. Joyce made the word elastic, both by abandoning at times its meaning, and by bringing out simultaneously *all* the meanings, dictionary or otherwise, it ever had in the English language or any other language. We will never find in Stein's writing a word such as Joyce's: (bababadalgharaghtakamminarronnkonnbronntonnerronntuonnthunntrovarrhounawnskawntoohoordenenthurnuk!) which can be "decoded" as an imitation of the sound of a thunderclap, composed of syllables of words meaning thunder from more than a dozen languages.[13] With patience, erudition and ingenuity Joyce can be understood. Stein claimed that Picasso once described Joyce as "an obscure writer all the world can understand."[14] For Stein this technique was merely a change of masters—Joyce was still bound by reference. Stein's writing derives its meaning from nothing external to the writing, but from her realization of what she presents in, rather than merely suggests by, her words. And that fact renders absurd any hermeneutic research into anything not presented in the words she writes down. "Miss Stein does not add to the already overwhelming dose of unassimilated facts and impressions which we all have to carry," the editors of *transition* announced and warned their readers not to attempt to "decode" her work as though it was a "species of modern Sanskrit." "Miss Stein has been reproached because she gave up adding to the great accumulation of human knowledge at an early age. Her greatness lies in this very fact. What is more a salutary than to be able to read without 'knowing' any more?"[15]

Stein discovered, during her experiment with what she called "the recreation of the word," that once anyone elects to use words, it is not possible to make no sense at all:

> I took individual words and thought about them until I got their weight and volume complete and put them down next to another word and at this time I found out very soon that there is no such thing as putting them together without sense. I made innumerable efforts to make words write without sense and found it impossible. Any human being putting down words had to make sense of them.[16]

These were the circumscribing limits which Stein imposed upon her writing. Stein's experiments constitute an essentially "immanent" approach to language, an exploration "within" language of the properties and potentials of language, an activity distinct from, but necessarily concomitant to, the use of language as a signifying system.

Stein's experiments with the signifying capacities of words, particularly in the 1911–1914 style of *Tender Buttons*, "Susie Asado," "Preciosilla," and "Portrait of Mabel Dodge at the Villa Curonia" which culminated in the lists of unrelated single words of *How to Write*, are similar to Tristan Tzara's techniques for writing a Dadaist poem:

TO MAKE A DADIST POEM
Take a newspaper.
Take some scissors.
Choose from this paper an article of the length you want to make your poem.
Cut out the article.
Next carefully cut out each of the words that makes up this article and put them all in a bag.
Shake gently.
Next take out each cutting one after the other.
Copy conscientiously in the order in which they left the bag.
The poem will resemble you.
And there you are — an infinitely original author of charming sensibility, even though unappreciated by the vulgar herd.[17]

These experiments bring out the distinction between reference and compositional game, between a pointing system and a self-ordering system. Even in the random arrangement of words, we can impose meaning — grammatical structures will be formed by chance and, in our predilection for meaning, we are able to construct analogies with grammatically correct statements. Although Stein experimented with ungrammatical writing, meaning (the position of a subject of enunciation) and significance (possible, plausible, or actual denotation) remains. But the semiotic process does not stop there. Instead of serving as the upper limits or goal of enunciation, the sentence-meaning-significance here acts as its lower limit or by-product. "Indeed, however empty this discourse many seem," Lacan observes

> it is so only if taken at its face value: that which justifies the remark of Mallarmé's, in which he compares the common use of language to the exchange of a coin whose obverse and reverse no longer bear any but effaced figures, and which people pass from hand to hand 'in silence.' This metaphor is enough to remind us that speech, even when almost completely worn out, retains its value as a *tessera.*
>
> Even if it communicates nothing, the discourse represents the existence of communication; even if it denies the evidence, it affirms that speech constitutes truth; even if it is intended to deceive. The discourse speculates on faith in testimony.[18]

The conveyance of thought has, as Stein says, nothing to do with writing; "write" and "right" have nothing to do with one another:

> It is only in history government, propaganda that it is of any importance if anybody is right about anything. Science well they never are right about anything not right enough so that science cannot go on enjoying itself as if it is interesting, which it is.... Master-pieces have always known that being right would not be anything because if they were right then it would not be as they wrote but as they thought and in a real master-piece there is no thought, if there were thought then there would be that they are right and in a master-piece you cannot be right, if you could it would be what you thought not what you do write.
> Write and right.
> Of course they have nothing to do with one another.[19]

The Materiality of The Matrix

Stein subjected her writing to a technical analysis more normal to linguistic rather than artistic investigation. "Gertrude Stein," she says of herself in *The Autobiography of Alice B. Toklas,* "always had a passion for exactitude" and a "definite impulse then and always toward elemental abstraction" (73). She scrutinized the shape and sound of words, parsed sentences, investigated the structure of narrative codes, analyzed the nature and function of nouns, verbs, pronouns, conjunctions, etc., and diagrammed the deep-structure (what she called "bottom nature") of characters as if they too were parts of speech. This desire to reduce every compositional component to its simplest paradigm is comparable to the way the early Cubists followed Cézanne's injunction to "treat nature by the sphere, cone, and cylinder." Each strata of her media (the visible configurations of word-sounds, the semantic units, and the representational narrative world itself) Stein brings to the surface and makes each in turn self-reflexively disclose its *mode of giveness.*

Stein was most preoccupied with the first stratum—the sensuous materiality of words. It is on this level—the materiality of the medium itself—that Stein's explorations have most in common with Cubist artists. The inclusion of words and letters in Cubist painting marked an important step in the articulation of the materiality of the flat two-dimensional canvas. As Georges Braque observed: "They were forms which could not be distorted because, being quite flat, the letters existed outside space and their presence in the painting, by contrast, enabled one to distinguish between objects situated in space and those outside it."[20] Stein gives her own version of the appearance of typography on the canvas: "Picasso in his early cubist pictures used printed letters as did Juan Gris to force the painted surface to measure up to something rigid, and the rigid thing was the printed word."[21] Both Braque's and Stein's comments refer to the materiality of the letter form. When the two-dimensionality of the painted surface is articulated—the existence of the canvas as an object is pointed out; but the physicality of the picture plane is only suggested until the medium of collage explicitly demonstrates it by having the *surface support actual objects.* Always the viewer is moving in and out of two realms of perception—what he "knows" to be the case, i.e., canvas, frame, paint, and what he is led to believe he is seeing—three-dimensional objects in space. Collage destroys the picture as illusionistic representation and draws attention to the concrete materiality of the canvas.

There is an important correlation between the introduction of typography into painting and the decrease in representation of analytic cubism. Pierre Guirraud in his book *Semiology* notes that "the poorer the mode of representation, the greater the codification of the signs."[22] It is just at the moment when the conventions of pictorial representation were breaking down—the figure is discernible but only barely—that the most highly codified sign system is introduced—that of language. The introduction of letters and words into painting asks that the viewer respond to an alien sign system—one that is wholly arbitrary, one in which meaning rests entirely on conventions of reception—and to make this response within the context of a sign system that is not considered to be arbitrary, that is, one that is thought to be able to provide visual counterparts to reality. In this way, the arrival of typography onto the canvas aligned the reading of the page and the painting. As if to humorously acknowledge the importance of this correlation for Stein, Picasso included a handpainted version of the calling card of "Miss Gertrude Stein" in *The Architects Table*, 1912 and later used Stein's actual calling card in a collage entitled *Still Life with Calling Card*, 1912.

In 1905 Picasso had made a series of wood-cuts—single line drawings of birds—which were almost identical to the Egyptian hieroglyphics he was studying at the time. Stein became extremely excited by what she understood to be the convergence of their respective art forms: "In the Orient calligraphy and the art of painting and sculpture have always been very nearly related, they resemble each other, they complete each other.... It was natural that the cubism of 1913 to 1917 revealed the art of calligraphy to him [Picasso], the importance of calligraphy seen as Orientals see it and not as Europeans see it.... In China the letters were something in themselves." This, according to Stein, Europeans never observed. "But for Picasso, a Spaniard, the art of writing, that is to say calligraphy, is an art."[23] Stein's own preoccupation with the "art" of writing made her acutely conscious of the look of a word or printed line on the page. At one point she announced, "I write entirely with my eyes. The words as seen by my eyes are the important words, and the ears and mouth do not count."[24] The possessive case apostrophe she refused to use because it spoiled the look of the word. Similarly, question marks, exclamation marks, and quotation marks "are ugly, they spoil the line of writing or the printing...."[25] For Stein these were shapes as well as symbols and should be judged accordingly. "The question mark is alright when it is all alone when it is used as a brand on cattle or when it could be used in decoration but connected with writing it is completely entirely uninteresting" (214).

Nevertheless, the semantic function is also a consideration in the inclusion or exclusion of words or punctuation marks. Periods are liked as much for their looks as for what they do. But the comma, "well at the most a comma is a poor period that it lets you stop and take a breath but if you want to take a breath you ought to know yourself that you want to take a breath" (221). Similarly, whole parts of speech are deemed functionally redundant or uninteresting. For a time she avoided nouns—"Things once they are named the name does not go on doing anything to them so why write in nouns" (210). Conjunctions are acceptable because they "work." Verbs and adverbs and prepositions are valued because of their potential for ambiguity.

> It is wonderful the number of mistakes a verb can make and that is equally true of its adverb. Besides being able to be mistaken and to make mistakes verbs can change to look like themselves or to look like something else. They are, so to speak on the move.... Then comes the thing that can of all things be most mistaken and they are prepositions. Prepositions can live one long life being really being nothing but absolutely nothing but mistaken and that makes them irritating if you feel that way about mistakes but certainly something that you can be continuously using and everlastingly enjoying [211].

As for using words as pure sound, Stein herself gives an account of the infinite resource of this component of language—one which she at times thought of as a temptation. "I found that I was for a little while very much taken with the beauty of the sounds as they came from me as I made them. This is a thing that may be at any time a temptation.... The strict discipline that I had given myself, the absolute refusal of never using a word that was not an exact word all through the Tender Buttons and what I may call the early Spanish and Geography and Play period finally resulted in things like Susie Asado and Preciosilla etc. in an extraordinary melody of words and a melody of excitement in knowing that I had done this thing."[26] Carl Van Vechten mentions in his preface to Stein's writings there is reason to believe these two poems paint a portrait and make an attempt to recapture the rhythm of the same flamenco dancer[29]:

> SUSIE ASADO
> Sweet sweet sweet sweet sweet tea.
> Susie Asado.
> Sweet sweet sweet sweet sweet tea.
> Susie Asado.
> Susie Asado which is a told tray sure.
> A lean on the shoe this means slips
> slips her.
> When the ancient light grey is clean it
> is yellow,
> it is a silver seller.
> This is a please this is a please there
> are the
> saids to jelly. These are the wets these
> say the sets
> to leave a crown to Incy.
> Incy is short for incubus.
> A pot. A pot is a beginning of a rare
> bit of trees.
> Trees tremble, the old vats are in bobbles,
> bobbles which
> shade and shove and render clean, render
> clean must.
> Drink pups.
> Drink pups drink pups lease a sash
> hold, see it
> shine and a bobolink has pins. It shows a
> nail.
> What is a nail. A nail is unison.
> Sweet sweet sweet sweet sweet tea.

If the poem is understood to be an attempt to limn the rhythms of flamenco dance, then the five emphatic beats with which the poem begins:

Sweét sweét sweét sweét sweét téa

may read as the stamping of the dancer's feet, punctuated by the click of the castanets and followed by the tripping rhythm:

Súsie//Aŝádò.

However, this poem is susceptible to various interpretations. Marjorie Perloff makes a case for the opening lines being the rapid, mincing movement of a

Japanese geisha girl gliding back and forth gracefully as she serves tea; further-more, she finds various semantic codes such as the Japanese sounding name "Susie Asado," "sweet tea," "slips hers" (pun on "slippers"), etc. to support this reading.[27] Obviously rhythm is not being used referentially either. "Susie-Asado" was the first Stein text set to music by Virgil Thomson. Thomson speaks of the freedom the poem's lack of reference gave the composer: "With meanings already abstracted, or absent, or so multiplied that choice among them was impossible, there was no temptation toward tonal illustration, say, of birdie babbling by the brook or heavy hangs my heart."[28]

Repetition

In the sound of words, in rhythm, and in repetition Stein found a regenerative potential for language. The poem for which she is best known—the rose poem—came about as a result of her frustration with the flatness of overworked nouns. As she said, "a noun is a name of anything by definition that is what it is and a name of anything is not interesting because once you know its name the enjoyment of naming it is over and therefore in writing prose names that is nouns are completely uninteresting."[29] There are ways of releasing a noun from this fixity and Making it New:

> But and that is a thing to be remembered you can love a name and if you love a name then saying that name any number of times only makes you love it more, more violently more persistently more tormentedly:

> When I said.
> A rose is a rose is a rose is a rose.
> And then later made that into a ring I
> made poetry and what did I do I caressed
> completely caressed and addressed a noun
>   [231].

Stein, in *The Autobiography of Alice B. Toklas* (137–138), mentions that the rose poem in circular form was printed in an early book (before 1914) by Carl Van Vechten and was applied to stationery, table napkins, plates, etc. by Alice. It is possible that Marcel Duchamp, whose name had been linked with Stein's in the scandal of the Armory Show and who met Stein in 1913, owes his famous female alias "Rrose Selavy" (Eros c'est la vie) to Stein's ubiquitous rose poem. Later, a contemporary artist, Carl Andre, exploited the plastic qualities of Stein's poem. "My plastic poem about the rose," Andre tells Hollis Frampton, "will not be printed in a blooming, petalled pattern":

roseroseroseroserose
roseroseroseroserose
roseroseroseroserose
roseroseroseroserose
roseroseroseroserose
roseroseroseroserose
roseroseroseroserose
roseroseroseroserose

I have typed the alphabet in consecutive and contiguous squares. I think you have seen the result. Painterly areas of various and contrasting values are generated. Miss Stein wrote: 'A rose is a rose, etc.' and Miss Stein is not to be put down lightly. The word 'rose' has a very different plastic appearance from the word 'violet.' The difference is, I think, worth exploiting.[30]

Andre, in priding himself on not shaping the poem into a representational rose, returns the poem to the traditional linearity of representational language. He did this perhaps to make more explicit the pun "rose/eros," a point which he claims Stein obfuscates.

The repetition of a noun will eventually cause its phonic property to override its semantic function. At the point the code becomes receptive to rhythm in opposition to meaning, language becomes invested with emotional significance. An important element of this cathected language is "the word perceived as word," a phenomenon in turn induced by the contest between rhythm and sign system. Stein fully understood the generative potential of repetition, particularly for writers writing in a "late" age:

Now listen. Can't you see that when the language was new—as it was with Chaucer and Homer—the poet could use the name of a thing and the thing was really there. He could say "O moon," "O sea," "O love," and the moon and the sea and love were really there. And can't you see that after hundreds of years had gone by and thousands of poems had been written, he could call on those words and find that they were just worn-out literary words. The excitingness of pure being had withdrawn from them; they were just rather stale literary words....

> Now listen! I'm no fool. I know that in daily life we don't go around saying "... is a ... is a ... is a ...." Yes, I'm no fool; but I think that in that line the rose is red for the first time in English poetry for a hundred years.[31]

This is Stein's refusal to sign the literary pact others have written for her, her refusal of what Barthes calls "this fatal character of the literary sign, which makes a writer unable to pen a word without taking a pose characteristic of an out-of-date, anarchic or imitative language...."[32] Repetition is her way of fighting against those "ancestral and all-powerful signs which, from the depths of a past foreign to him (sic), impose Literature on him (sic) like some ritual, not like a reconciliation" (86).

The Childish

Kandinsky in *Concerning the Spiritual in Art* (1912) touches on the potential of repetition which Stein would exploit:

> The apt use of a word (in its poetical sense), its repetition, twice, three times, or even more frequently, according to the need of the poem, will not only tend to intensify the internal structure but also bring out unsuspected spiritual properties in the word itself. Further, frequent repetition of a word (*a favorite game of children, forgotten in later life*) deprives the word of its external reference. Similarly, the symbolic reference of a designated object tends to be forgotten and only the sound is retained. We hear this pure sound, unconsciously perhaps, in relation to the concrete or immaterial object. But in the latter case pure sound exercises a direct impression on the soul. The soul attains to an objectless vibration, even more complicated, I might say more transcendent, than the reverberations released by the sound of a bell, a stringed instrument, or a fallen board. In this direction lie great possibilities for the literature of the future.[33]

This favorite game of children forgotten in later life recalls Kristeva's notion of the intonation, scansion, repetition, and rhythm which precedes the primary repression of desire in language. According to a number of psycho-linguistic studies of child language, concrete linguistic operations precede the acquisition of language and organize preverbal semiotic space according to logical categories distinct from the functioning of symbolic operations that depend on language as a sign system. This is a very different view from that of immanent semiotics, which explores meaning that is thought to be already there, and equally divergent from a Cartesian notion of language, which views thought as preconditioned by or even identical to natural factual data or else innate.

Studies of child language and certain kinds of speech disturbances such as aphasic regression render intelligible some of the peculiarities of Stein's style, in particular those characteristics most often pejoratively described as childish: the limited and simplistic vocabulary, the repetition of certain phrases or words which after a time take on different connotations because of the different contexts in which they occur, the manner in which these repeated words and phrases tend to dominate the entire passage, and the musicated language—often rather sing-song rhythms which result from this repetition.

Stein began what would be a life-long investigation of language while she was a student in William James' psychology class at Radcliffe. With Leon Solomons, Stein wrote two articles on the results of experiments they conducted in an attempt to realize unconscious or automatic writing by diverting the subject in the process of writing. These were published as "Motor Automatism" in the *Psychological Review* (September 1896 and May 1898). The psychological aspect of language was what motivated Stein to begin her career as a creative writer. She began by listening to the "sub-text" of everyday speech:

> I began to get enormously interested in hearing how everybody said the same thing over and over again until finally if you listened with great intensity you could hear it rise and fall and tell all that there was inside them, not so much by the actual words they said or the thoughts they had but the movement of their thoughts and words endlessly the same and endlessly different.[34]

In short, she is attending not to what people say, that is, their referential use of language, but to what she calls "the rhythm of anybody's personality." In *Melanctha* the characters repeat themselves over and over again in subtly differentiated versions of urban black speech:

> I don't see Melanctha why you should talk like you would kill yourself just because you're blue. I'd never kill myself Melanctha cause I was blue. I'd maybe kill somebody else but I'd never kill myself. If I ever killed myself Melanctha, it'd be by accident and if I ever killed myself by accident, Melanctha, I'd be awful sorry. And that certainly is the way you should feel it Melanctha, now you hear me, not just talking foolish like you always do. It certainly is only your way just always being foolish makes you all that trouble to come to you always now, Melanctha, and I certainly right well knows that.[35]

In an attempt to get at the "bottom nature" of her characters' language, Stein conducted an intensive analysis of what Freud specified as the two fundamental "processes" in the work of the unconscious: displacement and condensation. Roman Jakobson introduced these two processes into structural linguistics as the two axes of language—metaphor and metonymy, or selection and combination:

> The development of a discourse may take place along two different semantic lines: one topic may lead to another either through their similarity or their contiguity. The metaphorical way would be the more appropriate term for the first case and the metonymic for the second, since they find their most condensed expression in metaphor and metonymy respectively. In aphasia one or other of these two processes is blocked—an effect which makes the study of aphasia particularly illuminating.[36]

In normal speech both of these two processes are operative; the speaker is continually making selections from the "filing cabinet of prefabricated representations" and combining these linguistic units into sentences according to the syntactic system of the language he is using. In aphasia one or the other of these two operations is impaired. The study of the effect of this blockage has established several laws of language acquisition because, according to Jakobson, aphasic regression shows the child's development in reverse.

In aphasics suffering from a similarity disorder, that is, those with problems in the selection and substitution of words, Jakobson notes that certain key words such as the subject of the sentence tend to be omitted, while words with an inherent reference to the context, like pronouns and pronominal adverbs and words serving merely to construct the context, such as connectives and auxiliaries, are particularly prone to survive. It is difficult for aphasics suffering from this type of disorder to begin a conversation, but once the problem of beginning has been overcome, the flow of words tends to be of indefinite length—sentences are conceived as sequels to be supplied for antecedent sentences and the use of the same word over and over again causes a drastic reduction in vocabulary. Characteristics of the aphasic defect in the "capacity of naming" are apparent in Stein's early prose writing, for example in this segment of the portrait of Picasso:

> One whom some were certainly following was one who was completely charming. One whom some were certainly following was one who was charming. One whom some were following was one who was completely charming. One whom some were following was one who was certainly completely charming. Some were certainly following and were certain that the one they were then following was one working and was one bringing out of himself then something. Some were certainly following and were certain that the one they were then following was one bringing out of himself then something that was coming to be a heavy thing, a solid thing and a complete thing.[37]

Specific nouns are replaced by general ones such as "thing" or "it" or "one" because they are identifiable from the context and therefore appear superfluous to the patient, as they do to Stein:

> A noun is a name of anything, why after a thing is named write about it. . . . As I say a noun is a name of a thing, and therefore slowly if you feel what is inside the thing you do not call it by the name by which it is known. Everybody knows that by the way they do when they are in love and a writer should always have that intensity of emotion about whatever is the object about which he writes. And therefore and I say it again more and more one does not use nouns.[38]

Sign systems other than language depend in varying degrees on the processes of combination and selection. Jakobson cites the example of the "manifestly metonymical orientation of cubism, where the object is transformed into a set of synecdoches; the surrealist painters responded with a patently metaphorical attitude" (92). Guillaume Apollinaire in *Les peintres cubistes* (1913) noted the connection between the geometrical relational units of Cubism and grammar in writing:

> The new artists have been attacked for their preoccupation with geometry. Yet geometrical figures are the essence of drawing. Geometry, the science of space, its dimensions and relations, has always determined the norms and rules of painting. . . .
> The new painters do not propose, any more than did their predecessors, to be geometers. *But it may be said that geometry is to the plastic arts what grammar is to the art of the writer.*

Stein's refusal to name the subject of her sentence, her avoidance of nouns and adjectives and her abnormally frequent use of pronouns, copulas, adverbs, conjunctions and other syncategorematic words (words that cannot be used by themselves as a term, but only in conjunction wth other words: adverbs, prepositions or conjunctions; "all," "some" or "no"—which Jakobson describes as "purely grammatical relational units") may be understood as the verbal equivalent of the early Cubists' preoccupation with geometry, a preoccupation they inherited from Cézanne.

> Everything I have done has been influenced by Flaubert and Cézanne and this gave me a new feeling about composition. Up to that time composition had consisted of a central idea to which everything else was an accompaniment and separate but was not an end in itself, and Cézanne conceived the idea that in composition one thing was as important as another. . . . That impressed me enormously and it impressed me so much that I began to write *Three Lives* under this influence and this idea of composition.[39]

The abolition of the central idea of a painting like the omission of key words in a sentence produces a decentralized composition:

> The composition was not a composition in which there was one man in the centre surrounded by a lot of other men but a composition that had neither a beginning nor an end, a composition of which the corner was as important as another corner, in fact the composition of cubism.[40]

Stein claimed that this same principle of composition—the inner balance of equivalent components—should also govern sentence production: "Sentences are contained within themselves and anything really contained within itself has no beginning or middle or ending."[41] More specifically, Stein's over-use of nonreferential internally-relational words can be linked to the dominant technique of analytic Cubism called facetting—a modification of Cézanne's famous *passage* developed to reconcile the modalities of volume and plane. Those arbitrarily created facets or tiny overlapping planes were applied equally to the objects on the canvas as to the spaces between the objects. They did not serve to depict the object, but were purely relational in effect. Like Stein's overused syncategorematic language, facetting functions syntactically, not semantically.[42] Stein was fully conscious of the purpose of these nonmimetic relational units: "They were more important than anything else," she said. "They lived *by and in* themselves. He [Picasso] painted his picture not by means of his objects but by the lines."[43]

Once this contiguous mode of composition had been exploited to the point of near abstraction, Stein and the Cubists began to work along the vertical or metaphorical axis of their discourse. Stein began to write what she called poetry:

> In *The Making of Americans* ... I said I had gotten rid of nouns and adjectives as much as possible by the method of living in adverbs in verbs in pronouns, in adverbial clauses written or implied and in conjunctions.
>
> But and after I had gone as far as I could in those long sentences and paragraphs ... I then began very short things I resolutely realized nouns and decided not to get around them but to meet them, *to handle in short to refuse them by using them* and in that way my real acquaintance with poetry was begun.[44]

And she goes on to make the following very deft distinction between prose and poetry:

> Prose is ... the essential balance that is made inside something that combines the sentence and the paragraph. ... Now if that is what prose is and that undoubtedly is what prose is you can see that prose is bound

to be made up more of verbs adverbs prepositions prepositional clauses and conjunctions than nouns. . . .

　　But what is poetry. . . .

　　Poetry is I say essentially a vocabulary just as prose is essentially not.

　　And what is the vocabulary of which poetry absolutely is. It is a vocabulary entirely based on the noun as prose is essentially and determinately and vigorously not based on the noun [136].

In poetry, then, word selection is more important than in prose where words are linked contextually. Jakobson makes the same distinction between poetry and prose:

> The principle of similarity underlies poetry; the metrical parallelism of lines or the phonic equivalence of rhyming words prompts the question of semantic similarity and contrast. . . . Prose, on the contrary, is forwarded essentially by contiguity. Thus, for poetry, metaphor and for prose, metonymy is the line of least resistance [95–96].

Language forwarded essentially by metaphor or selection can, in extreme cases, result in the opposite type of aphasia—"contexture deficiency" or "contiguity disorder." The *combination* of linguistic units into a higher degree of complexity causes difficulty and the features of similarity disorders are reversed. "The syntactical rules organizing words into a higher unit are lost; this loss, called AGRAMMATISM, causes the degeneration of the sentence into a mere 'word heap'" (84). Word order becomes chaotic, words with a purely grammatical (i.e., connective) function like prepositions, conjunctions and pronouns disappear, but the subject tends to remain, and in extreme cases each sentence consists of a single "kernel subject word." This type of aphasia "tends to give rise to infantile one-sentence utterances and one-word sentences. Only a few longer, stereotyped 'ready made' sentences manage to survive" (86). This is a precise description of Stein's second mode of composition which she called poetry. In her early prose writing, the chief stylistic interest is syntax, but in *Tender Buttons* the central concern is diction, the selection of words based on association:

> I began to discover the names of things, that is not discover the names but discover the things the things to see the things to look at and in so doing I had of course to name them not to give them new names but to see that I could find out how to know that they were by their names or by replacing their names. And how was I to do so. They had their names and naturally I called them by the names they had and in doing so having begun looking at them I called them by their names with passion and that made poetry, I did not mean it to make poetry but it did, it made Tender Buttons.[45]

And nouns returned with a vengeance:

APPLE

Apple plum, carpet steak, seed clam, colored wine, calm seen, cold cream, best shake, potato, potato and no no gold work with pet, a green seen is called bake and change sweet is bready, a little piece a little piece please.

A little piece please. Came again to the presupposed and ready eucalyptus tree, count out sherry and ripe plates and little corners of a kind of ham. This is use.[46]

The return of nouns, however, did not result in a return to referential language, in part because the nouns used are not descriptive of the object to which they ostensibly refer. This phase of Stein's writing, as in "contexture deficiency" aphasia, tends to be characterized by what Jakobson calls "metaphorical mistakes": "To say what a thing is, is to say what a thing is like: . . . 'Spyglass' for 'microscope,' or 'fire' for 'gaslight' are typical examples of such quasi-metaphoric expressions" (72). Stein's "Apple" poem is intelligible (with some exceptions such as "carpet steak") as a series of quasi-metaphoric expressions relating to apples and various dishes made from apples. Stein describes the discovery of this mode of writing:

I became more and more excited about how words which were the words that made whatever I looked at look like itself were not the words that had in them any quality of description. This excited me very much at that time.

And the thing that excited me so very much at that time and still does is that the word or words that make what I looked at be itself were always words that to me very exactly related themselves to that thing the thing at which I was looking, but as often as not had as I say nothing whatever to do with what any words do that described that thing.[47]

The relationship between the word and its referent becomes much more ambiguous in other passages of *Tender Buttons* when the words are not made to combine with one another in normal syntactical structures:

CUPS

Cups crane in. They need a pet oyster, they need it so hoary and nearly choice. The best slam is utter. Nearly be freeze.

Why is a cup a stir and a believe. Why is it so seen.

A cup is readily shaded, it has in between no sense that is to say music, memory, musical memory.

Peanuts blame, a half sand is holey and nearly [182].

Sentences end with adverbs or adjectives or just when a subordinate clause is introduced. Stein's writing becomes mere "word heaps" with only "ready-made" or accidental syntax:

A NEW CUP AND SAUCER
Enthusiastically hurting a clouded yellow bud and saucer, enthusiastically so is the bit in the ribbon [165].

A CUTLET
A blind agitation is manly and uttermost [166].

Eventually Stein abandoned syntax altogether. In much of the writing that followed *Tender Buttons* she did away with the conventional horizontal format of the sentence altogether and made lists of words or phrases in vertical columns on the page.

Stein's statement about the arbitrary relationship between words and the object described is comparable to her statement on representation in painting—the interest does not inhere in the object depicted, but in the materiality of the work of art:

> . . . any oil painting whether it is intended to look like something and looks like it or whether it is intended to look like something and does not look like it it really makes no difference, the fact remains that for me it has achieved an existence in and for itself, it exists on as being an oil painting on a flat surface and it has its own life and like it or not there it is and I can look at it and it does hold my attention.[48]

More specifically, the structural premises governing Stein's second style of composition, or poetry, are comparable to those governing the second or synthetic phase of Cubism. Juan Gris, who began painting only in 1911, in the later, synthetic phase of Cubism, distinguishes between his mode of composition and Cézanne's. Like Stein, he sees the differences in compositional mode as analogous to that which distinguishes poetry and prose:

> Cézanne turns a bottle into a cylinder, but I begin with a cylinder and create an individual of a special type: I make a bottle—a particular bottle—out of a cylinder. Cézanne tends towards architecture, I tend away from it. That is why I compose with abstractions (colors) and make my adjustments when these colors have assumed the form of objects. For example, I make a composition with a white and black and make adjustments when the white has become a paper and the black a shadow: what I mean is that I adjust the white so that it becomes a shadow.
> This painting is to the other what poetry is to prose.[49]

Synthetic Cubism and the discoveries precipitating the shift to Synthetic Cubism—*papier collé* and collage—are characterized by the disappearance of the relational or "syntactical" (what Gris calls architectural) device of facetting:

objects are no longer assemblages of fragments, but are given their essential outline; color is reinstated, but not necessarily used to further the representation of an object; and *papier collé* and collage function polysemously on a number of levels simultaneously. They are colored, pictorial shapes which represent or suggest certain objects in the picture by analogies of color and texture or by the additon of keys or clues, and they exist as themselves; that is to say, one is always conscious of them as solid, tactile pieces of extraneous matter incorporated into the picture and emphasizing its material existence. Around 1913 to 1914 Picasso and Braque, as Edward Fry notes, "never tied their forms to a specific object, save when in collage a real object stood for itself and for the class of all similar objects. In the *papiers collés* and, later, in the fused signs of synthetic cubism, the forms chosen were invented, not copied from nature; and this product of intuitive invention differed fundamentally from the Cézannian composite form."[50]

In Braque's *Still Life With Guitar* 1912–1915, for example, the two strips of paper have a purely pictorial function; they are broad, flat planes of color (blue and brown) which serve to establish the basic composition of the picture. The blue strip with the hole serves to represent the central part of the guitar while the imitation wood-graining of the second strip mimetically depicts the wood from which the guitar is constructed. At the same time, they are fragments of paper attached to canvas. Thus iconic elements reappear on the canvas of this period, just as referential words returned in Stein's poetry, but in both cases the syntactical/semantic disruptions preclude the referent from signifying in the mode customary to their media.

During this phase of her writing Stein relied heavily upon "ready-made" or previously combined familiar lexical units: copy book phrases, nursery rhymes, fragments of plays and various forms of phatic language: formulatic language which functions as "filler" rather than transmitting information – The kind of "filler" we engage in when we say things like: "How do you do?" "Fine day isn't it?" etc. The same curiosity in exploring unorthodox technical procedures and the ability to see the aesthetic possibilities in the quotidian material of the verbal environment relate this aspect of Stein's writing to the collage and *papiers collé* of Cubism which in turn can be seen as the precursor to the Ready-mades of Dada, and to the Surrealists' *objets trouvés*. In Picasso's *Still Life With Violin and Fruit* (1913), *papiers collés* function alternately as ready-made and purely arbitrary signs. Fragments of newsprint from *Le Journal* are used to signify literally a newspaper on a table. Elsewhere on the canvas, newspaper fragments are given purely arbitrary significance and at the bottom, a large piece of newsprint functions both as an abstract compositional element and as a sign for the tablecloth. In the upper right hand corner "ready-made" fruit, five illusionistic color reproductions of fruit, are incorporated into the composition by being placed in a bowl and transformed only in so far as they are assimilated into a new context. The ready-made aspect extends to the implications of the newspaper captions: "La vie sportive" and "[App]ARI-TION."

Puns, collage, certain uses of *papier collé* and ready-mades function to convey meaning only in order to abolish it the more completely. They are succinct referential denials of reference. Octavio Paz, in his analysis of Marcel Duchamp's ready-mades equates the pun and the ready-made in terms of their gesture—the destruction of meaning and, what is the same thing, the idea of value:

> The Readymades are anonymous objects that the artist's gratuitous gesture, the mere fact of choosing them, converts into works of art. At the same time this gesture does away with the notion of art object. The essence of the act is contradiction, it is the plastic equivalent of the pun. As the latter destroys meaning, the former destroys the idea of value. The Readymades are not anti-art, like so many modern creations but rather *an-artistic*. Neither art nor anti-art, but something in between, indifferent, existing in a void.... It would be senseless to argue about their beauty or ugliness, firstly because they are beyond beauty and ugliness, and secondly because they are not creations but signs, questioning or negating the act of creation. The Readymade does not postulate a new value: it is a jibe at what we call valuable. It is criticism in action: a kick at the work of art ensconced on its pedestal of adjectives.[51]

The Pleasures of Merely Circulating

Puns produce another mode of textual irruption. By their semantic play they add a vertical dimension to the horizontal narrative progression:

> But, while the time-structure of the narrative is the product of an *irreversible, diachronic, cumulative synthesis*, the time-structure of the pun is the product of a synchronic, instantaneous unity; like metaphor, of which it is a species, the pun spawns a manifold, or polyphony, of meanings, simultaneously co-present. Being a cacophonous eruption on the linguistic surface, the singing of the pun inevitably disturbs the linear, unfolding temporality of the narrative progression. Together with pure sonorities and optical constructions, it produces nooks and crannies, bubbles, cracks, stains, and washes on the conventional plain surface of the linguistic canvas.... The good pun is not merely the dead trace, or pale shadow, of thought, but the living, self-moving motion of thought; it is language speaking by itself singing new meanings into beauty.[52]

Thus the pun by calling attention to itself as language causes a break in the production of meaning and brings into question the narratively depicted world, revealing the contingencies and lacunae in the depths of representation.

It is the break in the text through which the reader experiences language invested with pleasure, where the orderly linguistic purpose is subverted and the reader partakes in the production of signification.

As Barthes points out in his analysis of narrative plots, the proairetic and hermeneutic codes—codes of action, codes of enigmas and answers—are irreversible: their interpretation is determined linearly, in sequence, in one direction. What motivates us as readers to pursue the meanderings of what E.M. Forster describes as that "dull, unlovely worm of time"—the story, is the desire to know "what happens next." What motivates us to follow the unfolding of plot, based as it is on causality (the significant interconnection of events) is the expectation of meaning, the answer to the question "why?" which the plot posits. Ultimately, what motivates the reader is the expectation of the end, since for Barthes meaning (in the classical readerly text) resides in full predication, completion of the codes of signification. Inquiries into the function of the end, as Frank Kermode has shown in his study of formal closure, have to do with the human end, with death. Or as Kristeva puts it: "As long as the son pursues meaning in a story or through narrative, even if it eludes him, as long as he persists in his search he narrates in the name of Death."[53] In a convergent argument, Walter Benjamin claims that all narration is obituary in that life acquires definable meaning only at, and through, death: "The nature of the character in a novel cannot be presented any better than is done in this statement, which says that the meaning of his life is revealed in his death. But the reader of a novel actually does look for human beings from whom he derives the 'meaning of life.' Therefore he must, no matter what, know in advance that he will share their figurative death—the end of the novel—but preferably their actual one.... *What draws the reader to the novel is the hope of warming his shivering life with a death he reads* about."[54] Thus, the reader has quite literally become a *consumer* who feeds on the vitality offered by sacrificed characters. "Both the reading of novels and the analysis of character are acts of cannibalism at a metaphoric level; the ultimate aim of the activity is to suck the final marrow of meaning from the perfectly exposed innards of a perfectly executed figure."[55] It is just for this reason that Barthes rejects the realist epistemology in which the reader's role is that of consumer of the writer's product, and where both are motivated by a desire for the end. He favors instead the "writerly" text where the desire is not for the end but to put off the signified—the moment of closure, of ideological fixity—for as long as possible, to stay within process, the infinite play of meanings.

Stein makes the same choice. Her entire work can be seen as an attempt to circumvent the end, the closure which is implied in the capitulation to the "Law of the Father." "What is the use of being a little boy if you are to be a man what is the use," she whimsically asks. Once she extricated herself from any vestigial gestures of homage to a reality which has already been written for her, her writing becomes "a mode of Eros," or as one critic put it "a cubist

jou." Her whimsical statements cover her shrewd awareness of the consequences of doing otherwise: "Writing is neither remembering nor forgetting
neither beginning or ending. Being dead is not end it is being dead and being
dead is something."[56] This aphorism is the *modus vivendi* of her writing and the
rationale for her famous "continuous present"—for to circumvent closure it is
also necessary to give up the idea of origin; the teleological assumptions of narrative are dismantled along with its ideological presuppositions. "In writing the
thing that is the difficulty is the question of confusing time."[57] She was
bothered always by the fact that in any narrative there is both a time in which
the story takes place and another time in which the story is told—the difference
between living and narrating:

> I wrote a story as a story, that is the way I began, and slowly I realized
> this confusion, a real confusion, that in writing a story one had to be
> remembering. . . . It is this element of remembering that makes novels so
> soothing. But and that was the thing I was gradually finding out—
> realizing the existence of living beings actually existing did not have in
> it any element of remembering and so the time of existing was not the
> same as in the novels that were soothing.
> And yet time and identity is what you tell about as you create only while
> you create they do not exist.
> And so it is never necessary to say anything again as remembering but
> it is always said again because every time it is so it is so it is so (181).

Without closure there is no meaning. In *The Making of Americans* we are
confronted with the interminable, with a modern Scheherezade for whom
repetition is the stay of execution. The teleological assumptions of narrative
are dismantled along with its ideological presuppositions—for to circumvent
closure it is also necessary to give up the idea of origin. And the tale that is
repeatedly told is the story of a "text" that writes about itself in the act of
writing. The whole project is to repeat, "to go on now giving all of the description of how repeating comes to have meaning, how it forms itself, how one
must distinguish the different meanings in repeating."[58] And the reader's role
is to reread. "Those who fail to reread," as Barthes enigmatically puts it, "are
obliged to read the same story everywhere . . . rereading is no longer consump-
tion, but *play* (that play which is the return of the different)."[59] And as one
rereads *The Making of Americans* one reads this story:

> Once an angry man dragged his father along the ground through his own
> orchard. "Stop!" cried the groaning old man at last, "Stop! I did not drag
> my father beyond this tree."

"Every writer born," Barthes says, "opens within himself the trial of literature,
but if he condemns it he always grants it a reprieve which literature turns to

use in order to reconquer him."[60] But Stein never grants this putative father a reprieve. By the time one rereads *The Making of Americans* the "Law of the Father" is in a total shambles. "The tremendous cultural revolution implied by this interior revolution of technique tickles the very heart and liver of a man, makes him feel good," William Carlos Williams says of Stein's style. "Good, that is, if he isn't too damned tied to his favorite stupidities. That's why he laughs. His laugh is the first acknowledgement of liberation."[61] In this risible era of the New Right, libertarian laughter may be the only break, the only pleasure to be found in the plot being formulated for us. It may be that this revolutionary laughter is what really *enables* us to face anew—every year, every hour—what Hannah Arendt calls "the elementary problems of human living together."

Notes

1. John Cage, *Silence* (Cambridge, Mass.: M.I.T. Press, 1961), 93.

2. Kenneth Rexroth, *Birds in the Bush* (New York: New Directions, 1959), 10.

3. Jan Mukarovský, "Standard Language and Poetic Language," *A Prague School Reader on Aesthetics, Literary Structure and Style*, ed. Paul L. Garvin (Washington: Georgetown Univ. Press, 1964), 23.

4. José Ortega y Gasset, *The Dehumanization of Art*, trans. Willard A. Trask (Garden City, New York: Doubleday, 1956), 10.

5. Roland Barthes, "The Last Word on Robbe-Grillet," *Critical Essays* (Evanston: Northwestern Univ. Press, 1972), 199.

6. Gertrude Stein, "Composition as Explanation," *Selected Writings of Gertrude Stein*, ed. Carl Van Vechten (New York: Random House, 1946), 453.

7. This phrase is from David Michael Levin, "The Novelhood of the Novel: The Limits of Representation and the Modernist Discovery of Presence," *Chicago Review* (Spring, 1977), 88. Levin's essay is a central document in this context.

8. Kristeva includes a cryptic, but provocative footnote on this subject: "It seems that what is persistently being called 'interior monologue' is the most indomitable way in which an entire civilization conceives itself as identity, as organized chaos, and finally, as transcendence. Yet, this 'monologue' probably exists only in texts that pretend to reconstitute the so-called physical reality of 'verbal flux.' Western man's state of 'interiority' is thus a limited literary effect (confessional form, continuous psychological speech, automatic writing). In a way, then, Freud's 'Copernican' revolution (the discovery of the split within the subject) put an end to the fiction of an internal voice by positing the fundamental principles governing the subject's radical exteriority in relation to, and within, language." *Desire in Language* (New York: Columbia Univ. Press, 1980), 80.

9. Walter Benjamin, "The Author as Producer," *Reflections: Essays, Aphorisms, Autobiographical Writings*, ed. Peter Demetz (New York: Harcourt Brace Jovanovich, 1978), 235.

10. Walter Benjamin, *Illuminations*, ed. Hannah Arendt, trans. Harry Zohn (New York: Schocken Books, 1969), 254–255.

11. Gertrude Stein, *The Autobiography of Alice B. Toklas* (New York: Vintage Books, 1933), 119.

12. Gertrude Stein, "Poetry and Grammar," *Lectures in America* (New York: Random House, 1935), 237–238.

13. This was decoded by the editors of *transition*, 3 (June, 1927), 174.

14. *Autobiography*, 212.

15. "K.O.R.A.A.," *transition*, 3 (June, 1927), 176.

16. Gertrude Stein, "A Transatlantic Interview 1946," *A Primer for the Gradual Understanding of Gertrude Stein*, ed. Robert Haas (Los Angeles: Black Sparrow Press, 1971), 18.

17. Tristan Tzara, *Seven Dada Manifestos*, trans. Barbara Wright (London: Calder, 1977), 59.

18. Jacques Lacan, *Écrits*, trans. Alan Sheridan (New York: W.W. Norton, 1977), 43.

19. Gertrude Stein, *The Geographical History of America* (1933; rpt. New York: Vintage Books, 1973), 198–199.

20. Georges Braque, cited in John Golding, *Cubism: A History and Analysis, 1908–1914* (New York: Harper & Row, 1968), 93.

21. *Autobiography*, 92.

22. Pierre Guirraud, *Semiology* (London & Boston: Routledge and Kegan Paul, 1975), 40.

23. Gertrude Stein, *Gertrude Stein on Picasso*, ed. Edward Burns (New York: Liveright, 1970), 48–53.

24. Stein, *A Primer for the Gradual Understanding of Gertrude Stein*, 34.

25. Stein, "Poetry and Grammar," 215.

26. Gertrude Stein, "Portraits and Repetition," *Lectures in America*, 196–197.

27. Marjorie Perloff, "Poetry as Word-System: The Art of Gertrude Stein," *The American Poetry Review* (Sept.–Oct., 1979), 34. The scansion of the poem follows that of Perloff's.

28. Virgil Thomson, *Virgil Thomson* (New York: Knopf, 1966), 90.

29. Stein, "Poetry and Grammar," 231.

30. Carl André and Hollis Frampton, *12 Dialogues: 1962–1963* (Halifax: The Press of the Nova Scotia College of Art, 1980), 38.

31. Stein, *Writing and Lectures 1911–45*, ed. Patricia Meyerowitz (London: Owen, 1967), 7.

32. Roland Barthes, *Writing Degree Zero*, trans. Annette Lavers and Colin Smith (Boston: Beacon Press, 1970), 84.

33. Wassily Kandinsky, *Concerning the Spiritual in Art* (1912: rpt. New York: Witterborn, Schultz, 1947), 34. Italics mine.

34. Gertrude Stein, "The Gradual Making of *The Making of Americans*," *Lectures in America*, 38.

35. Gertrude Stein, *Three Lives* (New York: Random House, 1909), 226.

36. Roman Jakobson, "Two Aspects of Language and Two Types of Linguistic Disturbances," in Jakobson, Morris and Halle, *Fundamentals of Language* (The Hague: Mouton, 1956), 90. For a book length discussion of Jakobson's theories as they apply to Stein's writing see Randa Dubnick, *The Structure of Obscurity: Gertrude Stein, Language and Cubism* (Urbana and Chicago: University of Illinois Press, 1984).

37. Stein, "Picasso," *Selected Writings*, 293.

38. Stein, "Poetry and Grammar," 209–210.

39. Gertrude Stein, "A Transatlantic Interview," 15.

40. Stein, "Picasso," 119.

41. Gertrude Stein, "Lecture 2," *Narration* (Chicago: Univ. of Chicago), 20.

42. Both Wendy Steiner and John Malcom Brinnin discuss the parallels between analytic and synthetic cubism and Stein's stylistic changes. Wendy Steiner, *Exact*

Resemblance to Exact Resemblance: The Literary Portraiture of Gertrude Stein (New Haven: Yale Univ. Press, 1978). John Malcolm Brinnin, *The Third Rose: Gertrude Stein and Her World* (Boston: Little, Brown, 1959).

43. Stein, *Gertrude Stein on Picasso*, 43.

44. Stein, "Poetry and Grammar," 134. To name something is to cause it to enter the realm of signification. Stein devised various modes of "refusal" to undermine those activities which "give meaning." In *A Novel of Thank You* she makes naming a totally arbitrary activity in which "Everybody is named Etienne. Everybody is named Charles. Everybody is named Alice" (New Haven: Yale Univ. Press, 1958), 43.

45. Stein, "Poetry and Grammar," 235.

46. Stein, "Tender Buttons," *Writing and Lectures*, 181.

47. "Portraits and Repetition," 191–192.

48. "Pictures," *Lectures in America*, 61.

49. Juan Gris, cited in Herschel B. Chipp, *Theories of Modern Art* (Los Angeles: Univ. of California, 1968), 274.

50. Edward Fry, *Cubism* (London: Thames and Hudson, 1966), 39.

51. Octavio Paz, *Marcel Duchamp: Appearance Stripped Bare*, trans. Rachel Phillips and Donald Gardner (New York: Viking, 1978), 21–22.

52. Levin, 99.

53. Kristeva, *Desire in Language*, 151.

54. Walter Benjamin, "The Storyteller: Reflections on the Work of Nikolai Leskov," *Illuminations*, ed. Hannah Arendt, trans. Harry Zohn (New York: Schocken Books, 1969), 100–101.

55. This is a comment made by Dale E. Peterson in his analysis of Nabokov's *Invitation*: Literature as Execution," *PMLA*, Vol. 96, No. 5 (1981), 831. Peterson also provides an analysis of Benjamin's essay.

56. Stein, *The Geographical History of America*, 150.

57. Stein, "Portraits and Repetition," 189.

58. Stein, *The Making of Americans* (Paris, 1925); condensed ed. (New York: Harcourt, Brace, 1934), 294.

59. Barthes, *S/Z*, 16.

60. Barthes, *Writing Degree Zero*, 86–87.

61. William Carlos Williams, "A 1 Pound Stein," *Selected Essays of William Carlos Williams* (New York: New Directions, 1954), 163.

Why Gertrude Stein

Dick Higgins

The assumption about Gertrude Stein is that she's historically important, somehow, but also somehow beside the point. Her style is said to be her message, and elaborate theories of process are made up about this. *They say* that apart from her style, her work reads like "My Day," Eleanor Roosevelt's old newspaper column. *They say* it's vacuous, that no individual work stands out. Its interest is to the chroniclers who make lists of innovations, and her great achievement is "literary cubism." Socially, *they say*, she was a sybarite keeping a salon for the gilded expatriates from the USA who sparkled around France in the 1920's and 1930's, a great personality but not quite a serious writer, a curiosity who applied Jamesian psychology and Bergsonian philosophy to her own weird literary epistemology, perhaps she was a crazy feminist but certainly she had a charlatan element in her—that's what *they say*, the standardists and going thing people, who praise her with their lips while attacking her with their guts. Now I happen to be somewhere else: I see her as the most important writer between Matthew Arnold and Bertolt Brecht, I'd like to point out a few viewing points along the way to my opinion.

Just to poke into the Stein books that I published at Something Else Press, let's see what's there, not in depth (that'd take a pretty big book), but in probe. There are four to start with: *The Making of Americans, Geographies and Plays, Lucy Church Amiably* and *Matisse Picasso and Gertrude Stein*, and *A Book Concluding With As a Wife Has a Cow*. That was a good set to start with. It's also the nave of that female gothic cathedral that came to call on our time.

The Making is a "great novel," which, ostensibly, nobody can read; it was patronized and legendized, quoted and referred to a lot, abridged and issued in 1/4 length (with about 1/4 quality, though Stein was consulted about the abridgement), was crucified, dead and buried. On the third day—three decades later—it rose again in our unabridged edition and then in Harcourt Brace's shorter one, which most certainly didn't ascend into heaven, in spite of its charming passage about butterflies (irrelevant to the rest of the text), spied out

Reprinted from *A Dialectic of Centuries* (1978) by permission of the author. Copyright © 1978 by Dick Higgins.

by Bernard Faÿ in an early draft and edited into the wee version. The small version seems to be mostly about language and about the Hersland family. The large version is about thought, attacking the concept of national "experience" and differences, not by saying they don't exist but that by stroking and caressing the ideas can verge. Thinking becomes exciting as this process expands the reader's feelings about these cumulative details, as he or she duplicates the experience in his or her mind. Marathon readings of *The Making* have become an annual feature of the New York New Year's scene.

Geographies and Plays comes from the 'teens and early 'twenties while the "complete" version of *The Making of Americans* comes from 1909–1912. Actually, *The Making* will probably never be done "complete," since it exists in four different versions (at the Yale Library), dating from 1904 to 1916, quite different and totalling thousands upon thousands of manuscript pages (Stein wrote fast). But Stein was constantly working, thinking, planning the entire cosmology of the arts. She had a fragmented, grandiose concept of theater—a sort of instant theater, pageant-like but nonnarrative, like the more imagistic and disciplined sort of happenings. These were her plays. Spoken arias to be orchestrated among sets of imagistic characters. No symbols, climaxes, or authenticated archaisms. Plenty of costumes—and please, proscenium arches. Lots of arches, even, maybe. But an isolation of events, to be treated musically, and scored among the available voices. On Broadway *Four Saints in Three Acts* became a hit. Off-Broadway, likewise with *Dr. Faustus Lights the Lights* and *A Curtain Raiser*. People can feel this work, even in the version in which it has become best known, though they don't know why. Actually, such vintage "plays" as are in *Geographies and Plays* have never been done in a Steinian way, so far as I know. If you want to know the meaning of a word in Stein, look it up. Then mix up the various definitions and take any one at random—or look for a common denominator. Her plays are games, kid stuff, traditional theater, and goodness knows what else. Milking them for impact works with only a few (*Four Saints* and *Daniel Webster*—the last not currently available, it's in an old *New Directions* annual). The way to do them would be choreographically, not dramatically. Joy: no climaxes. And no production numbers. Just pure—coaxing, stroking.

The Geographies are stories that describe situations, environments: inventories of available events. They do not have anything to do, necessarily, with national things or geopolitics or topography. You can have a geography of the mind, and do: probably the finest of Gertrude Stein's philosophical writings is *The Geographical History of America*, a sustained inquiry in which she wonders who she is and how she knows it, based on the dame who went to market (in the nursery rhyme) her eggs for to sell, who fell asleep on the king's highway (so much for manly power), thieves came by and cut her petticoats away, and when she came by, back home, her doggie barked at her, and she knew "this couldn't be I, because my little dog didn't know me." The geographies in *Geographies and Plays* are like very fine prose poems that lead up to the *Geographical History*, quite interesting in their own right, but not so profound. "I know that I am I because my little dog knows me" is one heck of a lucid answer to Descartes, with his emphasis on himself: the earlier geographies are bridges between the "descriptions" from more experimental 'teens works (e.g., *Tender Buttons*, or the texts following the title text in *As a Wife Has a Cow a Love Story*).

Gertrude Stein didn't loathe blood and gore. Not by a long shot. She even revelled in it in her one mystery novel, *Blood on the Dining Room Floor*, which is filled with lots of mystery, suspicion and gooey mess, without any need whatever for suspense or explanation—a perfect refresher when you get tired of Rex Stout and Agatha Christie. But each of her novels is unique and fills a unique need. *Ida* is about identity, and does in fiction (art) what the *Geographical History* does in philosophy or psychology. The *Geographical History* ends: "When he is young a dog has more identity than when he is older./I am sure that this is not the end." (So much for men.) *Ida* ends ". . . They are there. Thank them./Yes." And you don't know who they are. *Mrs. Reynolds*, which Gertrude Stein wrote during World War II, and which is probably her greatest novel, is also about identity, is plotless, and deals with the slow movement of people and roles among themselves. It tells about Mrs. Reynolds (there is no Mr. Reynolds, really), Angel Harper (Adolf Hitler) who appears as a thunder cloud and goes away mysteriously—a procession passing by—and day by day, one relates to people as to the weather. But this particular sequence began in the almost unknown—even by Stein people—novel, *Lucy Church Amiably*, which Gertrude Stein called "A novel of rare and romantic beauty and which looks like an engraving." The whole work consists of minimally punctuated but commonplace sentences that cumulate lyrically into a very spacious and beautiful cloud. In the Gertrude Stein canon it holds about the same place as the Anna Lyvia Plurabelle section of James Joyce's *Finnegans Wake*, equally soft in tone and haunting, and written in the same year (1927). Nobody likes *Lucy Church Amiably*—it's too beautiful—if they have to read it to themselves. But try reading it aloud, with very clear breaks where Stein has put in sentence periods or paragraph breaks: the one is, per Gertrude Stein, emotional and the other logical or just plain sensible, but the reader can determine which. Read aloud, it is one of Stein's strongest works—in fact it is the best one to read aloud of all of them. Think of it as listening to falling water: Gertrude Stein did.

Matisse Picasso and Gertrude Stein (1909): this is the unmentionable book in the Stein canon. For one thing, it's about homosexuality, and for another thing, it's written in her most difficult, "cubist" style. For both reasons, it has baffled her (mostly male) critics.

A discreet title it has. But the title shows its sham immediately: each of the two "shorter stories"—and officially it's called *Matisse Picasso and Gertrude*

Stein with Two Shorter Stories — is longer than the title story. The first, *A Long Gay Book*, can pretty well speak for itself. It opens, as I've already said, with a powerful statement of how a very mature person, obviously loving children, feels on entering into a life in which her style and her sexuality will not be geared towards having babies. Many people know, from the *Autobiography* and elsewhere, that as a medical student she delivered a number of babies, that she wrote *A Long Gay Book* by watching couples and combinations and groups on the street and imagining about them. But until one has read the book, the fantasies sound abstract when one tries to describe them. The myth about *A Long Gay Book* is that it's uneven and unsustained. The fact is that it contains some of Stein's most fascinating writing and observation, and that only resistance to the subject matter has prevented people from seeing what a self-contained masterpiece it is. The opening pages, especially, are one of the mightiest texts in modern literature.

The second story in *Matisse Picasso and Gertrude Stein*, "Many Many Women" is a sort of sequel to "A Long Gay Book." It is purely about days and women. And identity, which is the touchstone of Stein's special cosmology. There are no men, other than by reference or implication, in the entire 80+ page novella. None of the personnel have names — they are simply and exclusively women. To see how positive her statement is, try the final two pages of the story. It's like brushing out your hair.

The third, "G.M.P.," is rather more bizarre. In it she tries to fantasize a love between Matisse and Picasso, including a very uncharacteristic (for Stein) string of symbols whenever she wants to avoid explicit sexual descriptions (as on page 264), and to draw a connection between this and the different kind of love that was shared between herself, Matisse and Picasso. No history, no recriminations: the love ended (she disliked Mrs. Matisse) and her politics weren't Picasso's. But love was there when that's what it was, and it's an unusual work in the Stein corpus, because of its symbols. The only other well-known one is *Four Saints in Three Acts*, with its Parsifal and holy-ghost imagery, references to passages in St. Theresa's autobiography and the writings of St. John of the Cross (who isn't even a character in *Four Saints*), all most unusual for a thoroughly unconverted Jew like Gertrude Stein. As a work, however, "G.M.P." registers as comparatively awkward, but it provides the beard for the book. And that too has its place in Steinian humor. In *Matisse Picasso and Gertrude Stein* we're spared the tiresome tea-party self-interrogations of the early novel, *Things As They Are (Q.E.D.)* (her other book with a purely initialled title besides G.M.P. — any connection?), and we don't get the full-fledged feminist eroticism of the later poem cycle, "Lifting Belly." But we do get frank exposition, a lot to say and a way to say it, joy and the view of things from inside things (as good cubism ought to be). Nobody would call this an easy book, but it's a heck of a human one and this is rare, and there's no excuse for not recognizing it as such. It needs reading more than talking about.

[On Stein's *Americans*]

Allen Ginsberg

After *On the Road*, a longer, more extraordinary piece of prose, *Visions of Cody* (1951), makes the breakthrough for Jack Kerouac's development just as Gertrude Stein's great prose experiment, *The Making of Americans*, stands for hers. A thousand pages of insane consciousness babble. I don't know if you know that text. Does anybody know of *The Making of Americans* by Gertrude Stein? That's actually I think one of the great prose masterpieces of the century. Stein had intentions very similar to those I've ascribed to Kerouac — she was a student of William James at Harvard, a student of consciousness, a psychedelic expert, so to speak, to join it to a familiar reference point for you; she was interested in modalities of consciousness, and she was interested in art as articulation of different modalities of consciousness, and she was interested in prose composition as a form of meditation, like yoga.

And, like yoga, she was interested in the language as pure prayer-meditation, removed perhaps even from its associations. To give an example (if this is too abstract and complicated an idea), like Alfred, Lord Tennyson, in order to get himself in an hypnotic state would repeat the name "Alfred Lord Tennyson; Alfred Lord Tennyson; Alfred Lord Tennyson; Alfred Lord Tennyson; Alfred Lord Tennyson; Alfred Lord Tennyson; Alfred Lord Tennyson; Alfred Lord Tennyson; Alfred Lord Tennyson; Alfred Lord Tennyson; Alfred Lord Tennyson; Alfred Lord Tennyson," until the sounds no longer had any association but were just pure sounds in a spacious physical universe, and he would get into a funny kind of ecstatic egoless state that way.

So Gertrude Stein was interested in using prose in the same way, that it both have a meaning and at the same time be completely removed from meaning and just become pure rhythmic structures pronounceable aloud. If you ever get a chance, you can listen to a record she made on Caedmon reciting some little prose compositions about Matisse and Picasso where she has little things like "Napoleon ate ice cream on Elba. Napoleon ate Elba on ice cream.

Reprinted from *Allen Verbatim* (1974) by permission of the author. Copyright © 1974 by Allen Ginsberg.

Napoleon ate ice on Elba cream. Napoleon ate on cream Elba ice. On Napoleon ice ate cream Elba. On Elba ate Napoleon ice cream. Ice cream ate Napoleon on Elba." Little formulas that go round, round the world, which is how she arrived at her famous statement which as you all know is "A rose is a rose is a rose." That's the end of long, long pages of circular prose that exhausts the word *rose* in many different syntactical combinations.

Her great book, *The Making of Americans*, is an examination of the consciousness of one single family. Very few people have read it through, including me—I haven't. I've read, you know, page upon page of it, and read aloud it's really exquisite.

Inventing Wordness:
Gertrude Stein's
Philosophical Investigations

Charles Bernstein

The Making of Americans fits well into a picture of the nineteenth century novel declaring, or dramatizing, the struggle between the public and the private: "official" morality versus the personal imperatives of justice, "private" experiences versus rigidly academic forms of expression. Indeed, *The Making of Americans* is very much a work of, or rooted in, the nineteenth century.

Stein's overall plan for the novel was to follow a family's history through three generations. Starting with "the old people [coming to] a new world" (*MA*, p. 1), she ended with her own generation. In this way she hoped to explain how "we" (for her then the present generation) got to where "we" are—"the basis of the existence in each one."[1] It was Stein's vision that each generation, living in its own time and making its own time, was different and that we could come to know ourselves by learning to hear the repeating of our history. She subtitled her novel, "Being a History of a Family's Progress."

A recurring structure of nineteenth century writing was the use of the family as a microcosm for the state or church or world. Thus the father would often carry the weight of earthly authority, law, official morality, convention, God. . . .[2] And often there would be a character who rebelled against (or felt out of connection with) these things by rebelling against (or withdrawing from) his family—the *ubermensch* or genius or idiot or outcast or possessed or homeless or holy man or woman. Leon Katz's studies of Stein's notebooks have revealed that Stein was explicitly concerned with problems of geniuses and saints (she liked to equate the terms) who were "unqualified and unlimited individualities, incapable of being known to others but capable of being self-known."[3] David Hersland, the last of the Hersland family talked about in *The Making of Americans*, was to come the closest to being such a "singular individual," one whose main problem, Stein wrote in her notebook, was "to run himself by his mind."

> Naturally some knew David Hersland had a brother and a sister and a father and a mother. Naturally some were certain that he was in

Hersland family living. He was like them, of course he was like them, why should he be unlike them when he had been living with them and had come out of them and had heard them and had seen them. . . . And sometimes it was a pleasant thing to him to be connected with every other one by such a thing by doing things in a way he was noticing other ones had been doing. Sometimes it was a pleasant thing to him to know then that everything means something, that he was a part of every one who was a part of him and sometimes he had very much family feeling in him, sometimes he had quite enough family feeling in him, very often he was naturally not having any family feeling (MA, pp. 862–3).

And so Stein moved into the twentieth century grounded in the nineteenth. The recurring motif of that century had been to represent (even allegorize) the family as setting limits that were acknowledged or transgressed; that is, to see family living as a microcosm of initiation into society. Stein's genius was to be able to express this solely in terms of language, by her prose compositon; for the David Hersland section is written in Stein's emerging modernist style.

For all Stein's talk about each one being a separate one, it remains to be registered that, for Stein, traditional prose and its established genres had lost the power to communicate this separateness. Indeed the very publicness and intelligibility of the established forms seemed to deny the overwhelming sense of privacy and distance from others. The nineteenth century had dramatized, and hence declared, the dialectic struggle between our inner lives and the external world. What is happening in the long "Beethovian"[4] paragraphs of *The Making of Americans* is the internalization of this dialectic into the prose composition itself.

> [In] writing *The Making of Americans*, I was completely obsessed by the inner life of everything including generations of everybody's living and I was writing prose, prose that had to do with the balancing the inner balancing of everything.[5]

Stein's focus became the words themselves; her declaration is that of *wordness*. The writing has become so dense that the meaning is no longer to be found in what the words represent, or stand for, but in their texture: the repetition, juxtaposition and structure of phrases, sentences, and paragraphs. One might say the words refer only to themselves, that there is no disjunction between what the prose refers to and the prose itself.

In the last sections of *The Making of Americans*, the dialectic becomes an investigation of (a struggle with) the limits of language. "To imagine a language," Wittgenstein writes, "is to imagine a form of life" (§19). The structure of language reveals the physiognomy, or over all topology, through which we see the world. To speak a common language is to "agree in judgments. [cf., §241, §242]. We are limited *to* language: for language provides the bounds of our intelligibility—of what can be meant. We see everything *through* our language: "*The limits of my language* mean the limits of my world."[6] As a result, the internalization of the dialectic into the medium of prose itself makes language function as family (and society) had in the nineteenth century dramatization. This is carried to its most radical end in Stein's later writing, particularly *Tender Buttons* and *How to Write*, where Stein composes a "grammatical" exploration of the limits of meaning—of sense and nonsense.

There is a temptation, I think, to confuse this style (the assertion of wordness) with private language. Schopenhauer has written that "style is the physiognomy of the mind and a safer index to character than face."[7] Stein, in the language of *How to Write*, would perhaps call this the different grammar of each personality—with the implicit recognition that though grammar is what individuates one person from another, it is also that which is *shared*.

Each one, then, has a different grammar, just as every good writer has a different style. The effort in much of Stein's early writing was to describe the particular grammar of each person; that is, to do portraits. The attempt of the portraits was to show each one as he or she is without telling stories. Each person, living in his or her own time, sounds different: has a different way of seeing quite apart from what is said. ("Essence is expressed by grammar. Grammar tells us what kind of an object a thing is" [§371, §372].) By listening to the different ways in which each one says things we can "know what they are," know the different worlds in which they live. Stein, then, is trying to describe what makes up a human personality (an individual consciousness or soul or form, a particular "repeating"). Her insight is that such individuating grammar is the most public and knowable because it fully discloses the person in the context in which she or he is living.

Still, one might feel that a peculiar grammar was, if not private, at least cryptic. And indeed interpreters of Stein have claimed this. Allegra Stewart sees Stein's descriptions of objects in *Tender Buttons* as a kind of code and proceeds to decipher them as if they were symbolic or occult or semiotic *signs*.[8] It is as if the words *stand for* something else—are the embodiment of something which really exists on another level. Thus, the words are seen as outer trappings (signs) that refer to and are separate from the real "inner" meaning. It is just this disjunction of outer and inner (similar to the disjunction between pain and pain-behavior) that I mean to refute by saying that the words "refer" only to *themselves* and that the meaning is internal to the prose. For if the unsayable "inner" meaning is being *translated* into the "outer" language it would be as if we already had a language full-blown prior to learning the one we speak: as if we had a form of life before we could speak and so were translating our pre-existing concepts into the public language.[9] That would perhaps be an explanation of a real private language, but it could not account for the fact that learning language is learning those concepts—that the limits of our language are the limits of our world. There is no escape into a prior and hence private language, a world *outside* language. Everything we know we know *through* our shared language, our way of life is formed by it: but we must learn it and speak it for ourselves.

The grammar that individuates is shared. The private dissolves into the public. In *The Making of Americans* Stein wrote, "I write for myself and strangers." She later abandoned this formulation but was discontent with the idea that one is audience to oneself. In *Four in America* she wrote, "I am not I when I see." (Stein acknowledges Flaubert's influence.[10]) The "I" drops out and writing becomes totally public in its intimate privacy.

> Here it can be seen that solipsism, when its implications are followed out strictly, coincides with pure realism. The self (*das Ich*) of solipsism shrinks to a point without extension, and there remains the reality coordinated with it.[11]

—All of my "inner" feeling is coming out in my "outer" repeating: everyone can be a whole one to me.

The words of *Tender Buttons*, like those of *The Making of Americans*, are not outer signs representing an inner world. *Tender Buttons* is not a cryptic code to be deciphered by industrious scholars or devoted disciples. —Though discipleship may be necessary in order to understand this work; for there is nothing to necessitate that one will understand any work of art—or any other person. Not *how* the world is, but *that* it is, is the Mystical. One must always interpret for oneself. Discipleship, if one calls it that, is a condition for all understanding, and all knowledge. Prose like Stein's will yield only as much as we are willing to give to it. We come to know what she is saying only when we undertake the task of understanding as if trying to make sense of ourselves.

Near the end of *The Making of Americans*, after the portrait of David Hersland and how he came to be "a dead one," Stein invokes the ontology of being-in-the-world, of "one being living."

> Any one can come to be a dead one. Any one can come to be such a one. Any one can come to be almost an old one if they have not come to be a dead one. Any one is such a one. . . . Any one is one being living, some are knowing all of this thing, some are not knowing all of this thing. Some are almost old ones, some are old ones, some are not old ones. Some are ones coming to be old ones (MA, p. 909).

Stein reminds us of the "very general facts of nature" that Wittgenstein says need mentioning in order to explain the significance of concepts (*Philosophical Investigations*, p. 230). She reminds us that we know we are "ones being living," that we can be certain that "being living is existing, that there is being existing, that there is being existing living" (*MA*, p. 890). She insists that each one has their own way of connecting what he or she says and means and thinks (*MA*, p. 782). She reminds us that people live in families, and grow old, and "come to be dead ones."

Notes

This essay is an unedited excerpt from *Three Compositions on Philosophy and Literature (Three Steins)*, my 1972 Harvard College undergraduate philosophy thesis. *Three Steins* provides a reading of *The Making of Americans* in the context of Wittgenstein's *Philosophical Investigations*. References to *The Making of Americans* (New York: Something Else Press, 1966) are indicated in text by "*MA*." References to the numbered sections of *Philosophical Investigations*, tr. G.E.M. Anscombe (New York: Macmillan, 1958), are preceded by §.

1. Gertrude Stein, "The Gradual Making of *The Making of Americans*," in *Writings and Lectures 1909–1945*, ed. Patricia Meyerowitz (Baltimore: Penguin, 1971), p. 85.

2. Examples range from *The Brothers Karamazov* to *Pride and Prejudice*, from Balzac's *Human Comedy* to Shelley's *Cenci*, from *Father and Sons* to *Wuthering Heights* to "Wakefield."

3. *The First Making of the Making of Americans* by Leon Katz (Unpublished Ph.D. dissertation, Columbia University, 1963), p. 283. Katz, in this quote, is using the language of Otto Weininger, author of the radically sexist philosophical tract *Sex and Character*. According to Katz, Stein read Weininger's book and was very interested in his "non-coordinate" characterology. Weininger wanted to define the "single and simple existence in a man"—a concept that is directly related to Stein's idea of "bottom being." Weininger writes that a man's "character . . . is not something seated *behind* the thoughts and feelings in the individual, but something revealing itself in every thought and feeling." His aim for his new psychology was to do "away with the study of sensations"—a motto that also attracted the attention of the young Ludwig Wittgenstein, who read Weininger's book with great interest. This "Viennese" (not to mention Viennese Jewish) connection to Stein's thought is largely unacknowledged and unexplored; it is also the most concrete link I've found between Stein and Wittgenstein.

4. See Stein's 1946 interview with Robert Haas, collected in *What Are Masterpieces* (New York: Pitman, 1970), pp. 97–104. In the interview, Stein says that she got from Cézanne "the idea that in composition one thing was as important as another thing. . . . After all to me one human being is as important as another human being and you might say that the landscape has the same values, a blade of grass has the same value as a tree." She says that, starting in *Three Lives*, she "threw away" punctuation and increased the length of her paragraphs "in an effort to get this evenness" of valuation. Writing *The Making of Americans*, "I felt I had lost contact with the words in building up these long Beethovian passages. . . . You had to recognize words had lost their value in the nineteenth century particularly towards the end, they had lost much of their variety and I felt that I could not go on, that I had to capture the value of the individual word, find out what it meant and act within it."

5. "Poetry and Grammar," in Meyerowitz, pp. 140–41.

6. Ludwig Wittgenstein, *Tractatus Logico-Philosophicus*, tr. D. F. Pears and B. F. MacGuinness (London: Routledge & Kegan Paul, 1961), 5.6.

7. Arthur Schopenhauer, *The Art of Literature* (Ann Arbor: University of Michigan Press, 1960), p. 11.

8. Allegra Stewart, *Gertrude Stein and the Present* (Cambridge: Harvard University Press, 1967). Stewart calls *Tender Buttons* a "mandella." This Wittgenstein remarks might serve as a cautionary note for much Stein criticism: "[The] mistake is to look for an explanation where we ought to look at what happens as a 'proto-phenomenon.' That is where we ought to have said: *This language game is played.* . . . The question is [one of] . . . noting a language game" (§654, §655).

9. I am here paraphrasing Wittgenstein's criticism of Augustine's picture of language in §32. – In speaking of *wordness*, I mean that Stein's prose has no background reference to recede into, it asserts its total internality or insideness; the concreteness of its composition is not separable from its meaning. Stein says she learned from Cézanne to treat composition itself as an "entity," as itself the reality rather than an imitation or representation of reality. To apply Weininger's terms, the meaning is not "something seated *behind*" the words, but something revealing itself *in* the words. – In both the theories of Quine and Saussure, it makes no sense to say what the *objects* of a language system are since language is a coordinate system in Quine or a system of differentials in Saussure. Strange as it may sound, such an "object" (or entity) is made possible in Stein's modernist composition by the fact that it does not name anything ("one does not use nouns"). The modernist composition's "objectness" consists of the assertion of its medium, or universe, or particular coordinate system. Its meaning, so to say, is its particularity: that it is just this "coordinate system" and not any other. This is why I say it exists primarily in relation to itself ("internality"): its particularity is coincident with its universe. This enactment of singularity in Stein's composition has parallels to her interest in the "singular" individual or genius (David Hersland) and also is the basis of her idea that the portraits "grammatically" portray the particularity of each person or object, what makes each one each one.

10. See the opening of the Haas interview.

11. *Tractatus Logico-Philosophicus*, 5.64.

Two Types of Obscurity in the Writings of Gertrude Stein

Randa K. Dubnick

Many critics have tried to deal with the difficulties of Gertrude Stein's writing by labeling it "meaningless," "abstract," or "obscure." But such judgments often are inadequate and misleading in their failure to make some important distinctions. In the first place, not all of Stein's writing is obscure. And within that part of her work which is obscure, there are two distinct styles which might be characterized as "abstract," each of which represents a linguistically different kind of obscurity. The first of these two styles developed during the writing of *The Making of Americans* and reached maturity toward the end of that book (as well as in some of the literary "portraits" produced during that same time). The second style is best represented by Stein's *Tender Buttons*.

Stein called the first style *prose* and the second style *poetry*. As will be seen, her definition of each category, and her description of these two obscure styles seem to suggest some of the dualistic distinctions that structuralist thought (from Ferdinand de Saussure to Roman Jakobson and Roland Barthes) has made about language. What might be fruitful, then, and what the structuralist vocabulary seems to make possible, is an examination of the nature and stylistics of each of the two distinct ways in which Stein's writing moves toward the abstract and becomes obscure. All of Stein's writing can be viewed as made up of variations and combinations of the two stylistic preoccupations represented by the participial style of *The Making of Americans* and the associational style of *Tender Buttons*. To understand the stylistics of Gertrude Stein's two basic types of obscurity, one must begin with an examination of these two works. Structuralist theories can aid in this examination by supplying a vocabulary as well as a framework that may identify the basis of her obscurity as her concern with the nature of language itself. This inquiry may lead to an understanding of the theoretical basis behind Stein's movement toward two kinds of abstraction. In this regard, a look at what was happening in painting, as Cubism also developed two obscure styles, may be helpful. The relationship

Reprinted from *Emporia State Research Studies* (1976) by permission of the author. Copyright © 1976 by Randa K. Dubnick.

between Stein's writing and Cubist painting, when seen from a structuralist's perspective, seems to be based on common emphases on certain linguistic operations over others. What one discovers is that Stein's comparisons of her writing to the work of the Cubists do not belie a misguided attempt to apply to language artistic theories which are irrelevant and inappropriate to it, as some critics believe: rather, those comparisons represent concerns about the nature of language itself, concerns which are, therefore, appropriately explored within the realm of literature.

Gertrude Stein, in one of her famous lectures, explains the radical stylistic difference between *The Making of Americans* and *Tender Buttons* in terms of the distinction between prose (the main concern of which is the sentence) and poetry (the main concern of which is the noun):

> In *The Making of Americans* . . . a very long prose book made up of sentences and paragraphs . . . I had gotten rid of nouns and adjectives as much as possible by the method of living in adverbs, in pronouns, in adverbial clauses written or implied and in conjunctions. . . . [R]eally great written prose is bound to be made up more of verbs adverbs prepositional clauses and conjunctions than nouns. The vocabulary in prose of course is important if you like vocabulary is always important. . . .[1]

However:

> . . . the vocabulary in respect to prose is less important than the parts of speech, and the internal balance and the movement within a given space.

On the other hand,

> Poetry is I say essentially a vocabulary just as prose is essentially not. . . . Poetry has to do with vocabulary just as prose has not. . . .
> And what is the vocabulary of which poetry absolutely is. It is a vocabulary entirely based on the noun as prose is essentially and determinately and vigorously not based on the noun.[2]

In asserting this different emphasis on, first, syntax and, then, diction, Stein seems to be touching upon what structural linguists differentiate as the horizontal and vertical axes of language (as formulated by Saussure, Jakobson, and Barthes, with somewhat varying terminology). The horizontal axis links words contiguously. It is

> . . . a combination of signs which has space as a support. In the articulated language, this space is linear and irreversible (it is the "spoken chain"): two elements cannot be pronounced at the same time (*enter, against all, human life*): each term here derives its value from its opposition

to what precedes and and what follows; in the chain of speech, the terms
are really united *in praesentia.*[3]

When Stein says that the key element in prose is the sentence, and that verbs,
prepositions and conjunctions (which function to hold the syntax of the
sentence together) are important in prose, she is implying an emphasis on the
horizontal axis of language.

On the other hand, the vertical axis of language links words by associations based on similarity and/or opposition, and has to do with the selection
of words.

> Beside the discourse (syntagmatic plane), the units which have
> something in common are associated in memory and thus form groups
> within which various relationships can be found: *education* can be
> associated, through its meaning, to *up-bringing* or *training*, and through
> its sound to *educate, education* or to *application, vindication.* . . . [I]n each
> series unlike what happens at the syntagmatic level, the terms are united
> *in absentia.*[4]

Stein characterizes poetry as concerned with vocabulary (and with the
noun in particular). Hers is an oblique statement of the obvious observation
that in poetry, word choice is of more concern than syntax, which is often suppressed, especially in modern poetry. The choice of a word from among a group
of synonyms on the basis of qualities like rhythm and rhyme, or the choice
of a poetic vocabulary from within an entire language, is an operation of selection. According to structural linguistic theories, the operation of selection
functions along the vertical axis of language.

As to Stein's remarks regarding the various parts of speech, Ronald Levinson points out in his article, "Gertrude Stein, William James, and Grammar,"[5]
that Stein's theoretical formulation of the functions of the parts of speech was
apparently greatly influenced by the theories of William James, who, in
Psychology, compared the "stream of consciousness" to a series of "flights and
perchings,"–the "perchings" being substantives ("occupied by sensorial im-
aginings"), and the "flights" being transitives ("thoughts of relating, static and
dynamic"), which depend on verbs, prepositions, and conjunctions.[6] As Levinson points out, Stein in her philosophy of grammar set forth in "Poetry and
Grammar" echoes some of James' theories, especially in the distinction she
makes between static words (nouns) and dynamic words (verbs, prepositions).
What is original is her use of James' theories as the basis of a distinction between poetry and prose. Here, prose is based on verbs, prepositions, and conjunctions (the "flights"): the words that support syntax. These words function
along the horizontal axis and have to do with contiguity: they combine to hold
the words of the sentence in relation to one another. Poetry, on the other hand,
is based on the noun or the substantive; the "perchings." Roman Jakobson's

linguistic analysis of aphasia indicates that these parts of speech have to do with the operation of selection (the vertical axis).[7] Thus, Stein's distinction between prose and poetry is based not merely upon stylistic or formal consideration, but rather on a distinction in emphasis upon what structuralists have since identified as two linguistic, and even mental, operations: similarity (or selection or system) and contiguity (or combination or syntagm).

Though one can see the germs of some of these ideas in James' theories as set forth in *Psychology*, Stein extends and applies them in her creative writing. James describes consciousness as a continuous flow, distinguishes between static and dynamic parts of speech, and discerns two types of association. The first is based on contiguity, meaning habitual association of things existing together in time and space. (This kind of association James identifies as performed even by animals.) The second type is based on similarity of entities not linked in space or time.[8] However, James does not extend this distinction from the realm of association and use it to bifurcate the whole of linguistic operations along these lines as do the theories of structuralism.

Stein's contribution is the creation of an aesthetic based on James' theories and on pragmatism in general, as Robert Haas points out.[9] Through this effort, she arrives at two types of obscurity which function, perhaps coincidentally, as practical illustrations of linguistic theories that were yet to be published at the time she was creating those two styles. (Even the first and most limited formulation of these structural theories in Ferdinand de Saussure's *Course in General Linguistics* was not published until 1916,[10] approximately four years after *Tender Buttons* was written, *circa* 1912.) Furthermore, her writing, which suppresses, first, the vertical axis at the expense of the horizontal axis, and, then, vice versa, foreshadows Jakobson's observations about the sublimation of, first, one of these two linguistic operations and, then, the other as it occurs in the speech of aphasic patients. Jakobson did not publish these observations until 1956 in "Two Aspects of Language and Two Types of Aphasic Disturbances."[11] Of course, in aphasia, the suppression of either of the two linguistic operations of contiguity and similarity is entirely involuntary and pathological, while Stein's theoretical writings indicate that the creation of each of her two obscure styles was quite consciously undertaken for certain theoretical and aesthetic reasons — all arguments about "automatic writing" to the contrary!

The key stylistic interest in *The Making of Americans*, and in other works of Stein's participial style, is syntax. Grammatically correct but eccentric sentences spin themselves out and grow, clause linked to clause, until they are of paragraph length. She asserts that nothing "has ever been more exciting than diagramming sentences. . . . I like the feeling the everlasting feeling of sentences as they diagram themselves."[12] Her long, repetitive sentences convey the feeling of process and duration, and of the time it gradually takes to get to know a person or come to grips with an idea. She felt that sentences were not emotional (i.e., the syntax or "internal balance" of the sentence is a given) but that paragraphs were. She illustrates this principle by reference to her dog's drinking water from a dish. The paragraph is emotional in that it prolongs the duration of the idea or perception until the writer feels satisfied. This feeling of satisfaction is subjective and not arrived at by following rules of grammar. By extending the sentence to the length approximately of a short paragraph, Stein was trying to achieve an emotional sentence. Many of the stylistic idiosyncrasies of her "participial" style function to extend the length of the sentence. What follows is a passage located near the end of *The Making of Americans:*

> Certainly he was one being living when he was being a being young one, he was often then quite certainly one being almost completely interested in being one being living, he was then quite often wanting to be one being completely interested in being one being living. He certainly then went on being living, he did this thing certainly all of his being living in being young living. He certainly when he was a young one was needing then sometimes to be sure that he was one being living, this is certainly what some being living are needing when they are ones being young ones in being living. David Hersland certainly was one almost completely one being one being living when he was being a young one. Some he was knowing then were certainly being completely living then and being then being young ones in being living then, some were quite a good deal not being one being completely living then when they were being young ones in being living. David Hersland did a good deal of living in being living then when he was a young one. He was knowing very many men and very many knew him then. He remembered some of them in his later living and he did not remember some of them. He certainly was one almost completely then interested in being one being living then.[13]

In this characteristic paragraph (consisting of only nine sentences), Stein uses many grammatical and stylistic strategies to extend the syntax and physical duration of the utterance. For example, one way to extend the syntax is to create very complex sentences, such as "Some he was knowing then were not quite completely being ones being living then, some were quite a good deal not being ones being completely living then when they were being young ones in being living" (*Making of Americans*, p. 801). It is characteristic of her writing that, although she may link clause to clause, she often will suppress the use of relative pronouns such as "that" or "who." This method makes it more difficult to divide the sentences into individual clauses, forcing the reader to take a more active role in struggling to follow the sentence structure. Another simple, but less orthodox, means of extending the syntax is by fusing two or more sentences through the comma splice: "He certainly then went on being living, he did this thing certainly all of his being living in being young living" (*Making of Americans*, p. 801). One should note, here, that the sparse use of commas also functions to make the reader work harder to follow the sentence. Another device for stretching the sentence almost to paragraph length is the mechanistic linking together of many independent clauses by a series of conjunctions:

> Some are certainly needing to be ones doing something and they are doing one thing and doing it again and again and again and again and they are doing another thing and they are doing it again and again and they are doing another thing and they are doing it again and again and again and such a one might have been one doing a very different thing then and doing that then each or any one of them and doing it again and again and again. (*Making of Americans*, p. 803.)

Stein's first style is full of participles that function as nouns or adjectives and verb forms as well, a use which critics have termed a philosophical choice. Participles prolong the time span to achieve a sense of duration and process. Moreover, the participle, and particularly the gerund, also help portray the pragmatic conception of the world as a constantly on-going event. However, it should be noted that when Stein substitutes, "When he was being a young one" for "When he was young," the sentence is lengthened by two syllables. Her substitution of the participle for a simpler form of the verb has the cumulative effect of substantially lengthening the sentence, especially in view of the fact that, as Hoffman points out, "Probably more than half her verb forms use some form of the progressive ending."[14] The Stein sentence is also lengthened by the fact that she so often insists on the "changing of an adjective into a substantive. Rather than saying 'Everybody is real,' [she] changes 'real' into 'a real one.'"[15] Again, this method has the cumulative effect of lengthening the duration of the reading or the utterance.

In *The Making of Americans*, Stein stretches syntax almost to the breaking point and simultaneously limits her vocabulary. She moves farther and farther away from the concrete noun-centered vocabulary of the realistic novel. In part, the movement is due to her subject matter. *The Making of Americans* is a monumental attempt to create a chronicle of one family which could serve as an eternally valid history of all people, past, present, and future. Herein, she presents people as generalized types, and uses the characters in the novel to represent all human possibilities. This method led her from the essentially conventional narrative which dominates the beginning of the book to the generalized and theoretical kind of digression dispersed throughout the novel, but especially prominent towards the end of the book.

Although the long passage cited earlier concerns David Hersland, Stein has supplied very little concrete information about him because she was trying to turn particular and perhaps personal facts (the Hersland family is considered to be autobiographical by most critics) into universally valid generalizations. This effort is reflected in the dearth of conventional nouns and the wealth of pronouns. This is a move towards obscurity in that the referent of a pronoun is more vague than that of a noun. Verbals are used instead of conventional nouns and adjectives: "alive" becomes "being living." The same phrase is also used as a noun: David Hersland is interested in "being living" rather than in life. Probably this construction reflects Stein's desire to emphasize the transitive linguistic processes over the substantive ones in prose.

Conventional verbs are replaced by participles, which prolong and deemphasize whatever action is being described. The participles contain very little concrete information. In the passage under discussion, there are only five participles, although each is repeated a number of times *(being, living, wanting, needing, knowing)*. The least specific participles are those most often repeated. *Being* and *living* each occur nineteen times in the paragraph.

There are few conventional adjectives in the passage, aside from the participles. As for adverbs, *certainly* occurs a number of times, here, as it does throughout the book. Some critics think that Stein, in this case, is attempting to reassure herself and her reader of the universal validity of her typology. In addition, the fact that she must say *some, many,* and *a good deal* more and more often is seen as her growing recognition of the limitations of what she is doing. The adverb *then* is prevalent in the novel, perhaps related to her attempt to bring all knowledge gained over the passing of time into the present moment. It is also natural that a style which extends syntax will contain many relational words, like prepositions and conjunctions.

The stylistic concerns of Stein's early prose, in both *The Making of Americans* and the early (pre–1912) portraits, are the extension of syntax and the simultaneous circumscription of vocabulary, which is limited not merely in terms of the quantity of words, but also in the degree of specificity allowed to appear. The result is a very vague and generalized portrayal of the subject matter. Thus, *The Making of Americans* fits very neatly her requirements for prose. It is concerned with syntax, and contains many verbs, adverbs and conjunctions, while it reduces the vocabulary, and for the most part eliminates conventional nouns in favor of pronouns and gerunds.

It is interesting to compare these observations about her prose style with Jakobson's observations about the two aspects of language as they relate to the speech of aphasics. Like Stein's writing, aphasia manifests two basic types of obscurity (although, of course, the obscurity in aphasia is pathological and involuntary, while that in Stein is a voluntary stylistic choice). Jakobson delineates two types of aphasia, each related to an inability to function in terms of one of the two linguistic axes which Roland Barthes has described as "system" (vertical axis) and "syntagm" (horizontal axis). Jakobson refers to these axes repectively as "selection" and "combination":

> Any linguistic sign involves two modes of arrangement:
> 1) Combination. Any sign is made up of constituent signs and/or

occurs only in combination with other signs. This means that any linguistic unit at one and the same time serves as a context for simpler units and/or finds its own context in a more complex linguistic unit. Hence any actual grouping of linguistic units binds them into a superior unit: combination and contexture are two faces of the same operation. 2) Selection. A selection between alternatives implies the possibility of substituting one for the other, equivalent to the former in one respect and different from it in another. Actually selection and substitution are two faces of the same operation.[16]

He points out further that "speech disturbances may affect in varying degrees the individual's capacity for combination and selection of linguistic units, and, indeed, the question of which of these two operations is chiefly impaired proves to be of far-reaching significance in describing, analyzing, and classifying the diverse forms of aphasia."[17] Some of Jakobson's observations regarding the language produced by patients suffering from an inability to perform the operation of selection are somewhat similar to what can be observed in the prose style of *The Making of Americans* and the early portraits. This similarity is not really surprising, since Stein is herein *voluntarily* suppressing the operation of selection by severely limiting her vocabulary and attempting to eliminate nouns. Jakobson describes some of the speech patterns of aphasics suffering from a similarity disorder as follows:

> ...the more a word is dependent on the other words of the same sentence and the more it refers to the syntactical context, the less it is affected by the speech disturbance. Therefore words syntactically subordinated by grammatical agreement or government are more tenacious, whereas the main subordinating agent of the sentence, namely the subject, tends to be omitted. ... Key words may be dropped or superseded by abstract anaphoric substitutes. A specific noun, as Freud noticed, is replaced by a very general one, for instances *machin*, *chose* in the speech of French aphasics. In a dialectal German sample of "amnesiac aphasia" observed by Goldstein, ... *Ding* "thing" or *Stuckle* "piece" were substituted for all inanimate nouns, and *uberfahren* "perform" for verbs which were identifiable from the context or situation and therefore appeared superfluous to the patient.
>
> Words with an inherent reference to the context, like pronouns and pronominal adverbs, and words serving merely to construct the context, such as connectives and auxiliaries, are particularly prone to survive.[18]

As it will be seen, some of Jakobson's observations about the language of aphasics with a contiguity disorder seem to indicate that this particular form of pathological obscurity shares certain characteristics with Stein's second stylistic interest, which she identified as poetry. For example, *Tender Buttons* represents a radical change from the early prose style of *The Making of Americans* and of other works to that which she called poetry. From prose, with its emphasis on syntax and its suppression of vocabulary, she moved to a concern for poetry with its emphasis on vocabulary and its suppression of syntax. This change manifests itself in a shift of linguistic emphasis from the operation of combination (horizontal axis) to the operation of selection (vertical axis).

Tender Buttons attained "a certain notoriety" in the press and attracted polemical criticism, perhaps because it seemed to "veer off into meaninglessness," at least in conventional terms.[19] But the work is more than a literary curiosity. Its marked stylistic change appears to have been a breakthrough that influenced the direction of much of Stein's future work. "... *Tender Buttons* represented her full scale break out of the prison of conventional form into the colorful realm of the sensitized imagination."[20]

In *The Making of Americans*, her concerns were those of imposing order upon the world by classifying its inhabitants into universal and eternally valid types, of creating a history of all human possibilities. This goal called for a language that expressed generalities in a very precise way. Her attempts to portray the "bottom nature" of a person, the essence which lay behind his superficial particularity, continued in her early portraits.

> Gertrude Stein had tried numerous techniques in her previous efforts to match her conception of a person with a style. She had generalized and reduced her vocabulary in order to make true statements, however simpleminded. She had constructed long, cumulative sentences on the model of This-is-the-house-that-Jack-built to convey the feeling of slowly becoming familiar with a person.[21]

However, by the time Stein wrote *Tender Buttons*, her attention was no longer focused on the universals of experience, but now on the process of experiencing each moment in the present tense as it intersects with the consciousness. In *The Making of Americans*, she had subordinated particularity and individual differences to the type, an approach which she eventually abandoned. "But by rejecting her knowledge of types, she was faced with each experience as a unique thing, with even its importance unprejudiced, as simply different."[22] She had simplified and generalized reality so as to impose an order upon it, but finally she "concluded that greater fidelity of representation might be achieved if she simply recorded the verbal responses her consciousness made to a particular subject, while minimizing her own manipulation of them."[23]

In her lectures (written with the hindsight of many years, which perhaps lent her stylistic development more coherence than it had in actual fact), Stein discusses her new desire to see the world and return to the sensual particularity of experience as it was immediately available to her consciousness. After doing her portraits, she slowly became bothered by the fact that she was omitting a looking at the world. "So I began to do this thing, I tried to include color and movement, and what I did is . . . a volume called *Tender Buttons*.[24]

The Making of Americans, with its historical orientation and its goal of classifying people according to type, necessitated remembering the past. Classification is based on resemblances, on similarities, which must be held over time in the mind. In her early portraits, Stein freed herself of the narrative and dealt with the presentation of perceptions one moment at a time, but these perceptions were not dealt with "in the raw." They had to be edited, selected, and generalized so that the person could be analyzed and presented in his essential reality. However, in *Tender Buttons*, she came to terms with the chaotic nature of real experience and "the existential swarm of her impressions."[25] The physical world is experienced as unique and immediate in each present moment as the consciousness receives data.

In any attempt to deal with Stein's writing, the word "abstract" is bound to come up. This term has been a problem in Stein criticism because it is not usually defined clearly. Even Michael Hoffman's book, *The Development of Abstractionism in the Writing of Gertrude Stein*, fails to come to terms with "abstract." Hoffman's definition of *abstractionism* is essentially the dictionary definition, "'the act or process of leaving out of consideration one or more qualities of a complex object so as to attend to others.'"[26] That Stein follows this approach, as any artist must, is obvious. However, this definition does not seem adequate to deal with important questions like Stein's refusal of verisimilitude. Because of the vague definition, Hoffman, thus, uses *abstract* to describe all of Stein's work without clarifying the distinctions between *non-representational, plastic, arbitrary,* and *abstract,* although he seems aware of the development of diverse styles in her writing. Stein's relationship to the Cubists, to whose work she compared her own, is an important question that cannot be examined without these kinds of distinctions. When Hoffman compares her work to that of the Cubists, he shares the common failure to be consistent and rigorous in his distinctions between the stages of Cubism as it developed over time.[27] John Malcolm Brinnin, in *The Third Rose*, alone saw that developments in the Cubist styles (analytic and synthetic) parallel stages in Stein's stylistic development as well.[28] This observation is potentially useful in clarifying the distinction between the two kinds of obscure writing that Stein produces.

Too often, the term *abstract,* when used in regard to Stein's writing, is taken to mean non-representational, which her writing almost never is. She never really abandons subject matter. In her early work, the subject matter was the representation of types of people, which appears to have led to an interest in the process of perception itself. In the style which *Tender Buttons* exemplifies, the subject matter is the intersection of the object with consciousness. As attention is focused on the process of perception, that process becomes as much a part of the subject matter as the object perceived. "As I say a motor goes inside and the car goes on, but my business my ultimate business as an artist was not with where the car goes as it goes but with the movement inside that is of the essence of its going."[29] In fact, Stein insisted on subject matter and disapproved of abstract art. That the Cubists' work was never abstract, i.e., never non-representational, is not always clearly understood, and confuses the comparison of Stein's writing to some of the work of those painters.

Subject matter is certainly not abandoned in *Tender Buttons*, nor does that book "signal an abandonment of control. Her practice was to concentrate upon an object as it existed in her mind. . . . Gertrude Stein perceived that [the object] was immersed in a continuum of sound, color and association, which it was her business to reconstitute in writing."[30] In *Tender Buttons*, the subject matter was not limited to a description of the objective world, but included mimesis of the intersection of the real world with the consciousness of the artist.

Nevertheless, it is possible to assert that the vocabulary of her early writing moves towards abstraction, if one means that it moves away from the concrete, that it is very general and contains few concrete nouns and verbs of action:

> He was one being living, then when he was quite a young one, and some knew him then and he knew some then. He was one being living then and he was being one and some knew he was that one the one he was then and some did not know then that he was that one the one he was then. (*The Making of Americans*, p. 952)

Tender Buttons has a less abstract vocabulary in that it contains many more concrete nouns, sensual adjectives, and action verbs than does her earlier style:

> The stove is bigger. It was of a shape that made no audience bigger if the opening is assumed why should there not be kneeling. Any force which is bestowed on a floor shows rubbing. This is so nice and sweet and yet there comes the change, there comes the time to press more air. This does not mean the same as disappearance.[31]

However, in a different sense, *Tender Buttons* taken as a whole is more abstract than *The Making of Americans* in that its words are used in a plastic, arbitrary way, and in that it is less concerned with traditional, discursive description.

> In the previous centuries writers had managed pretty well by assembling a number of adjectives and adjectival clauses side by side; the reader "obeyed" by furnishing images and concepts in his mind and the resultant "thing" in the reader's mind corresponded fairly well with that in the writer's. Miss Stein felt that process did not work any more. Her painter friends were showing clearly that the corresponding method of "description" had broken down in painting and she was sure that it had broken down in writing. . . .
>
> * * * *
>
> Miss Stein felt that writing must accomplish a revolution whereby it

could report things as they were in themselves before our minds had appropriated them and robbed them of their objectivity "in pure existing." To this end she went about her house describing the objects she found there in the series of short "poems" which make up the volume called *Tender Buttons*.[32]

As the concerns of Stein's writing gradually shift from an interest in orderly analysis of the world to an interest in the immediate perception of the world by the consciousness, her writing appears to deal more and more with the word itself: with the mental images called up by and associated with the word (signifieds), and with the qualities of words as things in themselves (signifiers). "Her imagination was stimulated then not by the object's particular qualities alone, but also by the associations it aroused . . . and by the words themselves as they took shape upon the page."[33]

Perhaps coincidentally, a similar shift in emphasis was occurring in the painting of the Cubists around the time *Tender Buttons* was composed.[34] Their earlier struggle, in Analytic Cubism, to see reality without the conventional and learned *trompe-l'oeil* of perspective focused their attention on the elements of composition and led them to the realization that the artist could use these elements arbitrarily rather than mimetically:

> . . . in the winter of 1912–13 a fundamental change came about in the pictorial methods of the true Cubists. Whereas previously Braque and Picasso had analyzed and dissected the appearance of objects to discover a set of forms which would add up to their totality and provide the formal elements of a composition, now they found that they could begin by composing with purely pictorial elements (shaped forms, planes of color) and gradually endow them with an objective significance.[35]

The Cubists had arrived at "the conclusion that they could create their own pictorial reality by building up towards it through a synthesis of different elements."[36] That the elements of signification might have an importance in their own right and be used arbitrarily by the artist to create not a mirror of reality but an authentic new reality (the work of art as *tableau-objet*) was an important realization for this group and a conclusion that Stein seems to have arrived at, perhaps independently. Stein now realized that words need no longer be merely the means to the expression of another reality, but may become freed of their normal mimetic function (still retaining their meanings and associations) and be used plastically by the writer. In her lectures, she describes her growing concern with the quality of language as a thing in itself:

> I began to wonder at . . . just what one saw when one looked at anything . . . [D]id it make itself by description by a word that meant it or did it make itself by a word in itself. . . .

> I became more and more excited about how words which were the words which made whatever I looked at look like itself were not words that had in them any quality of description....
>
> And the thing that excited me ... is that the words that made what I looked at be itself were always words that to me very exactly related themselves to that thing ... at which I was looking, but as often as not had as I say nothing whatever to do with what any words would do that described that thing.[37]

Like the Cubists, Stein abandons conventional description of an object, although she is still concerned with the object as her "model," but she inverts the traditional descriptive relationship of word to object. Rather than the word evoking the mental image of the object, the object evokes words (associations, etc.) which the artist arbitrarily assembles into an independent linguistic object related to, but not descriptive of, the model or referent. In Analytic Cubism, the artist abstracts form from the given object and creates a representation of the object (however unconventional) on canvas. In Synthetic Cubism, forms have their genesis in the artist, although he uses them to create an object on the canvas. The function of the painting is no longer to describe or represent another reality, but to exist as a thing in itself. In Stein's early works (*The Making of Americans* and others, of her participial style), words are used to abstract generalities about the world to analyze or describe it on paper. However, in *Tender Buttons*, the words are not conventionally descriptive of the object, but have their genesis in the writer and in the associations which the object evokes in him. The function of the writing is not to describe the given object, but to become an entity in its own right.

In *Tender Buttons*, with the new attention to the immediately present moment and the abandoning of traditional description, Stein turned from her earlier "portraits" of people to the treatment of inanimate objects and seems to have felt some bond with the painters of still lives. Dealing with human beings "inevitably carried in its train realizing movements and expression and such forced me into recognizing resemblances, and so forced remembering and in forcing remembering caused confusion of present with past and future time." Consequently, she turned from "portraits of men and women and children" to "portraits of food and rooms and everything because there I could avoid this difficulty of suggesting remembering more easily ... than if I were to describe human beings." Stein also felt that this was a problem she shared with the painters:

> I began to make portraits of things and enclosures ... because I needed to completely face the difficulty of how to include what is seen with hearing and listening and at first if I were to include a complicated listening and talking it would be too difficult to do. That is why painters paint still lives. You do see why they do.[38]

Indeed, as the Cubists turned from an analysis of a given reality on canvas to a synthesis of a new reality from the pictorial elements, the Cubists (Picasso especially) produced fewer portraits and more still lives. Perhaps the reason for this move is similar to the one that brought about the change in Stein's writing: dealing with inanimate objects allows the artist more freedom to treat the subject in an arbitrary manner. After all, the public expects a portrait to be a likeness of the model, who has the annoying habit of exhibiting his face in public, thus allowing it to be compared with the painting. But a still life is a small piece of reality that the artist arranges at will, and when he is finished, he can dismantle it, leaving the public nothing with which to compare the painting.

The new realization of Synthetic Cubism (that pictorial elements could be used arbitrarily) was marked by a return to color and texture in contrast to the predominantly grey paintings of Analytic Cubism. For Stein, the new interest in the sensory experiences of the present moment and the new-felt freedom in the use of words manifested itself in a richer, more sensual vocabulary, in contrast to the spare and spartan one of her earlier struggle to classify everyone into universal types. "The idea had entered her mind that lyricism contained a fuller measure of truth than could ever be encircled by making endless laboriously deliberate statements."[39] The evocative power of the word called for more "decorative" approach. Freed from her concerns with remembering and classifying, she began to concentrate on the present moment and all of the phenomena therein, including the words called up by those phenomena and their effect upon her conscious mind. Thus, instead of the genderless pronouns, verbs of being, prepositions and conjunctions, and the virtual elimination of concrete words in her earlier style, there is a renaissance of the particular: concrete nouns, sensual adjectives, and specific verbs.

This new interest in the word itself, and especially in the noun and the associative powers of the word, was what Stein considered the essence of poetry. In *Tender Buttons* and other works that she held as poetry, the chief linguistic operation is association (given various labels by structuralists such as substitution, selection, system) and choice of words. The association of words and concepts by similarity or opposition, and the selection of a word from a group of synonyms, are operations that function along the vertical axis of language. Interestingly enough, the *Tender Buttons* style also suppresses syntax (the horizontal axis) while it is expanding vocabulary. Construction of syntax becomes increasingly fragmentary until syntax disappears altogether in some of the more extreme passages.

In *The Making of Americans*, the chief stylistic interest is syntax, but in *Tender Buttons*, the central concern seems to be diction, the selection of words based on association (in terms of both similarity and opposition). The long sentence-paragraph is abandoned as more attention is forced on the noun:

...after I had gone as far as I could in these long sentences and paragraphs ... I then began very short thing ... and I resolutely realized nouns and decided not to get around them but to meet them, to handle in short to refuse them by using them and in that way my real acquaintance with poetry was begun.[40]

* * * *

I began to discover the names of things, that is, ... to discover the things ... to see the things to look at and in so doing I had of course to name them not to give new names but to see that I could find out how to know that they were there by their names or by replacing their names.... They had their names and naturally I called them by the names they had and in doing so having begun looking at them I called them by their names with passion and that made poetry ... it made the *Tender Buttons*.[41]

However, as Stein begins to abandon her extension of the sentence and enriches her use of diction, the result is not more conventional writing but rather a new style, equally obscure, if not more so. It is even harder to read, in the traditional sense, than her first obscure style, because, in part, there is a disjunction between the two axes of language in this second style. One word often does not appear to have any relationship to other words in the sentence except in terms of their existence as pure words (in terms of grammatical structure, or rhyme, or word play). Of course, words cannot be divorced from their meanings; thus, each word (signifier) calls up a mental image or idea (signified), but *Tender Buttons* cannot be read with a conventional concern for subject matter because one cannot use the total configuration of these mental constructs to reconstruct the "subject matter." Sometimes a sentence in *Tender Buttons* may appear to have a normal syntax and to be orthodox grammatically, yet the words selected do not relate to each other in a traditional and discursive way. "The change of color is likely and a difference a very little difference is prepared. Sugar is not a vegetable." (*Tender Buttons*, p. 9.) These sentences are grammatically correct, though their punctuation is not conventional. One may achieve the feeling that the sentence would be perfectly comprehensible if the context were supplied. Stein is using both syntax and diction, but because of the disjunction between the two axes of language, the sentence does not "mean" in a conventional way.

Sometimes in *Tender Buttons* Stein explores the patterns of speech, repeating syntactical patterns, at the same time somewhat arbitrarily plugging in terms from the pool of associated words in her vocabulary:

Almost very likely there is no seduction, almost very likely there is no stream, certainly very likely the height is penetrated, certainly

> certainly the target is cleaned, come to set, come to refuse, come to surround, come slowly and age is not lessening. (*Tender Buttons*, p. 70.)

She explores the rhythm and patterns of speech that are present, even when discursive meaning is not. Like "Jabberwocky," this passage conveys a feeling of speech, even though its words do not relate to each other in a conventional way.

In *Tender Buttons*, Stein's sentences become shorter as her emphasis shifts to diction and association rather than syntax. She explains in a lecture that lines of poetry are shorter than prose because

> ...such a way to express oneself is the natural way when one expresses oneself in loving the name of anything. Think what you do ... when you love the name of anything really love its name. Inevitably you express yourself ... in the way poetry expresses itself that is in short lines in repeating what you began in order to do it again. Think of how you talk to anything whose name is new to you a lover a baby a dog or a new land.... Do you not inevitably repeat what you call out and is that calling out not of necessity in short lines.[42]

Often in *Tender Buttons*, lines that appear to be sentences are not sentences at all: "Cutting shade, cool spades and little last beds, make violet violet when." (*Tender Buttons*, p. 54.) Obviously, this fragment promises to be a sentence until it is truncated by the period after "when," a word normally expected to introduce a subordinate clause. The disjunction between diction and syntax manifests itself in false predication. For example, how can shade, spades, and beds make violet? Here, each word is quite independent from those which precede and follow it in the speech chain, at least as far as the mental images or signifieds are concerned. (Obviously, however, there are relationships between some of the words in terms of sound.)

Stein uses punctuation in other ways to break up the continuity of the sentence: "This makes and eddy. Necessary." (*Tender Buttons*, p. 54.) Also: "Cream cut. Anywhere crumb. Left hop chambers." (*Tender Buttons*, p. 54.) She carries the disintegration of syntax even further, presenting a list within the horizontal structure of the sentence. (A list is usually a group of items associated with one another because they are similar in some way.) "Alas a doubt in case of more to go to say what is is cress. What it is. Mean. Potatoes. Loaves." (*Tender Buttons*, p. 54.) In some of her writing following *Tender Buttons*, Stein even entirely abandoned syntax and made lists of words or phrases in vertical columns on the page.

Again, one observes that some of the stylistic phenomena of Stein's second "obscure" style, emphasizing vocabulary and the noun while suppressing syntax, are strikingly close to Jakobson's observations about the language of aphasics suffering from a contiguity disorder, in which ability to use syntax becomes weakened or disappears, leaving the patient with *only* a vocabulary in extreme cases:

The impairment of the ability to propositionalize, or generally speaking, to combine simpler linguistic entities into more complex units, is actually confined to one type of aphasia. . . . the opposite of is actually confined to one type of aphasia. . . . There is no wordlessness, since the entity preserved in most of such cases is the word, which can be defined as the highest among the linguistic units compulsorily coded, i.e., we compose our own sentences and utterances out of the word stock supplied by the code.

This contexture-deficient aphasia, which could be termed contiguity disorder, diminishes the extent and variety of sentences. The syntactical rules organizing words into a higher unit are lost; this loss, called aggrammatism, causes the degeneration of the sentence into a mere "word heap. . . ." Word order becomes chaotic; the ties of grammatical coordination and subordination . . . are dissolved. As might be expected, words endowed with purely grammatical functions, like conjunctions, prepositions, pronouns, and articles, disappear first, giving rise to the so-called "telegraphic style," whereas in the case of similarity disorder they are the most resistent. The less a word depends grammatically on the context, the stronger is its tenacity in the speech of aphasics with a contiguity disorder and the sooner it is dropped by patients with a similarity disorder. Thus the "kernel subject word" is the first to fall out of the sentence in cases of similarity disorder and conversely, it is the least destructible in the opposite type of aphasia.[43]

In *Tender Buttons*, Stein's primary concern is words and their associations, and her selection of words often is imbued with a spirit of love and play:

Poetry is concerned with using with abusing, with losing with wanting, with denying with avoiding with adoring with replacing the noun. . . . Poetry is doing nothing but losing refusing and pleasing and betraying and caressing nouns.[44]

Sometimes the selection of words is obviously related to the object:

A Petticoat

A light white, a disgrace, an ink spot, a rosy charm.
(*Tender Buttons*, p. 22.)

Without too much effort, one detects the associations between word and object. Petticoats are lightweight and often white; a petticoat that shows is a disgrace which might provoke a modest blush. (Stein has been greatly overread, but it seems safe to identify the obvious and public association.)

Even when the associations of word to object are chiefly based on associated meanings, similarities of spelling and sound may play a role:

A Method of a Cloak

A single climb to a line, a straight exchange to a cane, a desperate adventure and courage and a clock ... all this makes an attractive black silver. (*Tender Buttons*, pp. 13–14.)

The "single climb to a line" might relate to the shape of the cloak, and the cane is related to the cloak as an object of apparel. (Both the cane and the cloak have a nostalgic, perhaps nineteenth-century flavor of elegance.) But the two phrases "A single climb to a line" and "a straight exchange to a cane," have identical rhythmic patterns as well. The "desperate adventure" and "courage" might be related to the connotations of "cloak and dagger." Black may be the color of the cloak which is "attractive"; perhaps silver was evoked by the sight of the lining of the cloak and the associated phrase, "silver lining." But clock seems to be associated with cloak because of the similarity in spelling and sound. In terms of association on the level of mental constructs (signifieds), Stein uses both association based on contiguity (defined by James as association of objects habitually found together in time and space, and identified by Jakobson as metonymy) and on similarity (which Jakobson identifies as metaphor.)[45] Both kinds of association are operations of selection which function along the vertical axis of language. But the metaphorical type of association seems to predominate in *Tender Buttons*, as one might expect, given that "metaphor is alien to the similarity disorder and metonymy to the contiguity disorder."[46] Moreover, the operation of association is stressed not only in terms of images and concepts (signifieds), but also in terms of the qualities of the words as words (signifiers).

Stein often plays with the qualities of words as *words* in *Tender Buttons* and chooses them on the basis of their associations with other words as signifiers. For instance, she often uses rhyme within the line: "... all the joy in weak success, all the joyful tenderness, all the section and the tea, all the stouter symmetry...." (*Tender Buttons*, p. 35.) Similarly,

Chicken

Alas a dirty word, alas a dirty third, alas a dirty third alas a dirty bird. (*Tender Buttons*, p. 54.)

and: "The sister was not a mister." (*Tender Buttons*, p. 65.)

She also associates words on the basis of alliteration: "The sight of a reason, the same sight slighter, the sight of a simpler negative answer, the same sore sounder, the intention to wishing, the same splendor, the same furniture." (*Tender Buttons*, p. 12.) She even uses onomatopoeia:

Chicken

Stick Stick call then, stick stick sticking, sticking with a chicken.
(*Tender Buttons*, p. 54.)

Playing with the sounds and meanings of words also leads to puns, as in the following, seemingly evoking the associations of Washington, Wellington, and veal Wellington:

Veal

Very well very well. Washing is old, washing is washing.
(*Tender Buttons*, p. 53.)

Additional punning occurs in the following:

Milk

Climb up in sight climb in the whole utter needless and a guess a whole guess is hanging. Hanging, hanging. (*Tender Buttons*, p. 47.)

She even plays with the spelling of words: "and easy express e. c." (*Tender Buttons*, p. 55.)

The devices used here are certainly traditional, or at least they seem so now: indirect associations of imagery, obliqueness, fragmented syntax, rhyme, rhythm, alliteration, etc. What is it, then, that so many have found upsetting? Perhaps it is the lack of discursive meaning or the fact that the "subject matter" cannot be reconstructed from the images like a jigsaw puzzle, but these may be inappropriate expectations with which to approach Stein's writing.

It is ironic that, in spite of Stein's intention in writing *Tender Buttons* to capture immediate experience while consciousness grapples with it, there have been so many problems in the reading of that book. One problem inherent in the work itself is the disjunction of the two axes of language making it almost impossible to read the work for conventional discursive content. Moreover, this problem leads to another: the effort of trying to "figure it out," to reconstruct the content, not only exhausts the reader, but overdistances him from the work itself. Such an effort is futile anyway, for *Tender Buttons* demands to be dealt with in its own terms. The reader is given none of the literary allusions that the reader of Pound, Eliot, or Joyce can hold on to. As for inventing glosses for the little pieces in *Tender Buttons*, Sutherland points out that it is possible and amusing to create them, but that "it is perfectly idle":

Such a procedure puts the original in the position of being a riddle, a rhetorical complication of something rather unremarkable in itself. It would be rather like an exhibition of the original table tops, guitars, pipes, and people which were the subject matter of cubist paintings. The original subject matter is or was of importance to the painter as a source of sensations, relations, ideas, even, but it is not after all the beholder's business. The beholder's business is the picture in front of him, which is a new reality and something else, which does not add up to the nominal subject matter.[47]

As Sutherland suggests, perhaps what the reader of Stein is required to do is to look *at* the work, rather than *through* it. One cannot look *through* it because it is an opaque, rather than transparent, style. If one does looks *at* the work, what does one see in *Tender Buttons?* He sees the word presented as an entity in its own right. By forcing the reader to attend to the word, Stein makes the word seem new, again. In this effort, she does not ignore the meanings of words, as so many critics have claimed. However by presenting each word in an unusual context, she directs attention not only towards its sound but towards its sense as the reader is forced to grapple with each word, one at a time. One is forced to attend to the word, and to language, with a sense of bewilderment and perhaps with a sense of wonder and discovery:

> Nouns are the name of anything and anything is named, that is what Adam and Eve did and if you like it is what anybody does, but do they go on just using the name until perhaps they do not know what the name is or if they do know what the name is they do not care what the name is.... And what has that to do with poetry. A great deal I think....[48]

The role of poetry, then, is to give the word back its youth and vitality:

> ...you can love a name and if you love a name then saying that name any number of times only makes you love it more, more violently, more persistently, more tormentedly. Anybody knows how anybody calls out the name of anybody one loves. And so that is poetry really loving the name of anything....[49]

Stein's fascination with language, both its sound and its sense, and her interest in exploring the way it works are certainly evident in *Tender Buttons*. Her intuitive grasp of the principles of its operation is manifested not only in her theories, but also in the very nature of the two so very different kinds of obscure styles that she created.

Richard Bridgman and Edmund Wilson are among those critics who attribute the relative unintelligibility of Stein's work to her need to write about her private passions and her simultaneous need to be discreet about the nature of those passions. As Stein herself might have said, "Interesting, if true." But the only relevance of this sexually motivated evasiveness is that it may have served as an impetus for her innovations with language. In *The Making of*

Americans (as well as in other works of the same style), she stretches the contiguity of the sentence as far as it will go without snapping, at the same time reducing to a minimum the vocabulary available for selection. In *Tender Buttons* and similar works, the available vocabulary becomes practically limitless while the syntax is shortened, destroyed, and even disintegrated into lists. As Jakobson's observations about aphasia indicate, conventionally intelligible language can only occur when both aspects of language are fully operative. Although one can only speculate that Stein's innovations grew out of a desire and a need to be unintelligible, one *can* say less uncertainly that her obscurity was a necessary consequence of the nature of her innovative experiments with language.

Notes

1. Gertrude Stein, "Poetry and Grammar," *Lectures in America* (Boston: Beacon Press, 1935), pp. 228–230.

2. *Ibid.*, pp. 230–231.

3. Roland Barthes, "Elements of Semiology," in *Writing Degree Zero and Elements of Semiology*, trans. Annette Lavers and Colin Smith (Boston: Beacon Press, 1970), p. 58.

4. *Ibid.*, pp. 58–59.

5. Ronald Levinson, "Gertrude Stein, William James and Grammar," *American Journal of Psychology*, 54 (January, 1941), 124–128.

6. William James, *Psychology: Briefer Course* (New York: Henry Holt & Co., 1892), p. 160.

7. Roman Jakobson and Morris Halle, "Two Aspects of Language and Two Types of Aphasic Disturbances," *Fundamentals of Language* (Netherlands: Mouton & Co., Printers, 1956), pp. 71–72.

8. See chapter entitled "Association" in James' *Psychology*, especially pp. 255–265.

9. Robert Haas, "Another Garland for Gertrude Stein," in *What Are Masterpieces* by Gertrude Stein (New York: Pitman Publishing Corp., 1940), p. 21.

10. Barthes, p. 9.

11. Jakobson and Halle, pp. 71–72.

12. "Poetry and Grammar," p. 216.

13. Gertrude Stein, *The Making of Americans: Being a History of a Family's Progress*, Complete Version (New York: Something Else Press, 1966), p. 801. Hereafter, references to this work appear parenthetically within the text.

14. Michael J. Hoffman, *The Development of Abstractionism in the Writings of Gertrude Stein* (Philadelphia: University of Pennsylvania Press, 1965), p. 133.

15. *Ibid.*, p. 138.

16. Jakobson and Halle, p. 60.

17. *Ibid.*, p. 63.

18. *Ibid.*, pp. 64–65.

19. Richard Bridgman, *Gertrude Stein in Pieces* (New York: Oxford University Press, 1970), p. 125.

20. *Ibid.*, p. 124.

21. *Ibid.*

22. Donald Sutherland, *Gertrude Stein: A Biography of Her Work* (New Haven: Yale University Press, 1951), p. 74.

23. *Ibid.*

24. Gertrude Stein, "Portraits and Repetition," *Lectures in America*, pp. 188–189.

25. *Bridgman*, p. 124.

26. Hoffman, p. 28.

27. In his chapter "Portraits and the Abstract Style," dealing with Stein's early portraits (1908–1912), Hoffman states that she wanted to use language "plastically" as the Cubists did. However, he fails to point out that neither Stein nor the Cubists created "plastic" art until 1912. Until that time, their art, although abstract, was mimetic. Cubist art did not become "plastic" until the development of synthetic Cubism (1912), nor did Stein's writing become "plastic" until she wrote *Tender Buttons* (1912). Hoffman further confuses the issue by referring to the fragmentation of forms by Braque and Picasso, a phenomenon related to analytic cubism. Moreover, he further confuses the issue by referring to what "the painters of the period" were doing and by examining Picasso's *Girl Before A Mirror*, but it is hard to see how this explanation could clarify what was happening in 1908–1912, since it was painted in 1932. See Hoffman, p. 170.

28. John Malcolm Brinnin, *The Third Rose: Gertrude Stein and Her World* (Boston: Little, Brown and Company, 1959), p. 134.

29. "Portraits and Repetition," pp. 194–195.

30. Bridgman, p. 124.

31. Gertrude Stein, *Tender Buttons* (New York: Claire Marie, 1914), p. 64. Hereafter, references to this work appear with the body of the text.

32. Thorton Wilder, "Introduction" to *Four in America* by Gertrude Stein (New Haven: Yale University Press, 1947), pp. viii–ix.

33. Bridgman, p. 124.

34. Bridgman, in a footnote on p. 125, indicates that it is unlikely that *Tender Buttons* was not composed earlier than 1912.

35. Douglas Cooper, *The Cubist Epoch* (New York: Phaidon Publishers, Inc., 1971), p. 188.

36. *Ibid.*

37. "Portraits and Repetition," pp. 191–192.

38. *Ibid.*, pp. 188–189.

39. Bridgman, p. 103.

40. "Poetry and Grammar," p. 228.

41. *Ibid.*, p. 235.

42. "Poetry and Grammar," p. 234.

43. Jakobson and Halle, pp. 71–72.

44. "Poetry and Grammar," p. 231.

45. See James' chapter "Association" in *Psychology*, as well as the discussion of the metaphoric and metonymic poles in Jakobson and Halle, "Two Aspects of Aphasia," *Fundamentals of Language*.

46. Jakobson and Halle, p. 76.

47. Sutherland, pp. 76–77.

48. "Poetry and Grammar," p. 229.

49. *Ibid.*, p. 232.

The Human Mind
& *Tender Buttons*

Harry R. Garvin

"The human mind" is the central notion in Gertrude Stein's theory of writing and reading. After using familiar Steinian terms to delineate the theory, I'll read two objects in *Tender Buttons* and suggest what happened in my consciousness while I was reading them. I hope a nice centennial bouquet comes forth.

During moments of actual composition, Gertrude Stein thinks she should "be one" with her human mind while unaware of an "audience" and of her own private self ("identity"). In the total consciousness during a concentrated span of *actual writing*, the human mind is the special "entity" that should dominate the rest of consciousness absolutely. No writer except Joyce has rivalled Gertrude Stein in meditating on levels of consciousness in process.

To achieve such a concentration while the hand is writing, Gertrude Stein thinks she must exclude not only personal identity and private feelings but also ordinary memory and practical intellect, associational emotions and ready-made resemblances—indeed, she must exclude all feelings prompted demandingly and too easily by past experiences and her "human nature." Further, the dominating human mind should not let the "subconscious" get into the consciousness. Gertrude Stein's term *subconscious* seems to refer to the Freudian and Jungian unconscious and also to the most emotion-laden levels of the Freudian "preconscious." Thus automatic writing, since it involves the subconscious, does not come from the human mind.

By such exclusions and by concentrating on clear words moving within her while she is writing down these words "one at a time," Gertrude Stein thinks she can free her human mind. This kind of freedom enables the human mind to "know" and thereby to create an "existence" (a "thing in itself and not in relation" to anything else) and to overcome ordinary time and achieve "movement" and masterpieces.

Thus Gertrude Stein's "refusal of the use of the subconscious" and of human nature springs from her desire to let her human mind dominate

Reprinted from *The Widening Circle*, I/4 (Fall 1973) by permission of the author. Copyright © 1973 by Harry R. Garvin.

consciousness during actual writing and bring forth words that are "exact and concentrated and sober."

Let us get a little closer to Miss Stein's self-discipline by considering her doctrine of "recognition." In her moments of composing she "waits" until her human mind feels, recognizes clear and exact whole words unpredictably forming and moving at varying speeds within her while she simultaneously "sees them as [she] writes them." No matter how subtle or intellectual her probing feelings are, they are recognized by her human mind as "one thing." She waits until in her consciousness she can feel fresh meanings in words, feel "the weight and form and completely existing being" of the words. (Concrete poetry is often a massive *visual* exaggeration, on the page itself, of this exquisite Steinian sense of words forming in her *consciousness*.) To recognize words in this way, she had to cut away the familiar associations and the cumulative excrescences of words. (The literary historian will have to remember Gertrude Stein when evaluating the originality, in theory and practice, of Robbe-Grillet, Nathalie Sarraute, and the avant-garde writers in France today.)

Though the human mind, by Steinian definition, always creates existences available to other human minds, only some of these existences are masterpieces. And a masterpiece at once implies that the human minds of readers can share the existences created by writers. The freely created existence, new and individual, can apparently be universal in the sense that the human minds of readers may be able to experience them, though never exactly. Gertrude Stein wishes "to say what you nor I nor nobody knows, but what is really what you and I and everybody knows." Like all who assert the supremacy of the artist over the audience, she yearns (sometimes secretly sometimes publicly) for at least a fit audience though few. She admits how hard it is for her to read other artists properly. Her deprecatory remarks on audience merely alert us to the dangers surrounding every human mind, a reader's as well as a writer's. Every human mind is, by definition, free and autonomous, and is the source of knowledge of the world and of the existences in other human minds.

Thus, the reader of Gertrude Stein's pieces must discipline his human mind austerely and intensely, in much the way Gertrude Stein had to while actually composing. That is the way I think her works should be read, especially her difficult portrait-pieces such as *Tender Buttons, Four Saints in Three Acts,* and *Four in America.* In any case, that is the way I should always like to read Gertrude Stein.

Let me now describe some of the meanings that can suggest the intuitive, "plain" feelings I had while silently reading two objects in *Tender Buttons.* Each time I read I moved intuitively, processively with the words; my descriptions below of my final reading of "Water Raining" and of "A Box" will deliberately not attempt here a critical interpretation or evaluation.

Water Raining

Water astonishing and difficult altogether makes a meadow and a stroke.

During the night, a sudden hard *(difficult)* rain with thunder (an etymological pun on *astonishing*) and lightning *(a stroke)* reveals *(makes)* a meadow. The stroke reveals both itself and the meadow. *Altogether makes* suggests the unity and suddenness of the whole scene.

A Box

Out of kindness comes redness and out of rudeness comes rapid same question, out of eye comes research, out of selection comes painful cattle. So then the order is that a white way of being round is something suggesting a pin and is it disappointing, it is not, it is so rudimentary to be analyzed and see a fine substance strangely, it is so earnest to have a green point not to red but to point again.

A box and its unopened contents are described in terms of surprise and paradox. Without further mention of the box or its unknown contents, she indicates that the contents will be unexpected. For kindness can result, surprisingly, in anger *(redness)* in another. A rude reply to a simple question brings not the expected turning away but a quick, irritated repetition of the question. Practical research comes from a fine eye (looking into a microscope, probably). Out of careful scientific breeding *(selection)* in order to increase the size of cattle comes painful calving. The four images are functional in that they all bring out the slightly ironic and surprising results of certain activities like opening a box and having expectations and hopes.

After this series of mild paradoxes, Miss Stein is ready for a generalized image and for a question and answer. The very order of things is surprising and ironic. *A white way of being round* — perhaps a large feeling, or an idea for a poem, or any thing that seems lovely, pure, complete — suddenly suggests a pin (small, ordinary, but here not sticking or nasty). But this surprise should cause not disappointment but a deep search into the pin *(so rudimentary to be analyzed)* in order to see this tiny, fine substance, or any fine thing, in so direct and natural a way that the thing becomes strangely clear. For it is most rewarding (pun on *earn-est*) to see ahead completely (steadily *have a green*) and purely, without faltering and without angry or irritating obstruction and stop *(point not to red)*. It is a pleasure to welcome surprise and paradox and to discover any thing completely.

I think all critical interpretations of *Tender Buttons* (including those by Freudian, Jungian, Hindu, or Buddhist critics) should be based at least initially on the critic's feelings in his own *consciousness* while actually reading each portrait. Indeed, a fully articulated theory and method for reading Gertrude Stein is a peremptory need in future Steinian studies and would surely become a perennial bouquet to Gertrude Stein.

I don't like to worry about the feelings I may be missing while I am reading a difficult Stein portrait, or about the inadequacy of my later description of these plain feelings. Every time I give some intuitive readings to a difficult Steinian piece, I can have fine adventures with ordinary words, can recognize nuances in her labyrinth of feelings. Many modern writers make the commonplace almost synonymous with the inauthentic; Gertrude Stein throughout her career celebrates the commonplace by seeing it in its strangeness and fineness, and she sees and hears great men and women in a finely ontological ordinariness. In the portrait-works, these celebrations of things and people lead us into extraordinary labyrinths. And often—especially in *Four Saints in Three Acts* and in *Four in America*—we find our own human minds forming simple words and metaphysical feelings.

Reading "Objects"
from *Tender Buttons*

Jackson Mac Low

I start reading "A CARAFE, THAT IS A BLIND GLASS." I go from word to word, seeing the shapes of the printed words, hearing the sounds inwardly, noting rhymes, assonances, alliterations. Where an image is suggested, I see it inwardly. I hear the alliteration "kind," "cousin," "color," with the near-alliteration "glass." The rhyme in "strange" & "arrangement." The alliteration of s's: "spectacle," "strange," "single," "system," "spreading." The assonance of short i's that binds the three sentences ("system," "this," "difference") as does the ending of each sentence with an "ing" (which is reinforced by the short e's in "resembling" & "spreading"). There are also the 2nd sentence's rhymes ("ordinary," "unordered") & the alliterative sequence "spectacle," "pointing," "spreading." The three sentences are a bound system of sounds.

But can I specify anything beyond the sounds? To use a phrase I first heard from Spencer Holst, it gives "the sensation of meaning," but can I connect the meanings of the words as readily as I find their sounds connected?

Beyond the obvious fact that the carafe is made of glass, I can see only certain connections of meanings: "a blind glass," "a kind in glass" (I didn't notice consciously the "blind"-"kind" rhyme before), & then "a spectacle" (something seen or to be seen, but also "spectacles" are "glasses"). Then "nothing strange," "not ordinary," "not unordered," "not resembling," & "difference" form a meaning sequence. Another sequence of meanings: "blind," "spectacle" (with the intervening "glass"'s causing the ambiguity of "spectacle," which might not have been as apparent without them), & "color," that seems to carry over to "arrangement," "pointing," "not unordered," "not resembling," & even to "spreading." The sequence "kind" (with its two meanings), "cousin," "nothing strange" seems opposed to "not ordinary," "not resembling," & "The difference is spreading.": a meaning movement from near-sameness to greater & greater difference.

"A single hurt color" is the most emotional phrase, altho "blind glass" with its implied oxymoron (glass is usually transparent—at least we first think of

Reprinted from *The L=A=N=G=U=A=G=E Book* (1984) by permission of the author.

transparency when we hear the word "glass" — & when it is made into spectacle lenses, it helps people to see better) is perhaps even more so. Maybe the "single hurt color" is the blackness of blindness. The whole poem suddenly seems to be about seeing!

But what of the "carafe" that starts it all? Why is it "a *blind* glass"? Ordinarily a carafe is one of the least "blind" — that is, the most transparent — of glass containers. It usually contains plain water. The OED defines it as "a glass water-bottle for the table, bedroom, etc." Its Romance forms (F. *carafe*, It. *caraffa*, Neapol. *carrafa* (a measure of liquids), Sp. & Pg. *garrafa*, Sicil. *carabba*) are related by some authorities to the Pers. *garābah*, a large flagon, & the Arabic *gharafa*, to draw or lift water.

Why, then, is *this* carafe a *blind* glass?

Is the whole poem then a "pointing" from the ordinary transparent carafe ("nothing strange") to one "not ordinary" — one that is "blind" — an orderly ("not unordered") movement "spreading" from transparency & clarity thru the "single hurt color" to the implied darkness & opacity of blindness, a movement condensed & made explicit in the title?

"The Complete Connection":
Two and Other Transitional Texts

Jayne L. Walker

In *Two* Stein directly thematized the opposition between the epistemological stance that governed the early sections of *The Making of Americans* and the radically different one that began to emerge in the David Hersland chapter. In a letter written in February 1912, she characterized this work as a "study of a man and a woman having the same means of expression and the same emotional and spiritual experiences with different qualities of intellect."[1] The Yale edition of *Two* subtitles it *Gertrude Stein and Her Brother*, but manuscript notes reveal that its original subjects were her brother Leo and her sister-in-law Sally. Stein had analyzed both of them in her notebooks and concluded that they were equally deficient as creative personalities, for opposite reasons. Leo's excess of rationality separates him from immediate experience. Sally is "more capable of first hand experience from sensitiveness but with that her intellect does not in any way connect" (unpublished notebooks). Stein began this long study in the austere, reductive style of the early portraits. But as she was exploring the contrasts between these two "qualities of intellect," her style began to change drastically. The more critically she distanced herself from the analytical stance that Leo represented, the more attracted she was to its polar opposite. By the end of the text, she had abandoned her previous "passion for simplification" in favor of what William James describes in "Reflex Action and Theism" as the "rival claims" of a "passion for distinguishing," which, in his words, "prefers any amount of incoherence, abruptness, and fragmentariness (so long as the literal details of the separate facts are saved) to an abstract way of conceiving things that, while it simplifies them, dissolves away their concrete fulness."

Tender Buttons (1912) was the culmination of this gradual process of redefining both the "real order" of the world and the artistic order of the text that models it. The works that span this period of transition between *The Making of Americans* and *Tender Buttons* contain a succession of different styles that trace this gradual epistemological break. While writing *Two*, Stein began to

Reprinted from *The Making of a Modernist* (1984) by permission of the author and the University of Massachusetts Press.

experiment with new ways of using language to model a "reality" unmediated by analytical thought. At the same time, she was still working on *A Long Gay Book* and two other projects she had begun after finishing *The Making of Americans*: *G.M.P.* and *Jenny, Helen, Hannah, Paul and Peter*. She began all of these texts in the early portrait style, and *Two* was the first that she finished. Continuing to work on the others, she completed the break with her earlier methods of representation and created a concrete, radically disjunctive style to celebrate her new delight in pure difference. *Two* is by far the most interesting of these texts, because it is the only one to present clear thematic motivation for the sequence of different styles that all of them contain.

In the portraits of artists and the notebook analyses that preceded them, Stein had begun to explore the temperamental qualities that lead to successful creative activity. She continued to develop themes as well as the techniques of these early portraits in *Two*. As in the portraits of artists, the patterning of the prose creates iconic models of the author's conception of the subjects' personalities. But the other early portraits are short texts; these techniques, sustained for more than a hundred pages, severely strain the limits of the reader's endurance of boredom. Probably this is the reason Stein's critics have had little to say about *Two*, despite its alluring subtitle.[2] Still, this far-from-"pleasurable" text rewards the reader's pain with some stretches of brilliantly innovative prose. And it is crucially important for understanding the aesthetic and epistemological issues that motivated the extreme changes in Stein's style between *The Making of Americans* and *Tender Buttons*.

The act of expression is central to her presentation of the two contrasting characters in this text: "Sound is coming out of them"; they are "expressing something." These endlessly repeated motifs dominate the first hundred pages of this long study in the portrait style. "Sound coming out of her comes out of her and is expressing sound coming out of her"—no more than that, except that "the sound coming out of her was the sound that was that she was one" (*Two*, 9, 15). This "sound" reveals the temperament of the speakers, not by communicating specific messages but by portraying the process by which they transform their experiences into expression. As in the portrait of Nadelman and in the characterization of David Hersland, the polarities of "thinking" and "feeling" are essential to Stein's portrayal of this process in *Two*. These motifs establish the fundamental contrast between the two characters, who are never named in the text. For the woman, "feeling is everything" (23). Representing the opposite extreme, the man "was expressing that if he had not been the one thinking sound sounding would not have been coming out of him. . . . [H]e was expressing that, thinking being existing, he was existing in being thinking" (50). As this long portrait goes on, a number of related motifs come to be associated with the man's exclusive reliance on rational mediation of experience: ordering, considering, deciding, convincing, concluding, judging, reasoning, understanding, and, especially, explaining and arranging. In contrast, the woman is presented in terms of receiving, accepting, doing, working, living, and loving.

Two consistently patterns its language to emphasize that the man's excess of rational control is a barrier that totally insulates him from direct experience: "he *judging* that something *was angering* him *was deciding* that he *feeling* that thing he *would be* one *deciding* that he *would* not *justify* that thing the thing he *was judging*" (43–44; my emphases). This sentence surrounds "angering" and "feeling" with verbs signifying intellectual mediation and subtly manipulates their tenses, to model the habitual process described elsewhere as "arranging what he had been feeling" (46). This constant rationalization prevents the man not only from feeling but also from doing anything:

> the sound coming out of him and sounding was expressing that in reasoning he was concluding and in concluding he had expressed the reason of his understanding that someone doing something was one having done that thing, . . . that thing that he would have done if he had done that thing. (36)

Again, Stein's characteristic syntactical maneuvers marshal her limited lexicon to convey acute psychological insights. In this passage the gerundial phrase "someone doing something" is submerged in a flood of "thinking" verbs. The first part moves backward in time from "*was* expressing" to "in concluding he *had* expressed the reason of his understanding." The object of these cogitations, "someone doing something," is no sooner expressed than it is transformed into the past and, finally, into the conditional past tense of fantasy ("having done . . . would have done if he had done"). In contrast to the male character, always "intending to be expecting to be doing what he could be doing," the woman is presented as simply "doing what she was doing" (56).

The following passage models the abrupt, jerky rhythms of the man's "sound," which manifest the discontinuity between his experience and his responses:

> Coming and not coming, enjoying and being charming, jerking and not jerking, gently and with enthusiasm, brutally and not completing, occasionally and continuing, steadily and explaining, excitedly and not deciding, deciding and beginning again, completing and repeating, repeating and denying, hesitating and terrifying, angrily and beginning, angrily and completing, concluding and denying, completing and undetermined, ending without beginning, continuing with realising, ending without experiencing, . . . sound is coming out of him. (7–8)

In contrast, the woman is frequently portrayed in polysyndetic sentences that model the simple continuity of her experience and her expression:

> She being that one she was expressing and expressing she was expressing
> this thing and expressing this thing she was feeling everything and feeling
> everything she was loving and loving she was being living and being
> living she was continuing and being continuing sound was coming out
> of her and the sound coming out of her was sounding and the sound
> coming out of her and sounding was telling and asking anything and
> telling and asking anything it was expressing that she being that one was
> one. [47–48]

Here and elsewhere in the text, Stein uses the *gradatio*, a classical figure of
thought that conventionally signals a chain of logical and chronological
causality, to reinforce the continuity of the various actions she associates with
her characters while obscuring the actual logic or chronology – if any – of their
relationship. Throughout *Two* Stein systematically used this and other syntactical constructions to create a sense of unity and continuity that defies conventional understanding.

In contrast to the fluid continuity that is both thematized and modeled in
the prose that describes the woman, a number of passages portray the disrup-
tion of simple "continuing" that the man's need for intellectual mastery entails:

> To continue, to commence to continue, to believe in continuing, to
> end continuing, to mean continuing, to expect continuing, to continue
> again, to explain continuing, to enlarge continuing, to restrict continu-
> ing, to deny continuing, to begin continuing is to arrange what can be
> arranged in arranging anything. [59]

Like the elder David Hersland in *The Making of Americans*, the man is constantly "beginning" ("Why does he always begin?"), while the woman's
endeavors are described as both "continuing" and "beginning again and again"
(76). The particular opposition that Stein intended to convey by means of
these two motifs of "beginning" is far from clear in the text. In *The Making of
Americans* she wrote, "It is hard to tell it about them because the same words
can describe all of them the one and the other kind of them" (178). In *Two* her
limited lexicon generally produces the contrasts she intended, but in this case
it is necessary to resort to her notebooks for clarification:

> logical processe not reinforced by experience [are] short and never sus-
> tained. . . . Sometimes it is very good if well started, it can never run long.
> It is impossible that it should, it either becomes sentimentality, logic
> chopping, idedistic conceptions, mania or it don't do on long. Real
> thinking is conceptions aiming and aiming again and again always get-
> ting fuller, that is the difference between creative thinking and theoris-
> ing. (unpublished notebooks)

This is the model of "creative thinking" that informs *The Making of Americans*, in which the author's "beginning again and again" is a process of repetition and accumulation. In *Two* the male character resists and tries to avoid repetition, while the structures of the prose insist on the reiterated pattern that characterizes all his new beginnings:

> Sound is coming out of him, he is not allowing any piece of that thing of sound coming out of him to be coming out of him again. He is not allowing that thing. He is stating that thing quite stating that thing. Pieces of sound coming again and again out of him are pieces that he has been changing, quite changing. [7]

Although repeating is "not interesting" to him, still, "[h]e was one and sound coming out of him was sounding and repeating coming out of him was repeating that in developing he could not be repeating" (54). Even this aversion is ironically subsumed under the cycles of repetition that define his character. A defect in this "listening" accounts for his refusal to accept the inevitability of repetition: "not being listening he was not hearing that repeating should be existing" (72).

Instead of resisting and attempting to reorder the natural flow of experience, the woman is described as "resonating" in harmony with it (11). From the beginning, the text emphasizes the "complete connection" between her experience and her expression:

> Feeling that sound sounding was coming out of her she was feeling that there was complete connection between sound sounding and sound coming out of her. She was feeling that there was complete connection between sound sounding and coming out of her and something being existing. [18]

Two begins with a simple opposition between the man's exclusive dedication to "thinking" and the woman's sole reliance on "feeling." But gradually the woman comes to represent an ideal synthesis of these two extremes:

> *She being one she is feeling. She being one and feeling is understanding. She being one and feeling and understanding is extremely thinking.* She being one and feeling and understanding and extremely thinking is being one who is some one.
>
> In listening and in listening sound coming out and sounding can be coming, in listening sound coming out of her and sounding was feeling in thinking being existing.
>
> In listening sound coming out of her and sounding was feeling understanding being existing. In listening sound coming out of her and sounding was feeling in agreeing to have thinking be continuing. In listening sound coming out of her and sounding was *feeling that understanding is creating.* (53–54; my emphases)

In the first paragraph of this passage, one motif of action after another is introduced as a predicate and then moved to a nominative position in the next sentence. This syntactical patterning gradually forges a union of "feeling," "thinking," and "understanding," and, finally, "creating."

The woman's "complete connection" becomes the ideal of creativity modeled in the language of the text, as its ever-longer sentences use the logical order of syntax to create associations that transcend its limitations:

> She would not have a decision and deciding that she would not be saying, she would be having a decision in meaning that reflection is interpretation and interpretation is decision and decision is regarding meaning and regarding meaning is acting and acting is expression and expression is not resisting winning and not resisting winning is submitting and submitting is leading and leading is declaration and declaration is beginning and beginning is intending and intending is deciding and deciding is creating and creating is not contending and not contending is destroying and destroying is submitting and submitting is decision and decision is creating and creating is leading and leading is reflection and reflection is exacting and exacting is decision and decision is meaning and meaning is progressing and progressing is not denying and not denying is feeling and feeling is thinking and thinking is arranging and arranging is continuing and continuing is rebeginning and rebeginning is submitting and submitting is deciding and deciding is creating and creating is reflecting and reflecting is meaning and meaning is deciding and deciding is believing and believing is continuing and continuing is leading and leading is expressing and expressing is meaning and meaning is feeling and feeling is submitting and submitting is deciding and deciding is creating and creating is following and following is leading and leading is following and following is deciding and deciding is creating and creating is submitting and submitting is meaning and meaning is expressing and expressing is accepting and accepting is submitting and submitting is following and following is feeling and feeling is meaning and meaning is creating and creating is doing and doing is continuing and continuing is expressing and expressing is leading and leading is following and following is expressing and expressing is meaning and meaning is expressing and expressing is leading and leading is expressing and expressing is following and following is creating and creating is expressing and expressing is meaning and meaning is doing and doing is following and following is creating and creating is leading and leading is expressing and expressing is meaning and meaning is expressing and expressing is feeling and feeling is following and feeling is leading and expressing is meaning and meaning is creating and creating is meaning and meaning is meaning. [90–91]

I quote this gargantuan sentence in its entirety to illustrate the powerfully hypnotic effect of this incantatory style. Repetition of the syntactical pattern "A is B and B is C and C is D" generates a chain of identities that eventually merges all of these motifs into an all-encompassing union. Earlier in the text these motifs were used to establish oppositions between two mutually exclusive ways of responding to experience, but the dynamic combinative process thematized and enacted in this passage embraces them all. Its cycle of identities culminates with the propositions, "expressing is meaning and meaning is creating and creating is meaning and meaning is meaning." The insistent affirmation that concludes this passage clearly reveals that Stein intended this new creative synthesis to produce an enrichment of "meaning" in her prose and not a denial of it. This point is worth emphasizing, because the passage in its entirety clearly reveals how radically she was beginning to subvert conventional logic in her pursuit of new meanings that transcend the limitations of rationality.

The elevation of the woman's "complete connection" between experience and expression into a new creative ideal was apparently not Stein's intention when she began writing *Two*. As I mentioned earlier, her notebook analyses clearly reveal that she regarded Sally and Leo Stein, the original models for this double portrait, as equally lacking the ideal balance of qualities that nurtures creativity. Her notebooks characterize Sally as a "mediumistic sensibility," extremely receptive to experience but lacking the intellectual power to produce original work (unpublished notebooks).[3] The early pages of *Two* attribute to the female character some of the negative traits Stein described in her notebook analysis of her sister-in-law: "not being then a strong one" (19); "suffering" (21); and extreme passivity (43). But as the passages quoted above illustrate, this character, with her "complete connection" between experience and expression, gradually came to represent Stein's own creative ideal as she continued to work on the text. But perhaps this was not quite as much of a deviation from her original plan as I have been suggesting. Although the title page of the manuscript identifies its subjects as "Leo and Sally," the notes she wrote on the text consistently refer to the man as Leo and to the woman as "Jane."[4] She assigned the name "Jane Sands" to Sally Stein in *A Long Gay Book* (notebooks, fragment #14). But in her notebooks she also sometimes used "Jane Sands" or "Jane Sandys" as pseudonyms for herself (notebooks-10, 6). Whatever her initial intentions, the text itself reveals the gradual process of reevaluation that eventually resulted in the idealization of this character.

While she departed so far from her original analysis of Sally's shortcomings, she never deviated from her focus on Leo's weaknesses. In fact, her relentless probing of the limitations of her brother's exclusive commitment to rationality seems to have impelled her to define her own creativity in radical opposition to the intellectual stance he represented. Although she cast it in the form of an anonymous study of contrasting personalities, *Two* was by far the most personal work Stein had written since *Q.E.D.* Her first intellectual model, her brother Leo had played a major role in shaping her ideas and tastes. He led her to Harvard and into William James's classes. A few years later she followed him to Europe and into the center of the creative ferment of avant-garde painting. In 1908 they shared the excitement of reading Weininger's *Sex and Character.*[5] During their early years in Paris, Leo's talk dominated their salon. He considered himself an artist, an aesthetician, and a philosopher. He proved incapable of sustained efforts in any of these fields, although he seems to have talked brilliantly about them all. Stein's notebooks reveal that Leo continued to be an important source of aesthetic insights and intellectual stimulation for her as late as 1909.[6] Soon after that, their relationship became strained close to the breaking point. Leo never recognized the value of his sister's work. He scorned it as absolutely, and perhaps as jealously, as he did Picasso's cubist paintings. In 1913 he described "cubism whether in paint or ink" as "tommyrot," the "intellectual product of the unintellectual."[7] Meanwhile, Stein had found in Picasso a continuing source of stimulation for her own work and in Alice B. Toklas a new source of emotional support. Although her final break with Leo did not occur until the fall of 1913, when he moved out of the rue de Fleurus apartment, her psychological separation was apparently completed in the process of writing *Two.*[8]

Significantly, the character Stein created to represent an idealized alternative to Leo's tyrannical rationality was a woman. This in itself signals a striking change in Stein's conception of her role as an artist and as a woman.[9] Beginning with Leo, all of her artistic and intellectual models had been male—James, Weininger, Cézanne, Matisse, and Picasso. A woman who was a serious artist in the first decade of this century was even more of an anomaly in France than in America or England. In Stein's circle in Paris, Apollinaire's mistress Marie Laurencin and Sonia Delaunay, the wife of Robert Delaunay, were the only female artists. Stein's *Autobiography of Alice B. Toklas* accurately reflects the attitude of that time by presenting these women primarily as appendages of the male artists and only incidentally as painters in their own right.

Stein herself, a woman artist who was also a lesbian, initially responded to the multiple social paradoxes of her identity by defining herself completely in terms of male models. In *Q.E.D.*, the most transparently autobiographical of all her works, her heroine paradoxically remarks, "I always did thank God I wasn't born a woman" (58). In this early text, each of the women involved in the romantic triangle is referred to at least once as a "man" (71, 80, 109). Stein easily transformed Adele into Jeff Campbell in "Melanctha." A few years later, she created David Hersland to portray a version of her own development. The invidious sexual stereotypes in Weininger's *Sex and Character* only reinforced this tendency to define herself entirely in masculine terms: "Picasso has a maleness that belongs to genius. Moi aussi, perhaps" (notebooks, 21). In this context, *Two*'s opposition between the sterile rationality of the male and the fluid creativity of the female in itself suggests a major change in Stein's conception of her role as an artist. While she was working on *Two*, she also wrote "Orta or One Dancing," her portrait of Isadora Duncan. The first text in this series to portray a woman artist, it attributes to its character the same creative fusion of "feeling," "thinking," "believing," "expressing," and "meaning" that characterizes the woman in *Two*.[10]

After she had completed more than one hundred pages of *Two*, Stein wrote a passage that reads as a virtual apotheosis of female creativity:

> [S]he is the one having a connection that expressing is the thing that rising again has risen, and rising is rising and will be having come to be risen. She is the anticipation of forfeiting what is not forbidden. She is the anticipation of conviction of remembering being existing. She is the anticipating of a new one having been an old one. She is the anticipation of expression having immaculate conception. She is the anticipation of crossing. She is the anticipation of regeneration. She is the anticipation of excelling obligation. She is the anticipation. She is the actualisation. She is the rising having been arisen. She is the convocation of anticipation and acceptance. She is the lamb and the lion. She is the leaven of reverberation. She is the complication of receiving, she is the articulation of forgetting, she is the expression of indication, she is the augmentation of condensing, she is the inroad of releasing. [107–8]

This exalted language incorporates both the rhythms and the traditional symbols of incantatory religious prose.[11] Its richly evocative imagery breaks the stylistic constraints Stein had rigorously enforced in her prose for a number of years.

Notes

1. Quoted in Mabel Dodge Luhan, *Movers and Shakers* (New York: Harcourt, Brace, 1936), p. 32. Stein's correspondence with Mabel Dodge, reprinted in this volume, contains some invaluable information about the chronology of her work during this time. On November 2, 1911, she wrote, "The long book is finished." In the letter containing the description of *Two*, Stein reported on the current state of her various projects: "I am working on four books now. One is a long gay book and has lots and lots of everything in it and goes on. It will be quite long. I have written about 120 pages of it. Another is a study of two, a man and a woman having the same means of expression and the same emotional and spiritual experiences with different qualities of intellect. That is going very well and slowly. Then I am doing one that will be published in a couple of months that consists of many portraits of women. Then I am doing another which is a description of a family of five who are all peculiar and are in a peculiar relation each one to every other one of the five of them. This one is just fairly begun." This letter is undated, but it refers to the futurist exhibition at Berheims, which took place February 5–12, 1912 (Umbro Apollonio, ed., *Futurist Manifestos* [New York: Viking, 1973], p. 220). This progress report reveals that in February 1912 *Many Many Women* was nearing completion; *Two* and *A Long Gay Book* were in progress; and *Jenny, Helen, Hannah, Paul and Peter* was just begun. Apparently, Stein had not yet begun work on *G.M.P.* The style of *Many Many Women* suggests that it was, indeed, the first to be finished, as Stein planned.

Two was the second of these texts to be completed, before June of 1912. A letter from Georgiana King in Yale Collection of American Literature, postmarked Madrid, June 18, 1912, informed Stein that she was returning the manuscript of *Two*.

2. Bridgman discusses it briefly, in *Gertrude Stein in Pieces* (pp. 112–14); Hoffman, in *The Development of Abstractionism*, equally briefly (pp. 156–61). In a conversation with Leon Katz at a very early stage of my work on Stein, he emphasized the importance of this text for understanding Stein's development during these years. More recently, in "Spreading the Difference: One Way to Read Gertrude Stein's *Tender Buttons*," *Twentieth Century Literature* 24, 1, (spring 1978): 57–75, Pamela Hadas uses this text to support her clever but inevitably reductive reading of *Tender Buttons* as a "personal story" of Gertrude Stein's break with Leo and her love for Alice.

3. Cf. notebooks-1, 14; C, 23.

4. Manuscript #35 in Yale Collection of American Literature.

5. Katz, "Weininger and *The Making of Americans*," pp. 8–9.

6. "Leo says Matisse's esthetic quality is clarity" (notebooks-13, 11). "When Leo said all classification is teleological I knew I was not a pragmatist" (notebooks, 11).

7. Leo Stein, *Journey into the Self* (New York: Crown Publishers, 1950), p. 48.

8. Mellow (*Charmed Circle*) discusses the dating of this event on p. 205. Based on his interviews with Alice B. Toklas, Leon Katz has been able to determine that, although Leo did not move out of the rue de Fleurus until 1913, the actual separation took place as early as the late spring or early summer of 1911, when Leo moved to Florence Blood's villa in Fiesole. This information, which I received only recently, confirmed my sense that *Two* was very much a part of Stein's process of separating from her brother.

9. Catharine R. Stimpson's essay "The Mind, the Body, and Gertrude Stein," *Critical Inquiry* 3, 3 (Spring 1977): 489–506, is the first serious effort to deal with the question of Stein's sexual identity as it manifests itself in her writing, in the context of her historical situation. Stimpson discusses the masculinization apparent in Stein's earliest texts and in *The Autobiography of Alice B. Toklas*, but she does not discuss this countermovement of feminization.

10. Manuscript notes indicate that Stein wrote this piece as a direct contrast to the portrait of Nadelman: "like Nadelman relation of ideas to impulse to temperament to morality" (#7 In Yale Collection of American Literature). Like the man in *Two*, Nadelman is portrayed as a man who fails as an artist because of an excess of "thinking."

11. Earlier in *Two*, manuscript notes clarify that Stein was contrasting her brother Leo's religious experiences with "Jane's." We know that Sally Stein was an ardent Christian Scientist. It is possible, as Leon Katz has suggested in correspondence with me, that Stein's initial intention here was to mimic Sally's religious rhetoric. But, whatever the author's intentional "meaning" (and, as I have been demonstrating in this chapter, Stein was deliberately loosening her conscious control of her writing in this text), the "significance" of this passage within the text, for the reader, is a celebration of those qualities of the woman's experience that the male character so strikingly lacks.

The Language of Modern Fiction: Gertrude Stein

David Lodge

Modern fiction may be characterized by an extreme or mannered drive toward the metonymic pole of language to which the novel naturally inclines, as well as by a drive toward the metaphoric pole from which it is naturally remote. A clear example of this double tendency is Gertrude Stein, a central figure in Modernist experimentation with language. Her writing went through distinct phases we can associate with the metonymic and metaphoric poles. This is from her early long novel *The Making of Americans* (1906–8):

> It happens very often that a man has it in him, that a man does something, that he does it very often that he does many things, when he is a young man when he is an old man, when he is an older man. One of such of these kind of them had a little boy and this one, the little boy wanted to make a collection of Butterflies and beetles and it was all exciting to him and it was all arranged then and then the father said to the son you are certain that this is not a cruel thing that you are wanting to be doing, killing things to make collections of them and the son was very disturbed then...

And so on. In "The Gradual Making of *The Making of Americans*," Gertrude Stein observed that her "sentences grew longer and longer," though of course they are artificially extended by absence of conventional punctuation. This too she noted in "Poetry and Grammar."

When I first began writing, I felt that writing should go on, I still do feel that it should go on but when I first began writing I was completely possessed by the necessity that writing should go on and if writing should go on what had colons and semi-colons to do with it, what had commas to do with it.

This both states and illustrates Jakobson's dictum that prose is naturally forwarded by contiguity; indeed it seems that Gertrude Stein was at this time deliberately and programmatically cultivating a kind of writing corresponding to the Similarity Disorder, or Selection Deficiency, type of aphasia of which Jakobson speaks. This type of aphasic has great difficulty in naming things; shown a pencil, he is likely to define it metonymically by reference to its use ("to write"), and in his speech main clauses disappear before subordinate clauses, subjects are dropped, while "the words with an inherent reference to the context, like pronouns and pronominal adverbs, words serving merely to construct the context, such as connectives and auxiliaries, are particularly prone to survive." Compare Stein in "Poetry and Grammar":

> A noun is the name of anything, why after a thing is named write about it. A name is adequate or it is not. If it is adequate then why go on calling it, if it is not then calling it by its name does no good. . . . Verbs and adverbs are more interesting. In the first place they have one very nice quality and that is they can be so mistaken. . . . Then comes the thing that can of all things be most mistaken and they are prepositions. . . . I like prepositions best of all. . . . When I was writing those long sentences of *The Making of Americans*, verbs active present verbs with long dependent adverbial clauses became a passion with me. I have told you that I recognize verbs and adverbs aided by prepositions and conjunctions with pronouns as possessing the whole of the active life of writing.

What she was after was to make "a whole present of something that it had taken a great deal of time to find out"—that is, to capture the living quality of a character or experience she had long observed or brooded over without giving the impression of *remembering* it. It was a technique of repetition, though she denied that it *was* repetition, and compared her method to the (metonymic) art of film, because "each time the emphasis is different just as the cinema has each time a slightly different thing to make it all be moving."

A little later, however, Gertrude Stein's methods changed, though a continuity of aim persisted. She began to write "very short things and in doing very short things I resolutely realized nouns and decided not to get around them but to meet them, to handle in short to refuse them by using them and in that way my real acquaintance with poetry was begun." She is here talking about her "still-life" studies of objects, collected in the 1911 volume *Tender Buttons*, of which this is an example:

APPLE

Apple plum, carpet steak, seed clam, coloured wine, calm seen, cold cream, best shake, potato, potato and no gold work with pet, a green seen is called bake and change sweet is bready, a little piece a little piece please.

A little piece please. Cane again to the presupposed and ready eucalyptus tree, count out sherry and ripe plates and little corners of a kind of ham. This is use.

She described her method as one of "looking at anything until something that was not the name of that thing but was in a way that actual thing would come to be written." In short, the technique was one of selection and substitution in Jakobson's sense, but the perception of similarities on which this operation depends was entirely private, and the result therefore inscrutable. Furthermore, the contextual relationships which should link the substitutions together into a chain are entirely neglected. The result is a writing resembling the speech of aphasics suffering from Jakobson's second disorder, Contiguity Disorder or Contextual Deficiency, where "syntactical rules organizing words into a higher unit are lost" and sentences degenerate into "a mere word-heap." Superficially, the result is a writing resembling that of the Dadaists and the later exponents of randomness like William Burroughs, with his "cut-up" method, developments Gertrude Stein might be held to have anticipated. However, where their aim is to affront human rationality, and/or to demonstrate the capacity of nature to generate its own meanings without human interpretation, hers is not. She still maintains the traditional stance of the artist, as one who by the exercise of a special gift or craft is seeking to bring her medium into closer and closer relation with her perceptions.

Hers is, indeed, an aesthetic of realization, a pursuit of the thing itself: "I had to feel anything and everything that for me was existing so intensely that I could put it down in writing as a thing in itself without at all necessarily using its name." This is essentially the Symbolist poetic—expounded by Mallarmé in terms of evocation and suggestion, by Pound in terms of the "image," by Eliot in terms of the "objective correlative." All poets—and Gertrude Stein herself noted: ". . . and here was the question if in poetry one could lose the noun as I had really and truly lost it in prose would there by any difference between poetry and prose." The answer must be no: apart from typographical layout, the sections of *Tender Buttons* are indistinguishable from Symbolist or Surrealist lyric poems. Prose, as Jakobson says, is forwarded essentially by contiguity, and narrative is inseparable from the combinative axis of language; to neglect this side of language completely removes the writer from the realm of prose fiction—and in Stein's case from the realm of meaningful communication, to an extent rare in Modernism. For even Joyce in *Finnegans Wake,* or, later, Samuel Beckett in "Ping" (1967), though they exemplify many of the features of writing pushed far toward the metaphoric pole (e.g. the disappearance of grammatically functional words, conjunctions, prepositions, pronouns, articles), still preserve through word-order a tenuous narrative and logical continuity. However, the point I want to stress about Stein's work is this: though *The Making of Americans* and *Tender Buttons* tend toward the opposite poles of metonymy and metaphor, they are both recognizably "modern" and both pursue the same general artistic aim—to render that elusive quality, "existence." Her use of repetition with slight variation in her earlier, metonymic prose has the effect of converting the dynamic into the static, the temporal into the spatial; this is entirely consistent with the aim of metaphor-oriented Symbolist and Imagist verse, or Pound's definition of the "image" itself; which "presents an intellectual and emotional complex in an instant of time." This instantaneousness is necessarily an illusion, given the sequential character of language; but it is an illusion easier to achieve in poetry than prose. Stein showed how prose might achieve similar effects.

A Note on Stein and Abstraction

Wendell Wilcox

The people for whom Gertrude Stein was a present influence have by now influenced a generation that followed their own and this puts her rather in the light of grandmother to our present writing. As such she has no need, surely, either in the personal or the literary way, of an introduction. In the last analysis her work is done, as she herself tells you in the last and loveliest of these poems.

To attempt to introduce her as a poet seems somehow equally futile after so many years, years in which she has produced variously and plentifully. It is easy however to think of her as a poet, especially if you think of poetry as the direct and passionate addressing of a single object, for no one has possessed more fully than she this power of concentrated, unswerving and single minded approach. In this sense even the long short story "Melanctha," which was one of her earliest works, becomes something of a poem. In fact in much of her prose you meet recurrence to and calling and re-calling upon a single person or thing, and the prose style which she has invented for her use, being patterned and rhythmic not in the sense of set patterns and meters, but in the sense of the play and movement between the words themselves, has in it a tone and quality which come close to poetry.

Whitman years before had brought poetry as close to the boundary line of prose as poetry could come without becoming prose. In Stein we find that prose has been brought across the line which he left, and I rather think that in her own mind the distinction was lost or, to speak more accurately, abandoned. In her work the two have become one. Sometimes we find her, as in these *Stanzas in Meditation*, giving a formal nod to the past of poetry by the occasional addition of meter and rhyme. This formal nodding is the only thing she holds in common with contemporary poets. Her prosody is most usually just the ordinary diction of her prose, and since by her style, her manner, and her approach to subject matter she has influenced in no way the poets but only the prose writers, it is far more natural to think of her as belonging to prose.

I rather think that the choice of which Miss Stein speaks in the last poem refers in part to the fact of her having elected to write in a manner which much of the time makes her concrete meaning inaccessible to the reader. For want of a better word we may call this manner abstraction. I cannot tell you exactly why she so chose or, for want of space, enumerate the contemporary impulses which contributed to it. Suffice it to say that this *was* her choice and that she made it not for the purpose of confounding the reader, as some suppose, but because it was part of her literary fate to do so. This abstraction is neither the least nor the important part of her work but it was her destiny that in parts of her writing she was to push abstraction to its farthest limits and by so doing not to end, but to culminate a tendency that has always been present in American writing.

A brief comparison of American and European writing will show the reader what I mean. You will find English authors constantly occupied with descriptions of the tangible whereas the early writers of our Eastern seaboard were concerned not so much with the actual happenings but with philosophizing and talking *about* the mental effect of these happenings. They describe the tangible as little as possible and then mostly for the sake of coloring, usually a little dark, the results on the mind and emotions. All through Hawthorne, Emerson, Thoreau, Melville and Henry James you will find this tendency to discuss effects and values rather than to stick to the tangible.

There are many reasons for this but chief among them was the separation from England which stood for us as a parent, which separation left us the feeling of being rootless and without real origin and so cleared the air for abstraction. Another was the effect of Puritanism on Eastern manners which prevented the actual description of sin but allowed a preoccupation with its effects. Sin became in Hawthorne faun ears under hair, dark flowers and scarlet letters. In Melville the primitive, inevitable but not quite mentionable became a great white whale. Gradually the fun and fascination of talking *about* and not mentioning spread to everything and reached its peak in Henry James where everything is thrown onto the mental plane and the sentence itself has become if not meaningless nearly unintelligible. In him the pleasure of writing about something in particular nearly disappears and the fun of writing, pure writing, emerges.

Stein takes the process a step further. In her mind as she writes there is almost always a subject but that subject is often as not her own private property. She writes about it but does not name it, or names it in such a way that its physical context cannot be guessed. The excitement is in words themselves, in the movement and interplay of the words.

Either you like this or you don't. More cannot be said on that point. It has its justification in the fact that for many of us the written word does not convey more (or different) than we already know. We have each of us our individual knowledge of life and the written word evokes and refreshes and makes lively that old knowledge but it does not tell us what the author knew. Not really. Even in the most concrete of naturalistic writing this lack of understanding of the author's real feeling about his matter is apparent to anyone. We have never seen the particular object which he describes. We have not seen the room in which he saw it nor the people who surrounded it when he saw it, nor can we know his emotional reaction to those people and it is all of these things that go to make up the personal meaning of the object he describes. When we read of this object we supply a like one from our own experience and its meaning and appearance are colored for us by our own knowledge of it, not the author's. The writer's particular excitement is conveyed to us through the medium of his words and these words in turn excite and revivify something we already know.

In abstract writing the words are given you more or less stripped of subject matter and it is through the author's excitement in them that your own excitement is roused. In the purest forms of abstract writing the excitement roused would I suppose be devoid of subject, at least theoretically, yet there are all degrees of abstraction. In the last of these Stein poems one feels fairly certain in every word what thing it is around which that word plays. This is fairly true too of the Spanish poem, but it is true only because the late war is close and because our mind leaps immediately to that and one assumes that that was where Stein's mind was too. In this light the meaning of it would be clear. Yet it is not necessarily clear. The meaning we give it is only accidental. You as a reader are free to do with it what you like. The poem exists in itself and in its words. It is not necessary to do anything.

The Impossible

John Ashbery

Stanzas in Meditation (1956) is the latest volume in the series of the un-published writings of Gertrude Stein which the Yale University Press has been bringing out regularly for the last decade. It will probably please readers who are satisfied only by literary extremes, but who have not previously taken to Miss Stein because of a kind of lack of seriousness in her work, characterized by lapses into dull, facile rhyme; by the over-employment of rhythms sug-gesting a child's incantation against grownups; and by monotony. There is certainly plenty of monotony in the 150-page title poem which forms the first half of this volume, but it is the fertile kind, which generates excitement as water monotonously flowing over a dam generates electrical power. These austere "stanzas" are made up almost entirely of colorless connecting words such as "where," "which," "these," "of," "not," "have," "about," and so on, though now and then Miss Stein throws in an orange, a lilac, or an Albert to remind us that it really is the world, our world, that she has been talking about. The result is like certain monochrome de Kooning paintings in which isolated strokes of color take on a deliciousness they never could have had out of context, or a piece of music by Webern in which a single note on the celesta suddenly irrigates a whole desert of dry, scratchy sounds in the strings.

Perhaps the word that occurs oftenest in the Stanzas is the word "they," for this is a poem about the world, about "them." (What a pleasant change from the eternal "we" with which so many modern poets automatically begin each sentence, and which gives the impression that the author is sharing his every sensation with some invisible Kim Novak.) Less frequently, "I" enters to assess the activities of "them," to pick up after them, to assert his own altered impor-tance. As we get deeper into the poem, it seems not so much as if we were reading as living a rather long period of our lives with a houseful of people. Like people, Miss Stein's lines are comforting or annoying or brilliant or tedious. Like people, they sometimes make no sense and sometimes make perfect sense or they stop short in the middle of a sentence and wander away, leaving us alone for awhile in the physical world, that collection of thoughts, flowers, weather, and proper names. And, just as with people, there is no real escape from them: one feels that if one were to close the book one would shortly re-encounter the Stanzas in life, under another guise. As the author says, "It is easily eaten hot and lukewarm and cold / But not without it."

Stanzas in Meditation gives one the feeling of time passing, of things happening, of a "plot," though it would be difficult to say precisely what is going on. Sometimes the story has the logic of a dream:

> She asked could I be taught to be allowed
> And I said yes oh yes I had forgotten him
> And she said does any or do any change
> And if not I said whom could they count.

while at other times it becomes startlingly clear for a moment, as though a change in the wind had suddenly enabled us to hear a conversation that was taking place some distance away:

> He came early in the morning.
> He thought they needed comfort
> Which they did
> And he gave them an assurance
> That it would be all as well
> As indeed were it
> Not to have it needed at any time

But it is usually not events which interest Miss Stein, rather it is their "way of happening," and the story of *Stanzas in Meditation* is a general, all-purpose model which each reader can adapt to fit his own set of particulars. The poem is a hymn to possibility; a celebration of the fact that the world exists, that things can happen.

In its profound originality, its original profundity, this poem that is always threatening to become a novel reminds us of the late novels of James, especially *The Golden Bowl* and *The Sacred Fount*, which seem to strain with a superhuman force toward "the condition of music," of poetry. In such a passage as the following, for instance:

> Be not only without in any of their sense
> Careful
> Or should they grow careless with remonstrance
> Or be careful just as easily not at all
> As when they felt.
> They could or would would they grow always
> By which not only as more as they like.
> They cannot please conceal
> Nor need they find they need a wish

we are not far from Charlotte's and the Prince's rationalizations. Both *Stanzas in Meditation* and *The Golden Bowl* are ambitious attempts to transmit a completely new picture of reality, of that *real* reality of the poet which Antonin Artaud called *"une réalité dangereuse et typique."* If these works are highly complex and, for some, unreadable, it is not only because of the complicatedness of life, the subject, but also because they actually imitate its rhythm, its way of happening, in an attempt to draw our attention to another aspect of its true nature. Just as life is being constantly altered by each breath one draws, just as each second of life seems to alter the whole of what has gone before, so the endless process of elaboration which gives the work of these two writers a texture of bewildering luxuriance — that of a tropical rain-forest of ideas — seems to obey some rhythmic impulse at the heart of all happening.

In addition, the almost physical pain with which we strive to accompany the evolving thought of one of James's or Gertrude Stein's characters is perhaps a counterpart of the painful continual projection of the individual into life. As in life, perseverance has its rewards — moments when we emerge suddenly on a high plateau with a view of the whole distance we have come. In Miss Stein's work the sudden inrush of clarity is likely to be an aesthetic experience, but (and this seems to be another of her "points") the description of that experience applies also to "real-life" situations, the aesthetic problem being a microcosm of all human problems.

> I should think it makes no difference
> That so few people are me.
> That is to say in each generation there are so few geniuses
> And why should I be one which I am
> This is one way of saying how do you do
> There is this difference
> I forgive you everything and there is nothing to forgive.

It is for moments like this that one perseveres in this difficult poem, moments which would be less beautiful and meaningful if the rest did not exist, for we have fought side by side with the author in her struggle to achieve them.

The poems in the second half of the book are almost all charming, though lacking the profundity of *Stanzas in Meditation*. Perhaps the most successful is *Winning His Way*, again a picture of a human community: "The friendship between Lolo and every one was very strong / And they were careful to do him no wrong." The bright, clean colors and large cast of characters in this poem suggest a comic strip. In fact one might say that Miss Stein discovered a means of communication as well-suited to express our age as in their own way, the balloons (with their effect of concentration), light bulbs, asterisks, ringed planets, and exclamation marks which comic-strip characters use to communicate their ideas. In *Winning His Way*, for example, she experiments with punctuation by placing periods in the middle of sentences. This results in a strange syncopation which affects the meaning as well as the rhythm of a line. In the couplet

> Herman states.
> That he is very well.

the reader at first imagines that she is talking about a group of states ruled over by a potentate named Herman; when he comes to the second line he is forced to change his idea, but its ghost remains, giving a muted quality to the prose sense of the words.

Donald Sutherland, who has supplied the introduction for this book, has elsewhere quoted Miss Stein as saying, "If it can be done why do it?" *Stanzas in Meditation* is no doubt the most successful of her attempts to do what can't be done, to create a counterfeit of reality more real than reality. And if, on laying the book aside, we feel that it is still impossible to accomplish the impossible, we are also left with the conviction that it is the only thing worth trying to do.

Stanzas in Meditation:
The Other Autobiography

Ulla E. Dydo

It is fifty-three years since Gertrude Stein, in a single summer at her country house, wrote both her most abstract, disembodied work and her most concrete, referential work. The first, *Stanzas in Meditation*,[1] was published posthumously and remains even today almost unknown. The second, *The Autobiography of Alice B. Toklas*, was published as soon as it was written, brought Stein the fame she had wanted all her life and remains her most popular book.

The language of the *Autobiography* may surprise by its cleverness and felicity, but it never calls attention to itself by its difficulty. The life and times of Alice Toklas and Gertrude Stein make easy reading. The difficult language of *Stanzas*, on the other hand, demands a reader's full and equal attention to every single word as word. The difference between books like the *Autobiography* and books like *Stanzas* is not a difference in subject matter or genre and not a difference in degree; it is a radical difference in kind. The two books do not even sound as if they were by the same author. Gertrude Stein herself was quite clear about this difference. The *Autobiography* was the first of a series of books which she characterized as her "open and public" books, or as "audience writing": books written to satisfy demands of an imagined or real audience. On the other hand, works like *Stanzas*—virtually everything Stein wrote up to 1932 and a good deal that she wrote after she became famous—she described as her "real kind"[2] of books: a literature of word compositions rather than a literature of subject matter. Not that the compositions lacked subject matter, but Stein believed that subject matter had no existence apart from its shape in compositions. The public books yield themselves easily to the reader interested in their subjects, but the other books refuse to give up their meaning if they are read by the conventions of representation of subjects or by the conventions of logical discourse about ideas.

Stanzas in Meditation raises two questions. The first concerns the nature of the stanzas: how are they to be read and what do they mean individually and

Reprinted from *Chicago Review* (Winter 1985) by permission of the author. Copyright © 1985 by Ulla E. Dydo.

as a complete work of poetry? The second concerns Stein's writing in 1932.³ Why should Stein at the same time have written a chronological narrative about known public figures and events and a work of pure word construction pointing only incidentally to identifiable subject matter? Why, in the summer of 1932, did she suddenly go in two opposed directions at once?

I undertook a detailed study of the stanzas in the hope of gaining access to this long work of poetry and to the Stein meditation. It was only in the process of this study that I unexpectedly, in the manuscript of *Stanzas*, stumbled upon evidence that suggested why the stanzas and the *Autobiography* were written in the same summer. Indeed, the evidence convinced me that the two works were related and could be understood only together. This essay tells of both the search for the text and the discovery of the context of *Stanzas*. It also suggests how text and context illuminate each other.

Stanzas in Meditation is Stein's longest work of poetry, and her most difficult. More disembodied than any work she had ever written and any she was to write, the stanzas were the purest word constructions she ever created. Using the last stanza (xv) of Part I as an example, I shall explain what that characterization means by considering *Stanzas* as a text in its own right. Later I shall look at the stanzas as context for the *Autobiography*.

I called *Stanzas* a *disembodied* work. The word is Stein's own. It appears in the draft of a letter written at the time she was composing the stanzas. The letter answers an inquiry by a Canadian researcher about her method of writing. She described her effort in her writing of that time to achieve

> exactitude of abstract thought and
> poetry as created by exactness and
> as far as possible disembodiment if
> one may use such a word, creating
> sense by intensity of exactness...

> (Draft letter to Lennard
> Bernstein Gandalac in answer
> to his inquiry of 27 May 1932, YCAL)

This tortured statement, one of the few where Stein tries to explain herself by precept rather than by example, speaks of her interest in the process of thinking rather than in the object of thought. The words *abstract* and *disembodiment* describe thought, not the objects that provoke thought or the results of thought. However, Stein always saw the artist's "first-hand experience" of objects as the necessary condition for all creation of *exactitude* and *intensity* in the work of art.

Here is the beginning of Stanza xv, the last of Part I.

> Should they may be they might if they delight
> In why they must see it be there not only necessarily

> But which they might in which they might
> For which they might delight if they look there
> And they see there that they look there
> To see it be there which it is if it is
> Which may be where where it is
> If they do not occasion it to be different
> From what it is.[4]

These lines cannot be read fast, nor can they be read expressively. Nothing concrete stands out in this passage, and no key words announce a subject or a theme. It is also virtually impossible to quote an excerpt, since the continuum of these lines—they make one sentence but they hardly feel like a sentence—offers no discrete statements that can be isolated. Certain phrases stand out because they are repeated, creating rhythm and sound patterns: "they might if they delight," "see there . . . look there . . . be there," "which it is . . . where it is."

In the process of perceiving something ("see it") the observers ("they") also perceive themselves ("they see . . . that they look . . . to see"). Voicing their gradual perception, including all the hesitations that are part of the process ("should they," "they might" and all the boxed-in "which" and "if" clauses), is more important than naming what they see. The parallel phrases with their minimal vocabulary create mirror effects and reflections in the reader's mind.

What is seen with delight (daylight?) is an abstract, disembodied landscape which appears in stark, single words distributed thoughout the stanza: hills, crops, ditches, clouds, sky, vines, some flowers and vegetables in a nursery rhyme, the weather, a bird. Seeing depends not only on light (sun, moon) and weather (clouds, sky) but also on the capacity to see.

> In one direction there is the sun and the moon
> In the other direction there are cumulous clouds
> and the sky
> In the other direction there is why
> They look at what they see
> They look very long while they talk along
> And they may be said to see that at which they look
> Whenever there is no chance of its not being warmer
> Than if they wish which they were.

Several questions are implied in these lines: is it necessary to sit in the landscape in order to see it? Are looking and seeing dependent upon sharing, caring and talking?

Line 20 asserts almost aggressively, "They care for it of course they care for it." Caring for it is affirmed so emphatically that one wonders whether they do care for it. By line 33 "each one has seen each one." Separate things have been seen separately by each observer.

> It is very well to have seen what they have seen
> But which they will not only be alike.

They see the same things, but are things the same? When they see what they saw before, is it the same as before? Are the two who see alike? Likeness and difference give way to liking it or not liking it as one line or phrase moves imperceptibly, almost without punctuation, into the next. At a later point, "no one / Is more able to be sure." The capacity to perceive on the part of each observer is in doubt. The stanza ends abruptly on a note of self-assertion: "I have my well-wishers thank you." The speaker—it is plainly Gertrude Stein—asserts her independence. The voice of this stanza changes in tone. The early sections create the lean flow of the perceiving process that Stein slowly and gradually traces in her disembodied words. But the stanza ends in an aggressive and personal voice that reflects a personality far more prominently than the earlier sections.

What is so difficult about reading such a stanza? It is precisely the lean, abstract language that offers no quick information, no stories and no referential center. Almost devoid of objects and color, the stanzas are starkly abstract. To say that they are abstract, however, is not to say that they have no meaning but that they must be entered through the words rather than through ideas or subject matter. Gertrude Stein makes meaning by constructing words. Meaning is not apart from words, ready in her mind to be fitted with words, but it is a part of the word constructions. Meaning is a function of words rather than words being a function of meaning.

One is never comfortably at home in a Stein stanza as one is in the well-furnished literature filled with images and metaphors that may be novel but that do not require new ways of reading. Reading the stanzas is like reading naked words, stripped of the "encrusted surfaces"[5] that habit has led us to expect and to recognize without the effort of thought. In the stark, naked words of this meditation, Stein allows no distractions from the movement of words that is the process of consciousness. The writing of these meditations was one of the most demanding tasks she ever set herself. They make slow and difficult reading of great intensity. She had never been as stern and absolute in her use of words as she was here.

A number of themes that are prominent in Stanza xv recur thoughout *Stanzas.* All derive from a single word, *like,* with which Stein composes many meanings. One is *being alike.* Another is *liking it* (i.e., what they have; the object of *liking* here is not usually specified, which emphasizes how unimportant the objects are compared to the process of liking). A third theme is *being liked.* Behind the play on the word *like* are also frequent echoes from *As You Like It,* a play that was especially important to Stein. Here are a few suggestive passages; some display the verbal felicity of aphorisms, as is to be expected from the great variety of constructions to which *like* lends itself:

Now I have lost the thread of how they came to be alike.

(V, vii)

I often think do they sound alike
Who hates that or a hat not I.

(IV, xx)

Or would it be a nuisance to like no one

(IV, xx)

Most certainly they like it because they like
                    what they have

(II, i)

They like whatever I like.

(II, xiv)

Thematically though not verbally related preoccupations emerge in these lines:

I have often thought that she meant what I said

(V, ii)[6]

They can place aisle to exile
And not nearly there
One in a while they stammer but stand still
In as well as exchange.

(II, xvii)

What is the use of union between this with this

(IV, xxiv)

Who is winning why the answer of course is she is

(IV, xxiv)

Plainly Gertrude Stein and Alice Toklas are quarreling. The fact that they are named only by pronouns—they, I, he, she—makes the quarrel starker and more abstract by placing emphasis on naked opposition rather than on dressed-up personalities.

A related recurrent theme concerns fame, sometimes linked with the hope for money. Fame—being liked by an audience—belonged to Gertrude Stein as a well-known writer; did Alice, who shared Stein's life but not her name, share in the fame?

It is very anxious not to know the name of them
But they know not theirs but mine
Not theirs but mine.

(III, viii)

Or may be very likely or not at all
Not only known but well known

(II, ix)

After all I am known
Alone
And she calls it their pair.

(III, xviii)

The innumerable quibbles reflect artistic and personal preoccupations as much as they embody Stein's fascination with the possibilities of the English language. Always personal problems are given form as writing problems, and words are used to construct equations of personal relations.

The minimal setting for these personal and verbal preoccupations in the stanzas is the pastoral landscape of Bilignin in the Rhone valley. This setting also shows that the stanzas were written in the country. And some minimal references to fruits, people and events allow exact dating of certain stanzas. The stanzas were written consecutively in the notebooks and are printed in the order of composition.

When inspiration lagged, as it frequently did, Stein sometimes set herself composition tasks, which kept her at her writing. For example, a large section of Stanza v of Part II is constructed with as many negatives as she was able to incorporate into her lines. Elsewhere there are constructions with prominent features of Shakespeare (they are not simply allusions that can be documented with footnotes). In some pieces Stein sets out to write in words of one syllable (*Madame Recamier, Listen To Me*) though she never considers herself bound by the rules she sets herself. Once a task gets her going, she feels free to abandon it. Another important form of self-discipline is evident in the fact that many of Stein's pieces are completely fitted into one of the French *cahiers* that she used as manuscript notebooks. Like a painter who paints within the given space of the canvas, Stein more often than not fits a composition into the space of a notebook, ending it on the last line of the last page. The challenge of this practice lay in the task of completing a composition within such a frame rather than merely stopping at the end of a *cahier*. Many Stein notebooks are spaces which she fills with word compositions. Form has to do with how to shape a given space.[7]

The text of the five parts of *Stanzas* is contained in six French notebooks. Part I begins in a thin brown *cahier* which is filled by the middle of Stanza ix, at which point Stein immediately continues in a second thin notebook of the same type. This notebook, filled to the end, completes Part I. Stein must have realized that the poems were developing into a larger work than she had expected when she began. For Part II she switched to a thicker notebook, which she filled to the end. Parts III and IV each fill another large notebook of the same type as that used for Part II. The result is that Parts II, III and IV are about the same length; Part I is shorter since the two thin *cahiers* together contain fewer pages than the larger *cahiers* used for Parts, II, III and IV. Part V is written in a hand-sewn dummy book filled to the end, but since it is fatter, Part V is longer. The uneven length of the five parts of *Stanzas* is simply the result of the size of the manuscript books.

It is known that Stein often derived word ideas from the texts or the illustrations on the covers of the French *cahiers* she used.[8] Many of her pieces used ideas or even phrases from these covers which offered information about

natural phenomena, great inventions, famous men, French history, first aid
and other instructive topics. The early stanzas, however, were written in plain
books with conventional, stylized line drawings and no text on the covers.
Such drawings never interested Stein and never entered compositions written
in these *cahiers*. Nothing in *Stanzas* points to the world about which the *cahiers*
usually told stories. The stanzas are self-contained word constructions with
minimal reference to that world. The last plain dummy notebook is a particularly fitting book for the final part of Stein's abstract word meditations.

While the stanzas do not reflect the world of the French *cahiers*, they do
reveal an unexpected context[9] which requires interpretation. Almost consistently throughout the handwritten text, the auxiliary verb *may* is crossed
out, and *can* is inked in above it in Gertrude Stein's hand. Of the two
typescripts, the first reproduces with almost no errors the original, unrevised
text. The second includes the revisions, but they are not executed exactly like
the revisions in the manuscript. Some of the changes are typed in from the
start, others are written by Gertrude Stein into spaces left open by Alice during
typing, and still others are inked in by Gertrude above the crossed out original
verb *may*. In some cases the revision destroys meaning, as when *may be* (*maybe*)
becomes *can be*. In others, it destroys rhymes (*may/to-day* becomes *can/to-day*).
What accounts for these changes since neither meaning nor rhetoric explains
the need for them? How must they be read?

The text printed in the Yale volume of *Stanzas* (and reproduced in *The Yale
Gertrude Stein* [1980], a selection from the Yale edition) is the revised text of
the second typescript, as seems entirely reasonable. But why has no one raised
questions about the revisions? In part because readers do not study Stein texts
with the careful attention they require. Many Stein students assume, wrongly,
that her writing is arbitrary. The opening line of Stanza xv was revised from

> Should they may be they might if they delight

to

> Should they can be they might if they delight

The substitution of *can* for *may* surely substitutes nonsense for sense. Stein's
sentences, however, are so different in construction and idiom from standard
English sentences that no one has noticed how very odd the revised text
sounds and that something in these revisions does not make sense.

It turns out that not only the auxiliary verb "may" is eliminated from the
stanzas but the *word* "may" or "May" in all its possible forms. Three times the
month of May appears in the text. In one case the revised text substitutes *today*
(II, iii), which preserves an end rhyme. In the second case, in mid-line, *day* is
substituted for *May* (I, vi; V, xvi). Nothing appears to be gained by the revisions. They cannot be literary revisions. What are they?

Within two days after arrival in Bilignin in the first week of May 1932,
Stein wrote a piece entitled "Here. Actualities," in which she recorded some

recent events. (Stein's title translates the French *Ici les actualitiés*, which is radio language announcing a news broadcast.) The piece tells of the discovery, about a week earlier, of the manuscript of Stein's first work (the novel *Q.E.D.*, not named) among the manuscripts in the Paris apartment. Stein describes the discovery as the culminating event in a "season of debuts" in the winter and spring of 1932. The debuts included the appointment of 29 February 1932 of Bernard Faÿ to a professorship at the Collège de France; the first communion in April 1932 of Paulo Picasso, Stein's godson; and the first show, from April 12 to 25, 1932, at the Galerie Vignon, of the painter Sir Francis Rose, a Stein protégé. The discovery of the manuscript of the early novel – Stein's literary debut – has historic significance. It makes news. Written in 1903, the novel records Stein's love affair with May Bookstaver, a young graduate of Bryn Mawr College (where Stein had friends) whom Stein saw in Baltimore and New York from 1901 to 1903. The relationship was complicated by a rival, another young woman, who claimed Bookstaver's affection more successfully than Stein. The story of the love affair is commented on in detail by Leon Katz in his introduction to *Fernhurst, Q.E.D. and Other Early Writings* (New York: Liveright, 1971).

What matters for *Stanzas* is the effect upon Alice Toklas of the discovery of the early book, which had not been typed or published and about which Alice Toklas had not known. In the *Autobiography* Stein suggests that she had forgotten the early novel – a rather unlikely suggestion. In "Here. Actualities" Stein asks whether the work was "hidden with intention." She adds, "There is no blindness in memory." The contradictions and the secretiveness surrounding the Bookstaver affair show that this relationship was not a matter of indifference.

Alice Toklas told Leon Katz in interviews conducted between November 1952 and February 1953 that she had not known about the affair with Bookstaver or about the early novel until the spring of 1932, when the manuscript was unexpectedly discovered.[10] What aroused Alice Toklas's jealousy was less the love affair itself than the discovery that, when Stein and Toklas had exchanged "confessions" upon falling in love, Stein had not told about the relationship with May (other names used are Mary, May Mary, M.M.). Stein had kept in touch with her friend, who in 1906 had married stockbroker Charles Knoblauch in New York, and she had kept May's letters. It is likely that the two women met in Paris when the Knoblauchs traveled. It was Mrs. Knoblauch who had placed the portraits of Picasso and Matisse with Alfred Stieglitz, who published them in *Camera Work*. She had also had in safe-keeping for many years copies of most of Stein's pieces and made efforts to place them with publishers.

Alice, who had known nothing about this relationship, was enraged. She destroyed – or made Gertrude destroy – May's letters, which had served as the basis for the early novel. She became, as she put it, "paranoid about the name

May." That paranoia appears to be the key to the revisions of the text of *Stanzas*. Alice Toklas must have initiated the elimination of the words *may* and *May* from the stanzas in the hope of purging the poems of Gertrude Stein of anything suggestive of May Bookstaver. When one considers the fact that Stein plays in piece after piece, especially in her work of the 1920s, with the names May, Mary and Mabel (the name of the third young woman in the triangle love affair), with the half-rhyme *Mary/Marry* and with puns like *may marry*, the implications of the relationship with May Bookstaver and of the discovery of *Q.E.D.* become far more significant than they have appeared. From the spring of 1932 on, Alice Toklas and Gertrude Stein quarreled intermittently for several years. On the American lecture tour, Gertrude Stein saw few old friends, and the two women were frequently at odds. The themes of quarreling, of liking one another and of identity in the stanzas reflect the tension between Stein and Toklas.

The purgation of *Stanzas* implied in the *may/can* revisions may have been punitive or conciliatory or both. The changes are inked into the manuscript and the typescript in Gertrude's hand. Alice did not normally write in the Stein manuscripts except to copy earlier Stein drafts, to mark page numbers, correct misspellings and occasionally to correct Stein's French. However, the women had for years habitually used the manuscript notebooks for personal messages. Gertrude frequently scribbled into her manuscripts private notes and poems that were meant for Alice and were carefully offset from the Stein compositions. These notes were either written like secret messages in very fine pencil in tiny handwriting, or they were otherwise separated from the rest of the text. Knowing that Alice would carefully read every word of a piece, Stein inserted love letters to her in her work. These were never meant to be parts of the compositions and were not typed by Alice. The *may/can* revisions have a private dimension very different from what is evident in the love messages concealed in earlier Stein manuscripts. One gets the impression that during the summer of 1932 each of the two women goaded and hurt the other wherever possible.

In Stanza xii of Part I, for example, Stein prepares to write the word *many*. But she ends up writing *may* and inks in, very carefully, as one would ink in a correction that must be legible, the letter *n* above the space between the *a* and the *y* of *may*. It is difficult to look at this revision as a casual correction of an error, especially as the original *may* and the correction are both unusually neatly written. The "misspelling" looks deliberate rather than accidental. That there was constant irritation connected with the name *May* is also clear from the fact that in several other pieces of the summer of 1932, the names *May* or *Mary* are pointedly manipulated. Phrases that look like innocent, ordinary forms of word play with occasional typing or proofreading errors turn out to conceal an explosive situation which only a cumulative study of the manuscripts can uncover and document. The revisions are personal and not literary. This argues for restoration of the original text of *Stanzas*. Ironically the editorial changes, meant to do away with May Mary and to conceal the story behind *Stanzas*, ended up by giving it away.

Gertrude Stein's sense of her own voice and of her power of speech was intermittent. What interfered with it was her own insecurity, the ridicule of others, the rejections by editors, the great and lonely struggle always to create her own language forms rather than to rely on the inherited conventions. She had struggled in her early years to find a voice and an identity as a writer. She received little praise from any audience for many years, found publication virtually impossible and was forced to pay for the printing of most of her own books. Only a few personal friends read her, supported her and expressed faith in her. She was ridiculed by her brother Leo, her closest companion throughout her early years and the one figure in her life who might have validated her enterprise.

When she was finally able to reject her brother, it was because she had received unconditional validation for what she was writing and what she *was*—from Alice Toklas. Alice allowed Gertrude Stein to hear her own voice, to affirm the reality of what she was trying to do with words, and to know who she was. For twenty-five years Alice's unqualified "yes" answered Stein's "Am I if I am" (V, lxxxiii). Alice was Stein's *alter ego*, allowing her life and work until a third person—a ghost—entered Alice's life from Gertrude's novel *Q.E.D.*, which had come to life.

In the spring of 1932, Alice withdrew her validation—at least temporarily. Her rage, visible in the intrusions into the meditations, must have left Stein uncertain of her own identity. As always, Stein looked for answers to the question of identity in the only way she knew—in words. It was in words that she could create her own autonomy. Words were a way to keep loss of love at bay, and since loss of love was a threat of death, words allowed her to keep death at bay. She wrote enormous numbers of pieces that summer. But mainly she separated her voice from Alice's by writing *Stanzas*—and the *Autobiography*.

The stanzas are an uneven series of fits and starts. Her voice, sometimes in control of her words and sometimes uncertain, moves from lyrical song to aggressive hostility to the contemplation of fame to self-defense. But it is always a voice that tries to shape stark words into speech. When she finally composed a book that would make her famous and earn her money—things she herself had always wanted—she wrote, in one of the last of the stanzas, that she wanted to renew the union and "once more to add feeling to feeling" (V, liii). She wanted to restore what had been theirs. "I need not hope to sing a wish / Nor need I help to help to sing..." (V, lxviii). She asked the central question: "The whole of this last end is to say which of two" (V, lxxxi). She concluded the stanzas reaffirming the union with Alice.

Why am I if I am uncertain reasons may inclose.
Remain remain propose repose chose.
I call carelessly that the door is open
Which if they may refuse to open
No one can rush to close.
Let them be mine therefor.
Everybody knows that I chose.
Therefore if therefor before I close.
I will therefore offer therefor I offer this.
Which if I refuse to miss may be miss is mine,
I will be well welcome when I come.
Because I am coming.
Certainly I come having come.
            These stanzas are done.

                                              (V, lxxxiii)

My reading, derived from the context created by the revisions of *Stanzas*, assumes that the last stanza refers at least in part to the relationship between Stein and Toklas. Yet there is nothing in these lines that directly points to the relationship. The lines refuse to be pinned down. They do, however, unmistakably speak of making a choice. The object of the choice, like the object of *liking* discussed earlier, is not named. Stein is interested in the process of making a choice, not in the object chosen. It is in this sense that the stanza is abstract and non-referential.

Wendell Wilcox, writing about *Stanzas* in a piece that accompanied a small selection of stanzas published in the February, 1940 issue of *Poetry*, said,

> I rather think that the choice of which Miss Stein speaks in the last poem refers in part to the fact of her having elected to write in a manner which much of the time makes her concrete meaning inaccessible to the reader. For want of a better word we may call this manner abstraction. I cannot tell you exactly why she so chose.... Suffice it to say that this *was* her choice and that she made it not for the purpose of confounding the reader, as some suppose, but because it was part of her literary fate to do so....[11]

Neither Wilcox's reading nor mine makes a claim to being the right one. Together they are reminders of the kaleidoscopic nature of the stanzas, which are never about one thing, but never about nothing.

In Stanza xiv of Part IV, Stein says, "This is her autobiography one of two." If *Stanzas* is Stein's own autobiography, the book whose voice is the voice of Gertrude Stein, *The Autobiography of Alice B. Toklas*[12] is Alice's book, written in *her* voice, *her* style, and *her* name. The *Autobiography* was not Gertrude's book. It was a public work, written for an audience and not for the sake of writing. In a letter to Carl Van Vechten written over a year after Stein's death,

Alice said that the *Autobiography* was the only work Gertrude wrote for her.[13] The implications of her statement are more complicated and less charming than they might appear to be. Once again the manuscript books tell a story.

In the Stein Archive there is a preliminary notebook for the earliest version of the *Autobiography*. The notebook, a French *cahier*, shows one of the rare illustrations and texts about an American subject: the story of a gold prospector during the Gold Rush is told to exemplify the law of talion, the Mosaic law of an eye for an eye and a tooth for a tooth. The story and illustration concern a greedy gold digger who tries to rob and kill a companion, but fails and therefore flees. Two others join the victim to pursue the culprit, catching him with a lasso. Vengeance is wrought when one of the captors—not the man he had tried to kill—puts a knife through him. A comment at the end of the story states that such customs no longer exist in America, where life is now more civilized than in the last century.

Can this *cahier* have been chosen accidentally by the Californian Stein? Is the *Autobiography* the ironic symbol of retaliation spelled out in the *cahier's* title, "Châtiment Mérité"? Is Stein getting back at Alice or Alice getting back at Stein? And what of the violence of the story? Are the two women indulging in acts of violence by means of words that sound peaceful, but are actually violent? Or is the book Gertrude's peace offering to Alice?

The preliminary notebook for the *Autobiography* begins with the same description of Alice's background that opens the book: her birth in San Francisco, a brief sketch of her mother's father, a pioneer who came to California in '49, and of her father's father, who left his wife "just after their marriage to fight at the barricades in Paris, but his wife having cut off his supplies, he soon returned...."

So far, except for minor differences in punctuation, the text is that of the first two paragraphs of the book. Having spoken of violence in connection with Alice's grandfather, Stein continues:

> I myself have no liking for violence but in spite of that
> which is what I wish to say I have had some occasions to
> feel what violence is and when I do feel so I can and have
> thoroughly tempted there which is what there is to do.
> Moreover nobody can doubt if it is not to be considered
> [word?] to have which is the result I have had that I have
> what I have and I always have as I always will had to have
> that which I have. In this way there can be no doubt, no
> doubt, that in no way there is any doubt that having to
> have that which I have I have had and I have that which I
> have....
>
> (YCAL)

Stein loses her way completely after the word *violence*. Bridgman says that her control over her material was uncertain and that it took her a long time to find

the right voice for the *Autobiography*.[14] Though it is true that Stein had difficulty finding the voice for her book, this passage tells a far more specific story.
Stein's voice in the *Autobiography* is Alice's voice. But using Alice's voice meant
doing violence to her own. Stein is concerned with violence between herself
and Alice Toklas, and she knows that Alice's peaceful appearance and wifely
occupations conceal a fierce and jealous rage. It is the violence of this concealment which throws Stein off course and leaves her uncertain about voice,
about tone, about sentences. This passage, with its repetitions and permutations of a few key phrases, is closer to what Stein does in the stanzas than to
what she attempts in the conventional narrative of the *Autobiography*. When
she finally rewrites the passage, it becomes the peaceful third paragraph:

> I myself have no liking for violence and have always
> enjoyed the pleasures of needlework and gardening. I am
> fond of paintings, furniture, tapestry, houses and flowers,
> even vegetables and fruit-trees. I like a view but I like to sit
> with my back turned to it.

The concluding sentence of this domestic idyll has its counterpart in a
sentence about scenery, best read in the context of Stanza xv, which opened
this essay:

> It is at one time no different between how many hills
> And they look like that caught in I mean
> For which they will add not when I look
> Or they make it plain by their own time.
> This which they see by
> They turn not their back to the scenery
> What does it amount to.
> Not only with or better most and best
> For I think well of meaning.

The familiar passage from the *Autobiography* about Alice sitting with her back
to the view makes full sense only in the context of the passage about not turning "their back to the scenery" from *Stanzas*. Each work is the context of the
other.

What does it amount to? What does it mean? What do "they see by"? Meaning, for Gertrude Stein, never amounts to any one thing. It cannot be added
up but must be seen in details, one and one and one. Seeing meaning is a
matter of one's capacity for seeing all of the "scenery" in the details which make
up the whole. Stanza xv ends with a lengthy composition of such scenery,
including the weather, the crops and the labor of digging and planting, with
well-wishing neighbors offering predictions of success. The excursion into
landscape returns Stein to the essence of meditation: the contemplation of

what she sees. Again and again in the *Stanzas* she describes what she sees, trying not to turn her back to it. In the *Autobiography* she renders the appearance and the public image, with the sort of peace-loving statements an audience likes to hear. In the stanzas she depicts the war, in all its disparate pieces. It is neither easy nor pretty.

This reading of Stanza xv is very autobiographical indeed. I do not believe that the two passages about scenery need to be read only autobiographically, but the fact that the *Autobiography*, a referential book in which every detail can be identified and annotated, picks up the same phrase as the stanza, a word construction with minimal referentiality, does suggest that the two passages are connected and concern the relationship of Gertrude Stein and Alice Toklas. The violence of the original draft passage in the *Autobiography* has been converted into a domestic scene, but Stanza xv ends with Stein's aggressive assertion:

I have my well-wishers thank you.

Notes

Research for this essay was supported by a Fellowship for College Teachers from the National Endowment for the Humanities and by Grant no. 13220 from the P.S.C.–C.U.N.Y. Research Award Program of the City University of New York. For permission to quote material from the Gertrude Stein papers, grateful acknowledgment is made to the Yale Collection of American Literature, Beinecke Rare Book and Manuscript Library, Yale University, and to the Estate of Gertrude Stein.

1. The Stanzas were published in the posthumous volume entitled *Stanzas in Meditation and Other Poems 1929–1933* (New Haven: Yale University Press, 1956) where they appear to be part of a longer collection. However, they must be considered as a self-contained work, parallel to the *Autobiography*. In this paper they are treated as a book and the title is underlined.

2. These words are used in a letter of 25 May 1934 to her agent, W.A. Bradley, who was negotiating with Alfred Harcourt for new book contracts after the *Autobiography*. Until 1932 Stein wrote no popular books, and the distinction between her "open and public books" and her "real kind of books" had not been made. But from 1932 on, Stein worried about "audience writing."

3. Given Stein's difficulties with publication, many of her pieces remained unpublished for years. Eight volumes of unpublished work were printed posthumously; they include early and late work but are not arranged in exact chronological order. Moreover, many of the books published during her lifetime were collections of pieces written over a period of many years, the dates of publication unrelated to the dates of composition. The important dates for Stein are the dates of composition, not of publication. Her work evolves literally from one piece to the next and can be fully understood only in chronological sequence. The most reliable guide to chronology is *A Catalogue of the Published and Unpublished Writings of Gertrude Stein* by Robert Bartlett Haas and Donald Clifford Gallup (New Haven: Yale Univ. Library, 1941), extended by Julian Sawyer ("Gertrude Stein: A Bibliography 1941–1948," *Bulletin of*

Bibliography, XIX, 6, 1948, 183–187). The *Catalogue* is keyed to appearance of the works in print in Richard Bridgman, *Gertrude Stein in Pieces*, New York: Oxford University Press, 1970, pp. 365–385). The Haas-Gallup listing was begun with Gertrude Stein's assistance and approval. Some of the dates given in the listing require revision. In the following pages, the dates printed in parentheses after titles of pieces, unless otherwise indicated, are the dates of composition, not of publication. Publication – especially of book-length collections – does not reflect Stein's development as a writer.

    4. All quotations from *Stanzas in Meditation* are taken from the autograph manuscript text in Stein's notebooks. This text sometimes differs from the printed text. The nature of the textual discrepancies is discussed in detail in this paper.

    5. James Laughlin visited Stein in September 1934 and in July 1935 – before and after the American tour. He wrote after visiting her a piece that speaks about Stein's language in words which probably echo her own. He summarizes Stein's belief that "anaemia of language" breeds "associative word linkages, which, by endless repetition in use, become so habitual . . . that they impede clear, free and original thinking." It is the artist's obligation to reject this system of "canned language." "He can stand his ground as an artist and fight back, regardless of the odds against him. He can stand his ground as an artist and fight back, wrestling with words till he bleeds sweat to draw from them the *purity and strength of meaning they still possess beneath their encrusted surfaces.*" (My emphases. "New Words for Old: Notes on Experimental Writing," *Story*, IX, 53, December 1936, 105, 110.)

    6. To outsiders, Stein and Toklas did not appear to be alike at all. "They never grew to resemble each other as often happens in such cases. Her [Alice Toklas's] personality was intact." (Bryher, *The Heart to Artemis*, New York: Harcourt, Brace and World, Inc., 1962) Interestingly, even a lesbian friend like Bryher assumes that the "wife" is in danger of merging into the husband's personality. Bryher stresses that Alice's personality remained intact but never questions Gertrude's personality or Gertrude's sense of herself. Yet it is Gertrude, not Alice, who worries about her identity and about *being alike*. In the stanzas the problem of who she is erupts again and again with anguish and pain.

    Other contexts speak of identity lightly and playfully. Stein, who liked to write her own name, frequently inscribed her manuscript books not only to herself as the author but also to Alice Toklas as wife, as beloved, as inspiration, as her other self. For example, the first of the two manuscript *cahiers* of *Daniel Webster A Play* (1937) shows on the cover, in the space for the student's subject, name, address, institution and class, the following notation:

> *Cahier de* Gertrude Stein
> *à* M   Alice B. Toklas
> *demeurant*   Here
> *Etablissement de*   Soi
> *Classe de*   Premier

Such playful, yet serious, inscriptions are common throughout the years. The brilliant invention of Gertrude Stein as the author of *The Autobiography of Alice B. Toklas* is also a form of concealment of Alice as the (king)maker of Gertrude Stein.

    7. Not only compositions but also letters are frequently fitted on a page or a series of pages. Enough Stein letters end on the last line of a page to make the reader familiar with the manuscripts feel that they are sometimes composed to fit on Stein's stationery, just as compositions are fitted into the *cahiers*.

8. Both Richard Bridgman in *Gertrude Stein in Pieces* and Wendy Steiner in *Exact Resemblance to Exact Resemblance* (New Haven: Yale Univ. Press, 1978) comment on Stein's use of the illustrations and texts of the *cahiers* in certain pieces. However, the *cahiers* require further investigation as contexts for Stein's work. Some of their characteristics are discussed in this essay.

9. The manuscript problems summarized here are illustrated in detail in my piece, "How to Read Gertrude Stein' The Manuscript of 'Stanzas in Meditation,'" *Text: Transactions of the Society for Textual Scholarship* I, 1981, pp. 271-303.

10. Details about Alice Toklas' reactions to the Bookstaver affair in this and the next paragraph were contributed by Leon Katz in his interviews with me, 1980-82.

11. Wendell Wilcox, "A Note on Stein and Abstraction," *Poetry*, LV, February 1940, 254-257.

12. The date of the *Autobiography* derives from Stein's own assertion (in *Everybody's Autobiography*, New York: Random House, Inc., 1937, p. 9) that she wrote the book in about six weeks in October and November 1932. The completion of the typescript is documented in letters to Stein's agent, William Aspenwall Bradley, to whom she sent the typescript from Bilignin in two sections in November, 1932 (Stein to Bradley, n.d., received by Bradley November 8, 13, and 25, 1932; Bradley to Stein, November 13, 21 and 26, 1932). When did she *begin* the work? Internal evidence in *Stanzas* suggests that Stein may have begun work on the *Autobiography* before October, perhaps as early as the spring of 1932. The *Autobiography* creates many fictions. The idea of the book as the easy product of a mere six weeks during the beautiful autumn of 1932 sounds like another of the fictions with which Stein surrounded herself, hoping to conceal the full truth of the matter from an audience eager for gossip about the private lives of public persons.

13. Letter to Carl Van Vechten, 13 November 1948 (YCAL).

14. *Gertrude Stein in Pieces*, p. 212.

Operas and Plays [A Review]

Richard Howard

"When I write something that somebody else can see then it is a play for me," wrote Gertrude Stein the year *Operas and Plays* was first published in a very limited edition (by herself), in 1932. By then—it was the year she went public, astonishing herself and the world by the success of *The Autobiography of Alice B. Toklas*—she had already produced one collection, one anthology, really, which included her first plays and operas, *Geography and Plays*; and three years after her death, *Last Operas and Plays* appeared in 1949. It all adds up to as large a body of work for (or against) the theater as any American writer has produced, and it still remains a problem to our more orderly manuals of dramatic history.

I am tempted to say that the three most *marking* dramatists in the literature of the United States are three women widely known for other achievements— Mae West, Martha Graham and Gertrude Stein. West created, or at least accrued, a "character," an image of the extenuated seductress so persuasive, and so comical, that Bertolt Brecht wanted to cast her as his Mother Courage. Miss Graham's dance dramas are the most convincing representations I know of the vastness of the unconscious, where as Edwin Denby once said, "folly is at home, easy to watch and hard to take." And Stein's plays (there are 77 of them) constitute—unperformed, derided, unexamined—what is surely the purest attempt to call attention to the theater experience which has ever existed. For all my suspicions that Richard Foreman, Robert Wilson and Meredith Monk have found hints and hopes in her texts, Stein's theater *oeuvre* is still something of a mystery to us, although she had said as early as 1913: "I do not want plays published. They are to be kept to be played." Perhaps the republication of this astounding volume will afford some remedy to our disease of neglect.

Perhaps. It would be preposterous to recommend the works in this book to anyone who intends to sit down and read a play—as we have learned to do in Western culture since Ben Jonson (though Shakespeare would have been astonished at the notion, I believe). Not to read a play as we can read Ibsen or Shaw or Pirandello. Nor even as we might, with a certain degree of temerity, read Beckett and Ionesco. The Stein texts are determined to rebuke any consecutive interest, any perusal which might attempt to be cumulative. Here, as an entirely characteristic example, is a bit of stichomythia from "The Five Georges" (1931):

George G.
...Do dictionaries always mean that they are and have been right.

George S.
May we be here.

George of England.
Be here while they last as they will be distributing better what she wants. What she wants.

George L.
Forget me as well as forget me not.

George M.
They pay or pair admirably compare.

George G.
He or she.
May be thoughtless.

George S.
Develop

One takes the absence of punctuation at the end as a command, and just in case one might have supposed that a more sustained hearing of a Stein song—a development, indeed—would reward reading, here is an aria from the opera "Madame Recamier" (1930), sung by the eponymous heroine:

By the time that they will go
Who goes in joining places to their plainly adding theirs.
They will attribute in it as it calls
Who makes it better that they come away
From relief of what it is most to have
In little measures which they can belie
In liking they must have more to reunite
It is as well that they can call it for them
It is a better name than after all a very little will do now.
Do or do not in all of it a pleasure....
When this they see they can as well as will remember me.

No, reading hundreds of pages of such stuff is madness, or at least is merely maddening. Evidently Stein's method of composition was to follow whim, her dramatic construction was doodling and her notion of theatrical economy was to juxtapose incompatibles. When enough had accumulated, she could recapitulate aggressively, and there is so much minute variation within repetition in these works that a mere reading does not promote ready investigation.

As Gertrude Stein instructed, what these plays require is performance. Moreover, we have evidence as to the requirements. The four successful Stein theater pieces—successful in the theater—are all based on works just as abstract and abstruse as any in this volume. In fact the most celebrated of all, *Four Saints in Three Acts* (1927), is in this volume, in its ur-text, just as Stein gave it to Virgil Thomson and Maurice Grosser to work with. Then there was "Wedding Bouquet," a ballet with words which Lord Berners had made out of another play in this volume, "They Must. Be Wedded. To Their Wife" (1931). This has been performed wherever Sadler's Wells appears, and always with great *éclat*. After Stein's death, Mr. Thomson's second opera, on her text *The Mother of Us All*, was first performed in 1947, and continues to be done in American opera houses from Santa Fe to Charleston. And most recently, Al Carmines' setting of *In Circles* ran in New York for several seasons consecutively. These triumphs on the stage suggest that, with music, choreography and the immediacy of performance ("to make the looking have in it an element of moving," as Stein said) the difficulties vanish. Or at least they can be transformed into something else—into a circus, into singing games, into something between voodoo and bullfighting.

Yet none of these triumphs—continuing triumphs, at that—were what Stein wanted. She had invented so many other kinds of literature—the first American novel of black life (in *Three Lives*), the first American novel of lesbian life (*QED*), the first cubist prose—and she had invented herself in the doing. Had she not invented a new kind of play, too? I think Stein was nervous about all the charm and entertainment that apparently had to be added to these works in order to put them over. She wanted them put on, not over: "it begins well but then it begins to get funny and one must not be too funny," she wrote her old friend Carl Van Vechten about *Four Saints*. She knew she had devised a theater of immediacy—often it appeared to be her means of the interpenetration of language and landscape—which depended on nothing but the moment, the hypertrophied consciousness of the present.

As opera, as antiphon, as ballet, as film, and ultimately as a theater of dialogue and persons—though without character and without situation—the playwriting of Gertrude Stein remains, as it rears itself up in this bewildering book, an enigma. These plays await their revelation in performance, not as a stream of consciousness (as Stein's teacher William James, who invented the phrase, might have elicited it), but as a fixed consciousness. What we have in this volume are the scripts for a particular kind of pageant. It is one I cannot myself recognize or even identify yet; but, judging from the way in which those with an audience once they are given physical incarnation on the stage, I should be very reluctant to say they are not successful or that they cannot succeed.

What Stein wanted was the continuous present entity, as opposed to the cumulative historical identity of traditional drama. The plays certainly do not work in the mode of our theater's main line; they are—or would be judged by a Chekhov (though not by a Maeterlinck), by a Giraudoux (though not by an Artaud)—static compositions, with no reality referred to but their own. They are, in terms of any conventional dramaturgy, impossibly hermetic, non-logical and self-indulgent. Yet they stand for a ludic theater you may never have experienced but can find intimated (surely the right word) and occasionally prodded into being by your infantilism, your affectlessness, your primitivism. And if you have the valor to approach them as possible moments in your experience (say, by reading aloud), they will disclose, I believe, a dimension of theater experience as rare as that fourth one which, for all I know, they may incarnate. As Stein says in her "drama of aphorisms," "They Weighed Weighed-Layed" (1930): "It is best to plant them one by one."

Last Operas and Plays

Leonard Bernstein

In the vast sea of critical material that has been written about Miss Stein in the last decades there are discernible two general currents of thought, both of which I feel have carried our attitude toward her extraordinary work somewhat off the course of direct appraisal. Critics have usually divided themselves into the pious, who revere her every detached syllable, and the cynical, who write patronizing pieces in mock Steinese and consequently feel exempt from further analytical responsibility.

Isn't it true, after all, that Miss Stein's real and valid contribution to letters has always consisted in the weight of her influence? The variety of fads and isms associated with her work has never for a moment diminished her unaccountable power of impressing other writers, to say nothing of musicians and painters. There is a very real basis for this; and once we accept it—and accept her as an artist's artist—we no longer feel guilty at never finishing her more protracted works, nor do we feel embarrassed at reacting to her utterances with pure innocent laughter.

For she was—let us admit once and for all—very funny. Her random distribution of labels—Act One, Act Twenty-Three, Scene Four, Scene One, Scene I, Scene One—has become a classic literary joke. The cagey final paragraph of *The Autobiography of Alice B. Toklas* is a masterpiece of wit and nonsense. It is a humor of destruction: a humor which, like that of the Marx Brothers, negates commonly accepted axioms of reality, and leaves the perceiver dangling, reeling, and grateful for the ictus that enables him to agree with organized chaos by the simple act of laughing.

But certainly her value far exceeds that of a mere comic. Reading over this valuable and fascinating collection of her works "for the theatre" I am struck more forcibly than ever by the depth of her experiment in words. It is always a dangerous thing for an artist to try to exceed the bounds of his esthetic medium. He has to be a kind of genius to get away with it. An artist has at his command patterns and orders that exist as a continuum in a specific

Reprinted from the original (May 3) draft of a review for the *New York Times*, May 22, 1949, by permission of the New York Times, Inc., and Harry J. Kraut. Copyright © 1988 by Leonard Bernstein.

medium; and to stray from these, or to try and mix them with others usually means a fiasco in the end—especially in the case of the two media of words and music. Words are fundamentally conceptual and *transparent* (that is, they allow the idea to show through without interference) and are only *secondarily* decorative; while music is basically abstract and opaque, made up of notes which have no conceptual meaning in themselves, and acquire meaning only in relation to one another. It takes a Berlioz or a Stravinsky or a Strauss to be able to conceptualize notes into anything like successful program music. And it takes a Stein to be able to musicalize words as successfully as she has.

Stein has come closer than any other writer except Joyce to the medium of music. The emphasis has changed, of course, throughout her writing life, and I suppose one's approach to her must vary with the individual work or period. She ranges all the way from bleak automatic writing (*An Exercise in Analysis*: 1917) through alliterative and tonal preoccupation (*Four Saints in Three Acts*: 1927) through suggested meanings and faintly philosophical maxims (*Doctor Faustus Lights the Lights*: 1938) all the way to the conversational practicality and conventional "meaningfulness" of *Yes Is for a Very Young Man* (1945). In all these degrees of meaning and non-meaning, of useful and useless repetition, of jokes and maxims, there runs the connecting stylistic quality that is Stein's: the childlike debarrassment of words of their associations, the astonishing simplicity of her phraseology, and the *musical* value of any succession of sounds that may occur to her.

But in the end, after reading so comprehensive a collection as this one—never quite reaching the end of some of the pieces and rereading others with real pleasure—we return to our original feeling that their ultimate value lies in their influence upon other writers. One can almost say that a whole school of American prose-writing could not have existed had Stein not existed first. As we read along we can sense the germination of stylistic aspects in Hemingway, Faulkner, Dos Passos, and in a host of poets of the twenties and thirties. Like so many extremist innovators, Stein precipitated a movement of which the really valuable contributions to literature were to be made by others, debtors to a woman who herself may never have written a page of lasting value except to critics and to other artists. It reminds one of Moses, who led his people in masterly fashion to the promised land, but was not himself permitted to enter it.

It reminds one also of Stein's opposite number in music, Virgil Thomson. I have often thought that the two were so very understanding of each other because they have this fate in common. Thomson's delightful, personal and inimitable settings of Stein texts (*The Mother of Us All* and *Four Saints in Three Acts*) seem to me to occupy exactly the same place in the history of music as do the texts themselves in literature. Without Thomson's music there could never have been the great movement in American music toward utter simplicity and hymn-like directness. With Thomson there came, as a reaction to the turgid, acrid music of the twenties, a new look, and a reinstatement of the tonic triad. But it has been, perhaps, for other composers to reap the harvest of this influence, and to create the pieces of music that we feel constitute the living body of the contemporary repertoire. Copland, for example, in coming under Thomson's influence, evolved a new and simpler style which has been perhaps the most influential force among younger American composers.

Stein and Thomson are both irreplaceable in the spectrum of contemporary art, whatever the public reaction may be. And whenever we find ourselves dismissing a Stein-Thomson opera as *chi-chi*, or pretentious, or slightly amusing, let us remember that, if not for this opera, *A Farewell to Arms* and *The Second Hurricane* might never have graced our world.

How the Curtain Did Come:
The Theatre of Gertrude Stein

Lawrence Kornfeld

Very Fine is my Valentine
very fine and very mine
very mine is my valentine
very mine and very fine
very fine is my valentine
and mine very fine very mine
and mine is my valentine.

Gertrude Stein

Since 1957 I have been the director of at least sixty plays. Six of these are by Gertrude Stein: *In a Garden* (1957), *What Happened* (1963), *Play I Play II Play III* (1965), *A Circular Play A Play in Circles* (1968), *The Making of Americans* (1972), and *Listen To Me* (1974). These six productions are "very mine" even though they are by Gertrude Stein and Al Carmines and Leon Katz and Myer Kupferman and especially the performers who acted and sang and danced them; but they were all very mine even though they were by the people who wrote them and played them. What happened in these productions was what happened to the people who did them; the words and music were not what happened: what happened was that the people who acted and sang and danced *were* the action the music and the dancing. Only *The Making of Americans* was a little different: it was a story about something remembered and continuous most of the time; a story that was about what it was saying it was saying (most of the time) so the actors had to often be pretending: they were pretending most of the time that they were other people being remembered and living in this time, but not themselves, I mean not themselves, the real actors on the stage, but people from another place. The other five productions are about what the actors singers and dancers did on the stage when they were on *that* stage at *that* time they were doing it. Many of them don't know this or don't believe this, but it is true and they are mistaken: they were only doing what they were doing at that moment on that stage, even though they repeated the same thing night after night and were not improvising.

Even though sometimes the actors thought they were pretending, except sometimes in *The Making of Americans*, they were not pretending. They were saying the words and singing and feeling many deep and beautiful things, and also fighting a lot, mostly with me, and sometimes with each other. Also, they moved around beautifully and were sometimes happy. Most of the time they were fighting with each other and with me; but they were always mine. When they spoke what they felt, and sang what they felt, even if I didn't know what they actually meant or felt, it was still all mine, and the more they fought the better it all was; and all this time I moved them around into pictures and pushed them into fights: fights on the stage, not fights with one another, although that happened too, but not on purpose, only because we were always very volatile. The pictures I made on the stage were always about fighting or not fighting. That is why I have the belief that if Gertrude Stein saw them she would find these plays mostly exciting and not boring; even though she said she didn't like plots, I know she liked fighting because I know that her life was a fight and her Susan B. Anthony in *The Mother of Us All* says, "Life is strife, I was a martyr all my life not to what I won but to what was done." What we did with our fighting was always joyous and tragic, that is, we felt many things around us, and our times are tragic and joyous. I am happy about the fighting, the strife, in the plays, but of course I am saddened by the fighting that was not on the stage, but that's what we were doing and it seems that what was happy and loving in these plays was when our fighting stopped for a while. For me, the real play is the process.

When I say fighting I mean strife; not just being angry, but also wanting something for yourself that belongs to someone else, or wanting to go toward a certain place and it's hard to get there. Fighting and strife are not only wars and painful affliction on the innocent, boxing and wrestling and the history of settlers and natives, and all of those aggressions that the body feels as pain and the mind feels as grief: fighting and strife as artists and other people who do creative things feel it, is about finding a way to that very certain special place that feels right.

Gertrude Stein's plays can be very boring if the director tries to make them all about the words of ideas, or the words of love, or the words of painting or the words about words. This is wrong. The director must fight the plays and then he will find out what the words mean, not what the words are about. Only Gertrude Stein knew what the words were about; we can manage to hear what they mean if we put up a good fight. Only Gertrude Stein cared what the words were about and maybe some of her friends for gossip cared, but I only care about what they will mean after we all fight over them.

What is it that happens when it seems to the actors that I am doing nothing and won't even tell them what to do, except move someplace or stand in a certain special place *just so*? This is one of my ways of fighting with the play: I know something and I won't tell it, but they, the actors, know I know something, so they fight and then the strife begins to fill up the spaces on the stage. Now, a director has to be very very careful with this technique because it could very easily look like, and in fact could very easily be, just plain stupidity. So much directing, even the kind where the director says many words and seems to be explaining much and helping everyone, is often really just stupidity disguised as style. So, if the director is not using lots of words and instructions, he must be sure that the simple facts he plants on the stage are fertile and can make a place for the actors to ripen with time and strife. I must go into this technique in more detail: the director does not actually make performances come from actors. (Teachers and coaches can but not directors, at least not this one.) Actors give their own performances inside a "landscape" that the director has helped actualize from the words and music and settings. To get a performance from an actor means really to *place him where he can do it*. So I'm always very busy making a place and putting actors into it; along the way I try to help them find out who they are there, and why they are there. The difficulty is that although I know what the place is, and I know who the person there is, I very often don't actually know what he's doing there! I often don't know how the place and the person are going to finally get together until the end of the rehearsal process, some four or five weeks later, and they've made a truce and are together.

This technique is best for plays by Gertrude Stein and other playwrights who write mostly for doing and landscapes, but must be used much less with playwrights who write mostly to tell stories. It can and must be used in all plays, but in plays that are about something that is being told from another place and time, and the actors are pretending to be people who they are not really like, then the director must use words and give instructions about how he understands the people in the play to behave. However, he should only do this if the actor either asks for advice or is doing something that the director believes is all wrong, or will lead to being all wrong. What is best in all kinds of plays is to let the written plays and the actors and the place find each other and fight out a truce and then repeat their existence every night to the audience. The director's part is not well defined in this process, and mostly he should mind his own business and make the place for everything to happen.

Of course the question comes up: what is place? Place is anywhere that anything can happen. For me place and the things in it have to have a certain "look" that makes me happy. It is the coming together of space, so that it appears to me as if it is an extension of my perception of myself and the world of my existence into the world of the play. I am told by some people that this place that I can make can be very pleasing and profound for them also; this I consider very good luck, because if they didn't like it, there isn't very much I can do about it. I should explain also what I mean by a "look": I don't mean decor necessarily; I have made things look right for me with elaborate sets and environments, and also with practically nothing more than lighting; sometimes I am very happy even without lighting; just people in the perfect place for them, and an audience looking at it. Of course I know also that the audience is part of this "landscape"; in my work they are the unknown factor every night: they re-interpret the play and change it every night; their synthesis is different every night because the energy of their perceptions changes every moment of the actual place and action that they are perceiving. Nothing changes on the stage, but everything changes in the theatre. I believe that it actually changes every night and is a different thing, but that which I have put on the stage remains the same (except of course for the wonderful and necessary growth that every play undergoes with running) although every eye renews it every night.

What are my six plays about? *In a Garden* was first. That's what it was about: my first fight. That the words the characters are saying are fighting words, and that the characters fight, is coincidental with my first fighting. *In a Garden* was about discovering fighting and trying to make it interesting. It was very interesting and the fighting was strong on the stage and in me. There wasn't much fighting with the singers because I was too young (and I thought at that time that I was only directing) but the music helped because I had to fight with it because I didn't, at first, like it. After the fight, I did. I don't remember much about this production except that at the end one person wore two crowns one inside the other, and that the boys were really dead, or would have been, if we hadn't been pretending.

That is the hardest thing about plays: pretending and reality. We pretend what is real and we really pretend, but what we pretend is not real and what is real is not a pretence. What happens on the stage is not an illusion, it is real, but it is pretending to be another kind of real thing. What I always try to do is find a way for everyone to pretend doing whatever they are doing, and that that pretence is actually the same thing they are pretending to be doing. It is like Judith Malina in jail pretending to be frightened when she was frightened. She didn't know it; Dorothy Day, who was watching her, did. People on a stage don't have to know it either. Actors don't like to hear this. They want to pretend that they know the final differences between real and pretend. I spend a lot of time fighting with them about this, but usually I'm the only one who knows there's a fight on; they usually think I'm directing. I know that the only time I'm directing is when I tell them when to go in or out of a door, or to move someplace, or to be angry or happy, or other simple things that they sometimes don't think of. What they do think of mostly are things like character and meaning.

They think that character is something inside them that they can find. They think that their confusion is character. Very few of them know that character is what happens between them, each one with each other one. Their confusion about meaning is that they think meaning is something that they will discover inside their heads that is the same thing as something they see outside their heads. This is wrong. Meaning is what they do with each other, and what remains after they have forgotten what the specific action was. Meaning is what is left over after doing something. So actors and other pretenders are always getting confused because they try to do something because of a meaning: how can you have something left over before you do something? You can't; they can't; and plays are more and more uninteresting because nothing happens, and nothing is left over for meaning. (This has come about because the plays are meaningless because the writers are filling them with pretended meaning when they are afraid to be active: hoping that "meaning" will fill up the empty places where characters should be having things happen, instead of pretending that they are really like something that in real life wouldn't even be commented upon. It's no wonder that only the silliest of musical comedies are a little bit satisfying sometimes, because no meaning gets in the way of the dancing.) Of course Gertrude Stein wrote about this a great deal, but she said it differently although I'm using some of her rhythms and words in my writing because I feel close to those plays writing like this.

What is the meaning of "happen"? I fought myself about this in *What Happened*. The title is just coincidental with what I was doing. This play is about doing things and not pretending to do them, or, if pretending, then the pretence was exactly what we were doing. *What Happened* was the most perfect production of the last twenty years. It had everything in it and it was very fine and very mine. It was always doing, and there was constantly something left over for meaning.

What Happened was about character and meaning, but it didn't say anything that audiences could talk about as characteristic or meaningful. People just felt good and then only some of them felt obliged to make up words that they probably hoped would be as historic as *What Happened*. But the fight was real, and this production remains important because it really happened.

Play I Play II Play III was the only one of the six plays that had no singing. It is about what happens to four people when someone tells them to be happy. This play is a ceremony for four people so that they would have something to do so that they could have something left over as meaning. It was very beautiful and had the least fighting of any of the plays, although the action was about fighting. It ended with all the characters singing "AH." It was the first time I was able to have characters who kept the same personality throughout the whole play. In *What Happened*, they sometimes went to delightful extremes and became other things for a while (and in plays by other playwrights the characters are always shifting around and being human), but in *Play I Play II Play III* they all five never strayed. It made it less interesting but more instructive, so therefore it was a complete success, although lots of people didn't find it as interesting as *What Happened*, or interesting enough to justify their effort to concentrate on what it was doing that was different from *What Happened* or other plays. Those who are not stingy with their

concentration generally enjoyed it. It had only one bad flaw: it had to be absolutely perfectly performed in order to be beautiful: one mistake and it wasn't
beautiful. The reason for this is that the characters were too consistent and
had no room for making mistakes. It all had to fit together. That's why it was
so right that the main prop was a cardboard box and everyone had to try to
get into it. It was a play about getting into a box and getting married and the
box had to be made into a home and not a container. Of course it was about
me, and I made the play for my Margaret. It was my perfect marriage
ceremony, but it had trouble being a perfect play.

Do you think I am overly concerned with perfection? You're wrong if you
think I am because perfection is only an accidental result of doing everything
you have to do. Perfection is not necessarily valuable, although having it is
often a sign that something valuable is present. But perfection as a goal is not
important. Perfection is not an essence, it is not a life food; perfection as a goal
is a marzipan apple.

Play I Play II Play III was not perfect, and it was too consistent with how
people are *thought* to behave. Life is about the fight of the limits of perfectability
against the freedom of doing everything that has to be done. After this play
I discovered this: not Perfection or Doing, not one or the other, but both:
Perfection and Doing are *not* mutually exclusive.

After this play I was eventually ready to do a play about the world, and
we did *In Circles*. It is the simplest of all six plays and the most popular. The
fighting during the making of it was not intense, it was like going to school.
The real fighting was something we all shared against the demands of the idea
of the well-made play. The fighting had mostly to do with the actors being so
good at what they could do, that they often pretended that they were pretending. They lost sight of the reality of pretence, and would often be compelled
to think of pretence as outside the realm of reality when, of course, pretending
is very real, and only unwelcome when it is not recognized as a real event.
Pretending is what we do when we are waiting for something else to happen;
it becomes real when it happens: the theatre is real because it happens after
it pretends to happen.

It was accidentally not a perfect play because some of the actors sometimes
forgot to tell the truth about what they felt, and they sometimes felt afraid to
pretend they were lying; instead they sometimes pretended that their lies were
truer than everything else they did. But then, since they didn't pretend to pretend, it all worked out beautifully, but imperfectly, which is alright; and it was
wonderful, and the music was so good to the words, and everything most of
the time was very fine and very mine, even when I was surprised at things that
would happen. It had a beautiful life as it grew and changed and became like
the world. *In Circles* was about the world as people live in it. By coincidence
the world practically was coming to an end almost, and therefore *In Circles* was
about the end of the world.

Nothing by Gertrude Stein reached me for some years because the world was ending, and the new one was unclear and I was making-do with other playwrights; (the world ending and beginning again being one of those activities that I reluctantly accept as an article of faith basic to going on again and again).

Then *The Making of Americans* was written by Leon Katz and Gertrude Stein in 1973 and 1906, and the continuity of my plays was interrupted, for *The Making of Americans* is not truly a part of my fighting, but is a faithful reproduction of Gertrude Stein's fighting, and it was my job simply to assist that fight of hers into the world of our time. Leon Katz and Al Carmines and I were Gertrude Stein's translators and this production was no fight, it was just very hard work. All of the fighting with the actors was the simple kind that is very common and has to do with remembering and imitating what was felt at another time, and fighting one's memories to make them clear, and also finding out what some difficult sentences really meant. It was a simple class of fighting, but a difficult species of remembering. The production, like the novel, is a masterpiece, and we are all proud of its beauty and its strength. It has characters and actions and doings things and so much left over for meaning that it fills the soul too much. It is not a perfect masterpiece and that is a blessing because it would then be smaller. Of all my works by any author it is most moving to me and least "mine," but so very very fine. It is separate from the others and doesn't give a hint about what was to come next, and last: *Listen To Me.*

Remember, *In Circles* is about the end of the world as the world, unaware of the end, suffers its happiness and sadness. Audiences thought it was about people coming together (that was what everyone wanted to see in 1968) but it was really about the end of things as people experience endings when they think that they are together pleasantly at the end of something that had happened to them together. It is about the world watching the ending of a play that it is the star of. *Listen To Me* (in which "the world is covered all over with people") the densest, yet most direct of our plays, brings down the curtain. It is a fight to the death: off-stage and on. Man and God are created and destroyed; characters are pure action and stasis; everyone pushes everyone around and the play pretends to be a play and *is* a play. It tells a hidden story that doesn't matter, and the fighting is bitter and at the end the only remaining character is an actor pretending to be Gertrude Stein saying "Curtain can come." The lights go out because there is no curtain, and this most bitter of plays ends in perfection: pretence and reality, theatre and life, actor and audience. One.

Unlike *What Happened*, some of the actors in *Listen To Me* continued to fight after the successful run. Most of them did not believe the work is a masterpiece, it is too much of an end of the world for them to have enjoyed doing it. They never really felt part of it because they were too much the being of it. *Listen To Me* was for the audience only. It was not, it turns out, very fine for the actors. It was fine and mine, a pet vulture that I love.

Listen To Me was a culmination of my work with Gertrude Stein and also a culmination of my work on a stage until I find a reason to lift the curtain again, and to lift the curtain means to discover the territory on both sides of that curtain. My fight is no longer for mastery or beauty, my fight seems to be for meaning, and what there is left to be done as actions, so that meaning can be left over. Discovery is dormant. Action is simple demand. Doing is necessary, like the first animals in history looking for water who accidentally discovered travel en route. So now maybe we should do the masterpieces that take skill and not much fighting: operas, Chekhov and the Greeks, and whoever speaks up to one at the moment.

In 1975 the world of the fought-out discovery is hibernating until strength returns and people are interested again in a good fight.

New York
April/May 1975

•••••••••

Post Script: New Haven, January, 1976. Beginning to fight again. Planning new production of Stein's *A Manoir* having found a reason to lift the curtain to begin again.

I begin again so often that I can begin again. (G.S.)

•••••••••••••••••

Thomson, Stein
and *The Mother of Us All*

Robert Marx

> *I will have nothing to do with opera, except as poetic theatre.*
> —Virgil Thomson

The Mother of Us All was the last collaborative work by Gertrude Stein and Virgil Thomson. The world premiere in New York during the spring of 1947, only ten months after Stein's death, was a successful but poignant event; it marked the end of a creative partnership that had not only revitalized experimentation in lyric theater and its stagecraft but also produced the first truly innovative and wholly remarkable American operas that reflected the experience and heritage of American culture.

In the past, many of the most stimulating European operas had come about through long-term collaborations between composers and dramatic poets (for instance Mozart and Lorenzo da Ponte, Verdi and Arrigo Boito, Richard Strauss and Hugo von Hofmannsthal). Stein and Thomson were part of this tradition. Their creative friendship lasted off and on for twenty years and resulted in numerous songs, a motion picture (never filmed, unfortunately), and two operas (the first was *Four Saints in Three Acts*). In the best sense the operas are works of poetic theater: the texts are musical in language and harmony, and each opera discards traditional conventions to generate its own panoramic world within the theater. Although sumptuously melodic they are not easy to sing, and mere vocal beauty in performance is not enough for success. Both operas demand the complete resources of the theater in an artful and delicate blend of choreography, design, and sound. But even when divorced from the stage (as on a recording) they retain their impact through the listener's imagination, for these are operas of contemporary sensibility and direct communication; simultaneously perceptive, charming, haunting—and great fun.

Until 1928, when Thomson composed *Four Saints in Three Acts*, American opera had failed to generate music of quality or earn the respect of audiences, critics, and musicians. The main reason was that American composers imitated (poorly, as it turned out) the successful musico-dramatic patterns and formulas of their European colleagues. The first opera by an American-born composer—William Henry Fry's *Leonora*, first given in Philadelphia in 1845—heavily relied on the style and technique of Donizetti and Meyerbeer. Subsequent nineteenth-century native works continued to follow the models of Italian, French, or German composers, depending upon which style was in vogue. The inferiority complex of American culture was at its height, and the desire of so many American opera composers to imitate European models was not only considered proper but was also necessary in order to elicit financial support for a production.

The star system of nineteenth-century opera production (which still exists) also worked against the growth of opera in the United States. Audiences usually went to hear stars, not specific works, and the great singers were entrenched in the operas of fashion (Rossini, Meyerbeer, Verdi, Massenet, Wagner, or Puccini) and considered it a waste to learn a new role in a language without proper operatic tradition. Artistic and social attitudes were against the American composer.

At the same time, as the population grew and reached westward, theaters (often optimistically called opera houses) were built all over the United States. Performances of popular European operas spread across the land, and sometimes there were even competitions or commissions for American works. (During the early twentieth century, for example, the Metropolitan Opera offered $10,000 in a contest for a new work by an American composer—a substantial sum at the time.) But the results were always the same: derived from European traditions and without a real stylistic connection to American speech, manners, or drama, these operas soon faded from the scene. Not until the fourth decade of this century did American opera produce results of originality, quality, and distinction with the first productions of Thomson's *Four Saints in Three Acts* (1934) and Gershwin's *Porgy and Bess* (1935).

Neither was staged in an opera house. After an initial showing in Hartford, Connecticut, Broadway was the scene of the spectacularly successful first production of *Four Saints*, and Gershwin's only opera was also performed on his native Broadway, even though the Metropolitan Opera had offered to produce *Porgy and Bess*. (Gershwin rejected the Metropolitan primarily because he felt a production there would be dramatically inadequate. However, a Victor recording of excerpts on four 78 rpm discs featuring two Metropolitan stars—Lawrence Tibbett and Helen Jepson—was made under Gershwin's supervision, and it gives some idea of what a Metropolitan *Porgy* might have been like: selections from this album were rereleased on an RCA lp *Porgy* anthology in 1976.)

After Thomson's first bold step Gershwin, Blitzstein, Menotti, and many others followed in the search for new and vital surroundings for serious musical theater. Thomson also validated the American theater as a working environment for the serious musician. Only after his initial efforts did classically trained American composers write incidental music for plays, background music for films, or operas that challenged dramatic concepts and musical traditions.

Virgil Thomson grew up in Kansas City, Missouri, where he was born in 1896. His ancestors, Scottish and Welsh, were early settlers in Virginia. They headed west in the nineteenth-century pioneer movement, settling down with family and slaves to farm the Missouri land in a region known as Little Dixie. During the Civil War the Thomson men fought—and some died—for the Confederacy, and the entire family, true to its heritage and adopted land, was staunch Southern Baptist. The moral and cultural patterns of the American Midwest—its Christian teachings and southern traditions—made up the environment of Thomson's youth. He was a precocious child, and although few in his family had artistic inclinations he was drawn to music at an early age, improvising on the piano before he was five. ("Always with the pedal down," Thomson remembers in his autobiography, "and always loud, naming my creations after the Chicago Fire and similar events.") At that age he began lessons, and when he was twelve he performed professionally as substitute organist for the Calvary Baptist Church in Kansas City. Thomson has written that "The music of religious faith, from Gregorian Chants to Sunday School ditties, was my background, my nostalgia," and this pervades much of Thomson's music, particularly the operas. His music is never far from this framework of midwestern tradition, and no matter how original Thomson's stylistic concept or how strong the French influence, the core remains a vibrant reflection of his youth's homeland—his "nostalgia."

Thomson continued his education in Kansas City, balancing musical studies with work on student literary magazines (his concise and brilliantly crafted prose would eventually make him one of the most perceptive and influential music critics of his day). On the American entry into World War I he enlisted in the Army (subsequently becoming a second lieutenant in the U.S. Military Aviation Corps), but the Armistice was signed just as Thomson was to be sent overseas. He resigned his commission and enrolled at Harvard University, where he continued musical studies in earnest while singing in the Harvard Glee Club and working as a church organist. Through his acquaintance at Harvard with S. Foster Damon, the Blake scholar, Thomson encountered two things that according to his autobiography changed his life: Erik Satie's piano music and Gertrude Stein's early prose work *Tender Buttons*. Satie, the mordantly witty scourge of French music, and Stein, the American writer who lived in Paris, were then scarcely known in the United States outside an intellectual circle that followed the growing avant-garde in France. But at Harvard, Thomson learned to revere all things French and to view France as his artistic destiny. "I came in my Harvard years," he wrote, "to identify with

France virtually all of music's recent glorious past, most of its acceptable present, and a large part of its future."

In 1921 he went with the Harvard Glee Club on a European tour. With scholarship aid he stayed on for a year in Paris, where he began work with Nadia Boulanger, the now legendary teacher of a generation of American composers (including Aaron Copland, Walter Piston, and Roy Harris), met Satie, and discovered the music of Les Six. This group of French composers (all disciples of Satie, they included Arthur Honegger, Darius Milhaud, and Francis Poulenc; at the periphery was the poet Jean Cocteau) sought to break the prevalent grip of Romanticism on music by turning for source material to music halls, cabarets, and jazz. The music of Les Six combined popular taste with the rigors of classical training and often took theatrical form—especially ballets, like Milhaud's *Le Boeuf sur le Toit*. These avant-garde productions, which blended the best of experimental choreography, music, and decor, remained a strong influence on Thomson. In the future he would insist that his operas be treated as "choreographic spectacles" and would continue the French line of musical experimentation by mixing hymns and popular ditties with the techniques of advanced musical expression.

In 1922, his scholarship expired. Thomson returned to Harvard. He spent the next three years in Cambridge and New York but yearned for Paris. He began to develop a reputation as an astute critic of contemporary music, having published essays in such influential journals as *The New Republic* and Nathan and Mencken's *American Mercury*. Thomson's criticism was controversial, and he developed important contacts in the American musical world. But the desire for an artist's life in Europe was strong. Announcing that he "preferred to starve where the food is good," Thomson left again for Paris in the fall of 1925. This time he would not study the music of others but create his own.

Satie had died, but Stein was alive and well, presiding over the most famous and stimulating *salon* in France. Anxious to meet Stein but wanting the acquaintance to come about informally, Thomson made no direct effort to see her. His friend George Antheil, whose music had begun to be known among Parisian intellectuals, was invited to a Stein at-home that winter and took Thomson with him. Stein was not pleased with Antheil, but she and Thomson got on, according to the composer, "like a pair of Harvard men." They corresponded briefly during the summer of 1926 and saw each other again at Christmas. Then, as a New Year's gift, Thomson sent her the manuscript of his setting of her early poem "Susie Asado." Stein, although musically illiterate, was pleased and wrote back:

> I like its looks immensely and want to frame it and Miss Toklas [Alice B. Toklas, Stein's companion for forty years] who knows more than looks says the things in it please her a lot and when can I know a little other than its looks, but I am completely satisfied with its looks.

This began a friendship that lasted, despite tensions and disagreements, until Stein's death.

Gertrude Stein was the youngest of five children born to German-Jewish immigrants. Her father, Daniel Stein, had as a child arrived with his parents and brothers in Baltimore in September, 1841. In 1862, in partnership with his younger brother Solomon, he opened a textile store in Allegheny, Pennsylvania, then a suburb of Pittsburgh (it is now incorporated into the city). Here Gertrude Stein was born on February 3, 1874. Although Daniel and Solomon prospered, they dissolved their business, and when Gertrude was less than a year old the family moved to Austria. The Steins remained abroad until 1879, living first in Vienna and then in Paris. Returning to the United States, they stopped briefly in Baltimore and in 1880 moved to Oakland, California, where Gertrude grew up in a prosperous household.

Devoted to her brother Leo, who went to Harvard, Gertrude enrolled at Radcliffe. She studied with the philosopher William James (elder brother of novelist Henry James), and was deeply influenced by his theory of pragmatism, which teaches that ideas are comprehensible only in relation to the immediate experiential consequences that precede and follow them. (This mode of analysis is strongly related to Stein's later experiments with abstract prose.)

Following James's advice Gertrude embarked on a career in psychology, leaving Radcliffe for Johns Hopkins University. But graduate work was both rigorous and boring, so she joined Leo, who was already wandering in Europe. They arrived in Paris in the fall of 1903 and settled in what was to become one of Europe's most famous addresses, 27 rue de Fleurus, where they began to assemble a spectacular collection of modern art. (The Stein heirs sold Gertrude Stein's collection for six million dollars in 1969.) Leo began a career as a painter and critic, while Gertrude commenced her formidable output of novels, poems, plays, and essays that would, after decades of public ridicule, have a significant impact on the development of modern English writing.

The Stein home became a center for art and artists, and by 1925 the apartment had become the focus of progressive movements in literature and art. Gertrude Stein had become the sun around which an entire body of American writers and artists (the "lost generation," she called them) revolved.

Music played less of a role than fiction or painting in the Stein circle, primarily because Gertrude's interests did not go in that direction. In her lecture on American drama she stated:

> I came not to care at all for music, and so having concluded that music was made for adolescents and not for adults and having just left adolescence behind me and besides I knew all the operas anyway by that time I did not care anymore for opera.

Thomson was able to change that attitude as Stein came to trust him. She was pleased with his settings, before the composition of *Four Saints*, of three of her poems: "Susie Asado," "Preciosilla," and "Capital, Capitals" (the last a conversation among four Provençal cities—Aix, Arles, Avignon, and Les Baux—set for male quartet and piano).

In choosing for his operatic collaborator an experimental writer like Gertrude Stein, Thomson broke with tradition. American opera composers had generally worked with versifiers who adapted the plots of well-known novels or plays. Dramatic originality was neither sought nor encouraged, and there was no experimental American opera that could use the work of a progressive writer. In rare instances American composers did work with poets of reputation—Horatio Parker's *Mona* (Metropolitan Opera, 1912) was set to a text by Brian Hooker, and Reginald de Koven's *Canterbury Pilgrims* (Metropolitan, 1917) had a libretto by Percy Mackaye; perhaps the most distinguished was Edna St. Vincent Millay's libretto for Deems Taylor's *The King's Henchman* (Metropolitan, 1927)—but there was no real precedent in the United States for the initial Stein/Thomson effort.

In Europe the situation was different. France alone had already seen the premieres of the narrated, acted, and danced theater piece *L'Histoire du Soldat* (1918; Stravinsky, Ramuz), the ballet *Parade* (1917; Satie, Cocteau, Picasso), and the opera *L'Enfant et les Sortilèges* (1925; Ravel, Colette, Balanchine). Thomson was following his own musical inclination toward lyric expression and his desire to make an impact with an American work in the theatrical sphere already developed in France. Progressive in her art and free of stale tradition, Gertrude Stein would prove to be the perfect collaborator. In his autobiography, Thomson has given the reason for his immediate attraction to her texts:

> My hope in putting Gertrude Stein to music had been to break, crack open, and solve for all time anything still waiting to be solved, which was almost everything, about English musical declamation. My theory was that if a text is set correctly for the sound of it, the meaning will take care of itself. And the Stein texts, prosodizing in this way, were manna. With meanings already abstracted, or absent, or so multiplied that choice among them was impossible, there was no temptation toward tonal illustration, say, of birdie babbling by the brook or heavy heavy hangs my heart. You could make a setting for sound and syntax only, then add, if needed, an accompaniment equally functional. I had no sooner put to music after this recipe one short Stein text than I knew I had opened a door. I had never had any doubts about Stein's poetry; from then on I had none about my ability to handle it in music.

Their first conversation about writing an opera together took place in January, 1927. Thomson suggested the subject matter: the life of the working artist, with possible references to Gertrude Stein and James Joyce in Paris, each holding forth before a group of disciples. As a gesture to operatic history, the contemporary references would be veiled as mythology. They agreed that Greek and

Scandinavian legends were not to be considered because they dominate so many earlier operas. Stein suggested the mythology of American history, perhaps with George Washington as central figure. Thomson vetoed the idea because he disliked eighteenth-century costumes, but twenty years later they did write their mythic opera about America—*The Mother of Us All.*

Discarding American history, they decided on the lives of the saints, particularly Theresa of Avila and Ignatius Loyola. Both these Spanish mystics were close to Stein: as a child she had been impressed with the San Francisco church dedicated to Ignatius, and with Alice B. Toklas she made an emotional pilgrimage to Avila, Theresa's birthplace. Stein worked for three months on the libretto, titled *Four Saints in Three Acts—An Opera To Be Sung,* and sent the manuscript to Thomson in mid–June.

The libretto—in four acts, not three, and with dozens of named and unnamed saints—bears no relation to anything else in opera. It is an abstract assemblage of words and images patterned after the techniques of Cubist painting.

The Cubist formula (as developed by Pablo Picasso and Georges Braque between 1907 and 1910) is essentially a revelation of structure. All planes lie on the surface of the canvas without naturalistic depth or perspective: the aim in part is to present all sides of the subject simultaneously. In Stein's prose the abstracted subject matter is traditional sentence structure. Words are placed together and separately as a sequence of sound patterns. Occasionally these make conventional sense as part of a narrative, but often the patterns are total abstractions, designed with great skill to convey Stein's desired sounds and rhythms through repetition and extreme textual compression. In Thomson's words, "She wrote poetry, in fact, very much as a composer works. She chose a theme and developed it; or rather, she let the words of it develop themselves through free expansion of sound and sense." Her innovative work re-created many of the new devices of the visual arts. There is a particularly strong parallel to the collage technique, for amid the varied images of her writing one might suddenly encounter snippets of a children's song or (in *The Mother of Us All*) quotations from the speeches of nineteenth-century politicians.

The dramatic structure of the *Four Saints* libretto has no logical pattern. In Act I, for example, scenes 3 and 4 play simultaneously, there are eight scene 5s, and scene 10 comes before and after scene 9. The presentation, seemingly random and disjointed, has its purpose and is dramatically potent. Stein's distinct and entirely artful collage of meaning and sound forces the reader to enter her world of dramaturgy. The images are often serious—the vision of the Holy Ghost (with its famous line "Pigeons on the grass alas"), a combined wedding and funeral procession—and the libretto, despite its wit, is not a stylistic joke. No matter how random, the images are always presented in relation to one another and endowed with poetry.

Four Saints presents a picture of religious benediction that Thomson calls "the community of peace." But at heart the work is about language: the relation of words to meaning and sound. With the text free of the common burdens of rhetoric, argument, and plot, the simple sounds of the words themselves are released, so we hear what James Mellow, the Stein biographer, calls "words at play, language in a state of beatitude."

The concept of a theatrical "landscape" in which all elements of sight and sound are perceived at once is crucial to an understanding of Stein's work. Instead of presenting a linear series of dramatic events that are progressive in their development of character and plot, Stein unveils a tapestry of images; as with the words themselves, all elements of the "landscape" are perceived simultaneously. What she called the "complete actual present," devoid of dramatic irony or hindsight, is her aim: an entire complex geography in which the theatrical image and the audience are in total emotional unity. Her dramas are about relationships, not situations. Relationships among characters, images, thoughts, and words are developed as she tries to "tell what happened without telling stories."

Four Saints in Three Acts is poetry composed for music, and Thomson, understanding the world of his collaborator, created a musical setting of great warmth and originality. He began work in November, 1927:

> With the text on my piano's music rack, I would sing and play, improvising melody to fit the words and harmony for underpinning them with shape. I did this every day, wrote down nothing. When the first act would improvise itself every day in the same way, I knew it was set. That took all of November. Then I wrote it out from memory, which took ten days. By mid-December I had a score consisting of the vocal lines and a figured bass, a score from which I could perform.

Act II was finished by February, 1928, the rest completed in midsummer. Stein allowed Thomson an opera composer's traditional rights. "Do anything with this you like," she told him. "Cut, repeat as composers have always done; make it work on a stage." But Thomson cut nothing. He set every word—even the stage directions, because he considered them part of the poetic continuity. Later, cuts were made, and Thomson devised two important new elements: he divided the role of St. Theresa (one part for soprano, the other for mezzo-soprano) and introduced two narrators, the Commère and Compère, a notion taken from French variety shows. In 1929 a vocal score was prepared, and Maurice Grosser, an American painter who was a close friend of Thomson's, wrote—with Stein's approval—a working scenario that would ease the opera's transition to the stage.

Many discussions were held about producing the opera. There were plans to have it done in Paris with Picasso sets; in Darmstadt, Germany, whose opera house specialized in unusual contemporary works; or in some other city. But none of these plans materialized, even though Thomson spent much of the next few years playing the piano score and singing all the parts for potential patrons. In time an American production was scheduled as a festival performance to coincide with the first Picasso retrospective held in the United States. It would take place in Hartford at the Wadsworth Atheneum, where a new wing was about to open that would display both the Picasso exhibition and the opera.

The production, which opened on February 7, 1934, became a legend in modern theatrical history. Not only was the sound of the opera (with its hymns and ballads) startling, but the stage picture was unlike anything seen before. Florine Stettheimer, an American painter who had rarely – if ever – exhibited her work, had designed beautiful costumes and brightly colored sets of cellophane and lace. As photographs of the production clearly show, her scenery, glittering in bright white light, perfectly supported Stein and Thomson's "landscape." The entire theatrical vision, with its choreographed movement by Frederick Ashton (later Sir Frederick Ashton, artistic director of Britain's Royal Ballet), evoked the spirit of Baroque religious art while parodying familiar opera poses. Most powerful of all was the all-black cast, recruited from church choirs in Harlem and Brooklyn. Few of the singers had previous theatrical experience, but as coached by Thomson and conducted by Alexander Smallens (then assistant conductor of the Philadelphia Orchestra) they were by all accounts superb in both voice and movement. Never before had a black cast been used in a work that had nothing to do with Negro life. Both *Four Saints in Three Acts* and *Porgy and Bess* owed much of their success to black performers, who had been excluded for so long from the mainstream of American theater. Thomson had chosen his company (over the objections of his librettist and designer) after seeing *Run Little Chillun*, a black musical on Broadway. The clarity of voice, freedom of movement, and potent theatrical energy of those performers were precisely what Thomson wanted for his opera.

In Hartford the opera was a major social event. Extra trains were run up from New York, bringing a distinguished audience drawn not only from music but from art, architecture, and publishing as well. The reception was so enthusiastic that it was decided to move the opera to Broadway immediately after its six performances in Connecticut.

For its Broadway run the chorus was enlarged and extra strings were added to the orchestra, but the production itself was not altered. Although the stage in New York was twice as large as that in Hartford, *Four Saints* retained its impact. The New York opening (during a blizzard) brought out another fashionable audience, including George Gershwin and Arturo Toscanini, and the response was even more exciting.

Most papers, sensing something unusual, had their music, dance, drama, and art critics cover the opening together. The reviewers generally agreed on the quality of the music, but the libretto puzzled many. The *Daily News* headline announced: "Virgil Thomson takes the glory, Gertrude Stein supplies the confusion: Music: 3 stars. Libretto: 0." Harshest of all was Olin Downes's review in the *Times:* "It is a text of palpable affectation and insincerity . . . a specimen of an affected and decadent phase of the literature of the whites." But in the weekly magazines and intellectual journals there was only high praise. Stark Young, the distinguished drama critic of *The New Republic,* called *Four Saints*

> the most important event of the season—important because it is theatre and flies off the ground, most important because it is delightful and joyous, and delight is the fundamental of all art, great and small.

Whatever the response, *Four Saints in Three Acts* was a show not to be missed. It ran for six weeks in New York and two in Hartford and Chicago for a total of sixty performances in its first year—a record at the time for a contemporary opera. Thomson became famous overnight. When Stein saw the production in Chicago, she declared herself satisfied:

> Anyway I did write *Four Saints in Three Acts* an Opera to be Sung and I think it did almost what I wanted, it made a landscape and the movement in it was like a movement in and out with which anybody looking on can keep time. . . . Anyway I am pleased. People write me that they are having a good time while the opera is going on a thing which they say does not very often happen to them at the theatre.

To help coordinate this production and engage the technical staff, Thomson had hired John Houseman, at that time quite inexperienced in the theater. They worked well together, and Houseman became Thomson's other major artistic collaborator. He went on to become an influential director and producer in New York (Orson Welles's Mercury Theatre productions on Broadway in the 1930s); Hollywood—*Citizen Kane* was probably his most famous film—and Broadway in the 1940s; directing the American Shakespeare Festival Theatre in Stratford, Connecticut in the 1950s; and finally becoming the head of the drama division of the Juilliard School. Thomson has composed incidental music for a great many of Houseman's productions, and in a return gesture, Houseman staged the first production of Thomson's third opera, *Lord Byron* (to a text by the playwright Jack Larson), at Juilliard in 1972.

Thomson remained in New York after *Four Saints,* working primarily on Houseman films and plays. Relations had been tense with Gertrude Stein, for they had disagreed about royalties, and she had begun to purge many of the younger artists around her. By 1936 matters were cordial again, but there was no talk of further collaboration. Thomson, always more comfortable in Paris, returned there in 1938 and remained until the Nazi occupation. His *The State of Music,* a cogent analysis of the economics of modern concert life, had been published in 1939. On the basis of this widely recognized book and his experience as a composer, Thomson was named chief music critic of the *New York Herald Tribune* in 1940 almost immediately on his return to the United States.

He stayed on as the *Tribune's* music critic until 1954. A fervent partisan of contemporary music, Thomson never hesitated to wage war on the established musical institutions, particularly the New York Philharmonic. Thomson loved the music he wrote about; his articles were always elegant, sharp, and influential, and he, Edwin Denby (the dance critic) and Stark Young were the best journalistic critics of their generation. Thomson's reviews, collected in four volumes, remain a model for younger writers.

During his critic's career, Thomson continued to work as an active musician. He began to accept assignments conducting his own music and that of his colleagues with some of the best American and European orchestras. By 1940, in addition to *Four Saints in Three Acts* and incidental music for the theater, Thomson had written two symphonies, dozens of vocal pieces, chamber music, film scores (*The Plow That Broke the Plains* and *The River*, both directed by Pare Lorentz), and a ballet on an American theme (*Filling Station*). While at the *Herald Tribune*, Thomson wrote more stage and film music, flute and cello concertos, two books of piano études, numerous songs and chamber scores, and *The Mother of Us All*.

Among Thomson's varied musical works, perhaps the most unusual are his "portraits" (generally for piano, although some are for chamber groups or full orchestra). The subject would pose for Thomson as if before a painter while the composer, without piano, would create a portrait in music. Most of the subjects were close to Thomson, and the diverse list includes Pablo Picasso, Aaron Copland, and New York's Mayor Fiorello La Guardia.

In 1938 Orson Welles had asked Thomson to write incidental music for a staging of John Webster's *The Duchess of Malfi*, one of the most poetic and theatrical Jacobean tragedies. Eventually the production was called off, but Thomson, excited by the play, asked Edwin Denby to prepare a shorter version of the drama as a libretto. Denby did this with the help of Maurice Grosser, and that summer, in France, Thomson set to work. He had outlined an entire act before renouncing the project, finding that the blank-verse text, even reduced, left no room for expansive musical treatment. In the 1950s Thomson would consider setting Gertrude Stein's *Doctor Faustus Lights the Lights* (which she wrote in 1938 for British composer Lord Berners, but which he never used). This project, one of Thomson's most promising, never grew beyond the planning stage.

World War II cut Thomson off from France and Gertrude Stein. In 1945, the year the war ended, the Alice M. Ditson Fund of Columbia University offered him a commission for another opera. He wired Stein to ask if she would be interested in working together again, and her reply was positive and eager.

They met in Paris in October, 1945. Fascinated by the language of senatorial oration, Thomson suggested a work about political life in nineteenth-century America. Stein, possibly thinking about the opera on American history that she had wanted to write twenty years earlier, immediately accepted the suggestion and chose Susan B. Anthony, the women's-rights activist, as her central character. The opera would be called *The Mother of Us All.*

Stein began work that same month and finished the domestic scene that opens the opera before Thomson left for New York in November. Immersing herself in the subject, Stein did a great deal of research on nineteenth-century American life at the American Library in Paris, and then wrote to the New York Public Library for additional material. She sent the finished libretto (which differs in the order of its scenes from the text set in the opera) to Thomson in March, 1946. In April he wrote to her:

> The libretto is sensationally handsome and Susan B. is a fine role.... The whole thing will be much easier to dramatize than *Four Saints* was, much easier, though the number of characters who talk to the audience about themselves, instead of addressing the other characters, is a little terrifying. Mostly it is very dramatic and very beautiful and very clear and constantly quotable and I think we shall have very little scenery but very fine clothes and they do all the time strike 19th century attitudes.

In May, his critic's responsibilities over for the season, Thomson was back in France and met with Stein about revisions in the text. The libretto was to be her last completed work, for on July 27, 1946, she died of cancer. Thomson began work on the vocal score that October in New York. By mid–December he had completed all but the final scene. He spent a month playing the opera for others, as he had with *Four Saints,* and in January, 1947, Thomson (now secure about what had already been composed) wrote Susan B.'s final monologue. He prepared the orchestral score in the spring, and the opera opened at Brander Matthews Hall at Columbia University on May 7, 1947.

The opera was conducted by the composer Otto Luening and was staged by the choreographer John Taras. The cast included two young singers: Dorothy Dow in the role of Susan B. and Teresa Stich as Henrietta M. In the 1950s and 1960s Miss Dow made a distinguished career in Italy, where she specialized in Wagnerian repertory as well as twentieth-century opera, creating several roles in the latter category, including Renata in the stage premiere of Prokofiev's *The Flaming Angel* in Venice in 1955. Miss Stich became famous as Teresa Stich-Randall and attained success especially in Austria, where she was eventually accorded the coveted title of *Kammersängerin* at the Vienna State Opera.

The production was successful, though not one for history books like the first *Four Saints.* Using Columbia students for many singers and for the technical staff prevented the opera's full realization, but the essential quality of the work came through. Reviews were favorable, and the opera was given a special citation by the New York Music Critics Circle. In *The New York Times*, Olin Downes ended a generally positive review by stating:

> The question that remains is whether this very literary style of opera . . .
> gives the composer enough opportunity for his score to stand as a unit
> in itself and keep its place in the repertory. It remains to be seen.

The question has been answered by history, for in the thirty years since its premiere *The Mother of Us All* has been given over a thousand times in nearly two hundred different productions.

The "landscape" of *The Mother of Us All* is somewhat different from that of *Four Saints*. Less abstract and more narrative, with recognizable characters and even the semblance of a plot, the libretto reflects the tendency of Stein's writing in her later years toward a more accessible and entertaining idiom.

Although Stein was not an ardent feminist, it is not surprising that she would choose Susan B. Anthony as her central figure. Not only was Anthony a woman of independence and strength who had a major impact on political events in the United States, but her very long life (1820–1906) would serve perfectly as the fictional central point around which an array of characters from America's past could circulate. It is also possible that Alice B. Toklas had something to do with the choice, for as a young girl in San Francisco she had met the feminist and was greatly taken with her. In a letter dated April 5, 1957, she wrote that Anthony was:

> . . . the first great woman I met and she made a lasting impression on me.
> She was beautiful and frail and quite naturally dominated the group of
> women she had been asked to meet.

Susan B. Anthony's career was one of strife and dedication. She was a pioneer crusader for women's rights in the U.S., whose work, along with that of her colleagues Elizabeth Cady Stanton and Anna Howard Shaw, led to laws that granted women full suffrage. Although by 1850 Anthony was organizing women's political conventions, in the early part of her life she was principally concerned with the abolition of slavery. But in 1866 the Fourteenth Amendment to the Constitution was passed, granting (as part of the Reconstruction) voting rights to all "male inhabitants . . . twenty-one years of age and citizens of the United States." Shocked and disappointed that the world "male" had been written into the Constitution, Anthony put all her energy into obtaining the vote for women.

Much of her work was done through writing, including her four-volume *History of Women's Suffrage*, but she also used political action. In 1872 she led a women's march on the polls in Rochester, New York, to test the voting laws.

The women were refused. Anthony was arrested and convicted on minor charges but refused to pay the fine and continued her struggle. At the time of her death there was still no Constitutional amendment granting nationwide women's suffrage, but some states (beginning with Wyoming in 1890) had begun to grant women the vote. Not until 1920 was the "Anthony Amendment" (first introduced in Congress in 1878) made a part of the United States Constitution as the Nineteenth Amendment.

The opera deals with much of this history, particularly the Fourteenth Amendment, which elicits Susan B.'s ironic outburst (Act II, scene 2) "Yes, it is wonderful" that because of her work for civil rights the word "male" was written into the Constitution. But in addition to Susan B. Anthony there is an entire gallery of American characters, used with total abandon and anachronism to create a diversified and purposely disjointed portrait of long-ago American life.

Most of these figures had nothing whatsoever to do with Susan B. Anthony and lived during different times. But Stein threw them together as part of her "landscape": Daniel Webster, the New England elder statesman and senator from Massachusetts (1827–41, 1845–50), delivers excerpts from his speeches and court cases; Andrew Johnson, the seventeenth president, argues with the abolitionist Thaddeus Stevens; Anthony Comstock, father of American censorship laws, wanders into view, as do John Quincy Adams (the sixth president) and stage star Lillian Russell (the last two, unlike the preceding personalities, could never have met, since Adams died in 1848 and Russell was born in 1861). Most humorous is the appearance of Ulysses S. Grant, who will not tolerate loud noises and talks about his military successor of a century later, Dwight D. Eisenhower.

Such anachronisms have more than charm; they have precise dramatic purposes. Act I, scene 2, for example, is a debate between Susan B. and Daniel Webster. As far as one knows, they never met, and Webster died before Anthony reached her fame. But the scene is built entirely of snippets from each character's actual public addresses, and the crosscutting of these fragments, which become a series of non sequiturs, emphasizes the frustration of Susan B.'s cause and the incomprehension of its opponents.

A number of the opera's characters are taken from Stein's life: the American playwright Constance Fletcher, the French painter Jean Atlan (renamed Herman in the opera), and Donald Gallup, the Yale librarian who would edit Stein's posthumous works. There are two mysterious narrators (replacing the Commère and Compère of Four Saints), Gertrude S. and Virgil T. The stage marriage of Jo the Loiterer to Indiana Elliot is a reference to the marriage of Joseph Barry, a journalist who knew Stein after World War II. Barry, who was once arrested for loitering, was about to marry a practicing Catholic, and there was much talk about whether the wedding should be civil or religious—the same situation that occurs in the opera.

With the display of so much of her personal life in the libretto, there is little doubt that Stein meant her portrait of Susan B. and her companion Anne to reflect her own life with Alice B. Toklas. The incorporation of her private world into a work of fiction had been an aspect of Stein's writing for many years. (In *Four Saints* there is a passage that describes her own difficulties beginning the opera, and her lengthy novel *The Making of Americans* is about her own family.) Toklas disputed this autobiographical analysis, saying that the portrait of Susan B. and Anne was no more than an heroic evocation of Susan B. Anthony and Anna Howard Shaw. But Stein had always wanted to be historical—she identified with these mythic figures (including St. Theresa) and drew such thinly veiled self-portraits on the assumption that she too, in time, would become a mythic personality.

As with *Four Saints*, Maurice Grosser prepared a scenario (reprinted here with the libretto) that described possible tableaux for the work and facilitated its staging. For *The Mother of Us All* the changes—devised by the composer himself—were more substantial. Two scenes are deleted (the first a dialogue between Susan B. and Anne about who will join the fight for women's suffrage, the second another debate between Susan B. and Daniel Webster), and one scene is presented out of sequence (the domestic dialogue that opens the opera was originally after what is now Act I, scene 2—the political meeting). The place of the intermission—which was before the current Act I, scene 3—was also changed. These major textual revisions are defensible, for Stein's structure would have created an extremely brief first act and a very long second act.

The score of *The Mother of Us All* exemplifies Thomson's musical language: melodious and warm, it evokes an old, imagined world of nostalgia and security. It seems to stimulate memories of experiences we have never had, of small-town American life in times long gone. All the tunes (except "London Bridge Is Falling Down") are original, even though we seem to remember them from a distant Sunday band concert or schoolroom chant. Thomson's skill is such that he can make us believe in his own nostalgia, what he called

> A memory-book of Victorian play-games and passions . . . with its gospel hymns and cocky marches, its sentimental ballads, waltzes, darned-fool ditties and intoned sermons . . . a souvenir of all those sounds and kinds of tunes that were once the music of rural America.

This is a singer's opera, for the emphasis is on the expression of the words. The phrasing and rhythms are designed to communicate the text. There is almost no ornamentation in either vocal or orchestral lines, and the musical flow always matches the spoken cadences of the words. So long as the singers have a true sense of verbal expression, there is never any problem understanding a text set by Virgil Thomson, for his music supports perfectly what he calls the verbal "trajectory." As with *Four Saints*, the French influence is clear, particularly in the harmonies of some orchestral passages. But the vocal lines are resounding Americana, and the whole work comes off as a Kansas City Fourth of July parade resonantly marching down the Champs-Elysées.

Thomson's music sustains this "political fantasy" with a sure grasp of theatrical technique and contrast. He was right to question Stein about the great number of characters who address the audience instead of each other, but the characterizations are clear and secure. The text (like so many opera librettos) portrays most roles in two dimensions, allowing the music to give them emotional depth and range. The various couples of the opera, for example, are all clearly defined through music in a way not matched by the words. Daniel Webster and his love Angel More (a ghost who wanders across the stage with tiny wings spread from her shoulders) sing in pompous tones that perfectly match the ornately oratorical statesman and his aristocratic lady. Jo the Loiterer and Indiana Elliot sing with a direct simplicity that recalls Masetto and Zerlina in Mozart's *Don Giovanni*. John Adams and Constance Fletcher (always flirting, but never able to marry) are a third contrasting pair of lovers, whose lilting music sustains the comic mode.

Susan B. Anthony's long final monologue, with its melody as solid as an inscription in granite, is an emotional summation of all the flowing warmth of the score. But smaller moments of delicacy and wit stand out. Thomson concludes Act I, scene 3 (a loud and hectic mixture of characterizations), by allowing Jo the Loiterer's guilty question "Has everybody forgotten Isabel Wentworth?" to become a gentle whispering coda to the whole boisterous pageant. Lillian Russell's tipsy catch phrase "It is so beautiful to meet you all here" is musically scattered about the stage like leaves in the wind. And the giddy trumpetlike Chorus of "V.I.P."s (Webster, Johnson, and Stevens) always makes a comic impact.

Carl Van Vechten, the American music critic, photographer, and novelist who became Stein's literary executor, summarized Thomson's music in an essay on *Four Saints:* "The music is as transparent to color as the finest old stained glass, and has no muddy passages." So much *is* transmitted like light in this score, for the elements are blended with all the skills of a vibrant colorist (nowhere more than in the impressionistic harmonies describing a snowy winter scene or in the snare-drum beat of an old-time political rally). The opera fulfills what earlier composers called *dramma per musica* (drama *through* music, not just alongside it), and as the text is filtered through song it gains color and emotional resonance without losing its magical sense of nostalgia or its melancholy pathos of an era lost to time.

The orchestration is full and effective, but throughout the opera the orchestra serves in a secondary role—setting the mood, adding tonal color, and primarily supporting the voices. In 1949 Thomson prepared an orchestral suite from *The Mother of Us All*, and three of its four movements are heard on this recording: "A Political Meeting" (in place of the overture), "Cold Weather" (before Act I, scene 3), and "Last Intermezzo" (Act II, between scene 1 and scene 2).

The opera's few musical motives are not used "dramatically" to extend the plot or reveal character. Rather, Thomson uses his lovely, flowing melodies to recall an earlier mood or unify the "landscape." The wedding hymn, for example, which is first heard in the orchestral prelude to the Act I finale, winds through the scene, musically coalescing a sequence of arias and ensembles. When it is restated alongside Daniel Webster's love song during Susan B.'s final monologue, the two melodies together evoke layers of complexity and emotion as she sings of her sacrifice to a cause:

> But do we want what we have got, has it not gone, what made it live, has it not gone because now it is had, in my long life in my long life Life is strife, I was a martyr all my life not to what I won but to what was done. Do you know because I tell you so, or do you know. My long life, my long life.

Is political action worth the emotional sacrifice? Does that sacrifice lead to true intellectual comprehension and social change, or simply to mere agreement? The opera poses serious questions, and the "memory-book" — both text and music — has more than pictures of simple gaiety.

Because of its humane complexity and the unity of its artistic vision, *The Mother of Us All* remains an astonishing work of American musical theater — probably the finest of its kind. It never fails to make an impact, no matter what is done to it. It has been performed in opera houses and church basements; with full orchestra, a single piano, or any number of combinations in between; with a cast of thirty professionals or with eight amateurs doubling on all the parts. It is indestructible.

Portrait, Patriarchy, Mythos:
The Revenge of Gertrude Stein

Neil Schmitz

I may say that only three times in my life have I met a genius and each time a bell within me rang and I was not mistaken, and I may say in each case it was before there was any general recognition of the quality of genius in them. The three geniuses of whom I wish to speak are Gertrude Stein, Pablo Picasso and Alfred Whitehead.

She always was, she always is, tormented by the problem of the external and the internal. One of the things that always worries her about paint-ing is the difficulty that the artist feels and which sends him to painting still lifes, that after all the human being essentially is not paintable.
                                          The Autobiography of Alice B. Toklas

There are three portraits of Gertrude Stein in *The Autobiography of Alice B. Toklas*: the monumental Gertrude who sits heavily in Picasso's celebrated portrait, her somber face distorted by Picasso's struggle with it, Alice B. Toklas's loving profile of the wronged and denied genius who rang her bell in 1907, Gertrude's Alice's Gertrude, a cunning self-portrait always framing the significance of Picasso's portrait, and a third, the self-effacing portrait of the *I* who at last seizes Alice's discourse, announces the writer's presence, and cleverly declares our innocence. This unknown Gertrude Stein, the peer of Picasso and Whitehead, who has lurked all along inside Alice's prosaic *I*, emerges, as it were, only to disappear. "I am going to write it," she asserts in the penultimate line of the text, "as simply as Defoe did the autobiography of Robinson Crusoe."[1] The allusion is deftly figured. Nearly everyone who matters in the history of modern art knows Gertrude Stein, knows the establishment at 27, rue de Fleurus, or the house in Bilignin, knows the pictures on her walls, her dog, knows Alice B. Toklas, they are all cited and catalogued in the *Autobiography*, the already famous and the merely promising; and yet within this charmed convivial circle, receiving F. Scott Fitzgerald, dismissing Ezra

Reprinted from *Salmagundi*, 40 (Winter 1978) by permission of author and publisher.

Pound, feeding Picasso, Gertrude Stein is inconsolably alone in her thought, marooned. To apprehend this solitude, the disembodied *I* that signifies Gertrude Stein, we must turn from the easily flowing style of Alice's narrative, from the social externality of the historical person, into the massed utterance of all those unpublished, unread novels, plays, meditations, poems, into the scripture, the true activity of Gertrude Stein's mind. *I am not here.* It is the final statement of the *Autobiography*, the consummate stroke, and this is the trick, the act of revenge, upon which the text is turned.

Neither Picasso's portrait nor Alice's in the *Autobiography* constitutes Gertrude Stein. Picasso's portrait, which now hangs in the Metropolitan Museum of Art in New York, is primarily the resolution of an artistic problem. One sees clearly enough in the strangely constructed face at once Gertrude Stein as Enigma and the thinking of *Les Demoiselles d'Avignon* and *Three Women*. Though she would remark in her later study, *Picasso* (1938), that the portrait "is the only reproduction of me which is always I, for me,"[2] this singular aptness is not, as we shall see, its proper significance in the *Autobiography*. As for Alice's profile, it is an advertisement humorously realized. Through the ruse of her appropriated voice, Gertrude Stein constantly refers us to the outlying mysterious *oeuvre* that justifies her place beside Picasso and Whitehead, the writing in which she, not Alice, speaks. Yet this voice is never abused or strained in its speech. Indeed Alice's daftness is the perfect foil for quick cuts. It is the droll wife who speaks, who domesticates the swash buckle of Ernest Hemingway and Ezra Pound, who looks bemused upon the large male ego. In that role, the role of the observant wife, Alice evidently saw a good deal. The allure of the *Autobiography* is just this: what Gertrude's Alice saw, the promise of intimate portraits, the promise of revelation (sixteen beguiling photographs are carefully sprinkled through the first edition), but if we lose ourselves in these anecdotal sketches, these private views, we lose as well the story that weaves these stories—Gertrude Stein's metaphorical escape from the meaning of Picasso's painting, from Picasso himself, through Alice's portrait, her devotion, into the self-possessed (and shorn) *I*.

This story concludes: *I am not here.* The *Autobiography* tricks those who did not see Gertrude Stein's significance as a writer, who missed her identity when they contemplated the beauty of Picasso's painting, who saw her as Picasso's creature, and it tricks the form itself. *The Autobiography of Alice B. Toklas* is the story of a fiction about Gertrude Stein. By redoubling her subjectivity, Gertrude Stein parades the egotism that creates autobiography, makes each hagiographical incident in the narrative, each laudation of the self, a calculated affront, and conceals until the last her presiding smile. As it is posed and solved by the Cubists, the question of portraiture, the problem of the external and the internal, is one of the central topics in the text, but what Gertrude Stein had already shown, and could not show here, was her own solution as a literary artist. Impersonating an autobiographer, revealing his alibi, she could, however, begin from the inside an ironic demystification of traditional narrative, restate the problem of the external and the internal in discourse through her final and surprising use of the Crusoe myth, and send rippling back over Alice's simplicities a confusion. Revenge is not, therefore, too strong a word to use in characterizing her formal strategies in the *Autobiography*. She is not the lady in the portrait. The book her publishers solicit can only be written by Alice. Indeed she parodies this arrangement by using a cleverly posed photograph of the author as her frontispiece. Alice is framed on the threshold in the illumined background. She stands directly facing the camera, one hand on the door latch, as though she were about to enter. In the foreground, in profile, partially obscured by the darkness, a writer sits at her desk, pen in hand. The photograph is appropriately entitled: *Alice B. Toklas at the door, photograph by Man Ray*.

It is, after all, Picasso's celebrity that gives the *Autobiography* its assured public in 1933–34, a dependence that perversely establishes Gertrude Stein not as a pre-eminent artist, Picasso's peer, but as a chronicler, the peer of Janet Flanner. From that position she looks askance at the spectacle of artistic success. Edmund Wilson's apt phrasing of this attitude: "Success, for her, seems to imply some imposture and deterioration,"[3] also describes her own ultimate celebrity as the eccentric writer who wrote amiable nonsense about roses. Drawn contractually into a mode of discourse (historical narration) she had already disparaged and abandoned in her previous writing, Gertrude Stein's "success" as an autobiographer is in fact an imposture, but here, as it is not in *Everybody's Autobiography* (1937), imposture is seized as an opportunity. It is Alice who shrinks Leo Stein to the vague reference, "her brother," who gradually erases Henri Matisse, who condescends to praise an oafish Hemingway. And yet these settled scores do not adequately reflect the substance of her animus in the *Autobiography*. Because of its complexity, that issue is delicately treated. Gertrude Stein genuinely admired Picasso's genius, understood it with a precocity that is still striking, owed him a great deal, and yet obviously his splendor obscured her own. He had painted her definitive likeness, captured her, rung her bell as she had rung Alice's bell. The risk of becoming Picasso's Gertrude as Alice is Gertrude's Alice is certainly before her in the *Autobiography*. And it involves crucially the question of her role, her place in the "heroic age of cubism," the very issue of her identity. The long struggle to free herself from the patronizing dominance of Leo Stein, to become independent, takes a subtler turn in her alliance with Picasso. He is at once her fraternal animus, a short Spanish Lincoln, and a towering presence in her life, the brilliant male colleague whose ugly work, unlike her own, is seriously regarded and accepted as beautiful. His virile splendor as an artist is the veritable sign in the *Autobiography* of her own neglect and isolation, her awkward standing as a curious woman. That splendor also defines her task: once again, to declare her difference.

Clarification of her difference begins with Alice's description of her arrival in Paris at the start of Chapter 2:

> This was the year 1907. Gertrude Stein was just seeing through the press *Three Lives* which she was having privately printed, and she was deep in The Making of Americans, her thousand page book. Picasso had just finished his portrait of her which nobody at that time liked except the painter and the painted and which is now so famous, and he had just begun his strange complicated picture of three women, Matisse had just finished his Bonheur de Vivre, his first big composition which gave him the name of fauve, or a zoo. It was the moment Max Jacob has since called the heroic age of cubism (*ABT*, p. 7).

The order and equivalence of these events speaks for itself; Gertrude Stein figures prominently in the citation, but there is also, less visibly, a focusing of the subject that cubism heroically considers in its first phase. All these works essentially deal with the form and nature of women. When Alice first sees the canvas of *Three Women* in Picasso's studio, she is taken aback: "I felt that there was something painful and beautiful there and oppressive but imprisoned" (*ABT*, p. 27). *Three Lives,* we are told, is written beneath a Cézanne portrait of a woman, a Cézanne that diverts Gertrude Stein from a translation of Flaubert's *Trois Contes* into the first notable exercise of her experimental style. What Alice says of Picasso's painting can also be said of *Three Lives.* And this coincidence does not escape us. "She was then in the middle of her negro story Melanctha Herbert, the second story of Three Lives and the poignant incidents that she wove into the life of Melanctha were often these she noticed in walking down the hill from the rue Ravignan" (*ABT*, p. 60). That is, from Picasso's studio. As Gertrude Stein poses for Picasso, she composes the Melanctha section in *Three Lives.* Cézanne, Picasso's master, is her master, and here are the two pupils—the one painting, the other writing—equally placed in the situation of learning.

In rethinking the conventions of classical painting, particularly the anatomy of the human figure, the cubists wisely begin with the most familiar, the most given, of such figures—the woman. This portentous image is the first broken. Gertrude Stein not only understood the method at work in this iconoclasm, she also grasped its metaphysical dimension. As Picasso subverts the tyranny of the subject in his painting, collapsing its story, its reference, by removing the orientation of one-point perspective, Gertrude Stein similarly attacks the episteme presupposing traditional narrative. But the point she stresses in this comparison is difference. Indeed critics who strive to cross the analogy and discuss her work as an application of cubist technique invariably emerge with lame readings of the text. L.T. Fitz's examination of *Three Lives,* for example, imposes the flat surface of cubist painting, its "total lack of a focal point," on the Melanctha section and ends up merely straining the analogy.

"Every page is literally as important to the work as every other page," Fitz tells us, "just as every part of a cubist painting is as important as every other part."[4] Richard Bridgman's interpretation of *Three Lives*, on the other hand, traces a Jamesian angle in her style, examines the text as an experiment with literary discourse, and is therefore shrewdly alert to the linguistic complexity that underlies the pictorial sameness Fitz beholds in Gertrude Stein's repetition. Bridgman also shows us how the "programmatic conception of style"[5] in 'Melanctha' complicates the feeling and theme of an earlier novel, *Things As They Are* (1903); how, in brief, the lesbian strife in that novel is transformed into heterosexual conflict in *Three Lives*. The logic and significance of this transformation, first considered under the spell of the Cézanne portrait and then worked out in her mind as she sat for Picasso, as he painted her portrait, effectively constitutes Gertrude Stein's initial confrontation with the designating force of grammar in writing, her first systematic questioning of the rules of discourse. If Picasso asks in the painting of this period: what is the thing seen? — her question was just as momentous: what is the thing spoken?

Melanctha Herbert's passion for clarity reveals its futility through her disclaiming repetition of *certainly*. Only her feelings are certain, and these she can not express. What she wants, and what Jeff Campbell wants, is the assurance of definition, the simplicity of male/female, and they do not find it. Melanctha's unspeakable feelings presumably obstruct this resolution. Their conversations are carefully orchestrated: each insistent *I*, each mistaken *you*, asserts the speaker's contrary isolation, and all the while the adverbs throb with the desire to be understood. What *it* is that tortures Melanctha and deters Jeff Campbell is left unsaid. It is, this *it*, a large and resonant Jamesian *it*. Meaning appears through the acoustical side of their discourse, through the dissonance of their tones. We do not see in the Melanctha section of *Three Lives*, we listen, and what we hear is the agitation of refusal. These Jamesian echoes are pronounced: Melanctha and Jeff do in simplified sing-song the intricate duet of May Bartram and John Marcher in "The Beast in the Jungle." In this period, 1903–1907, Chapter 3 in the *Autobiography*, Gertrude Stein also encounters Guilliame Apollinaire whose artistic sympathies are noted in James R. Mellow's *Charmed Circle, Gertrude Stein & Company*: "each had a highly developed aural sense of language, and in certain of their poems . . . the structure of the lines was carried by repetitions, percussive phrases, natural pauses, the sense of sound."[6] Yet these are the features of her style, its finish; the style itself, as the whole of her written being, is the result of a protracted meditation on the nature of identity, a meditation that becomes at last an act of faith. Gertrude Stein sociably works in the climate of experimentation then so brilliantly expansive in Paris, Alice faithfully records the heroic *gestes* in the *Autobiography*, but her distinctive approach to writing is not simply plucked from influential currents in the air. It is drawn from the visceral center of her doubted being.

Three Women, Three Lives, Les Demoiselles d'Avignon, The Making of Americans. How did one portray women? What is a woman? Picasso's conception in these paintings breaks the familiar externality of the feminine form, strips the conventional pose of its Vesalian musculature, and discloses a dreamlike monstrosity inside the form, "something painful and beautiful there and oppressive but imprisoned" (*ABT*, p. 27). Gertrude Stein painstakingly analyzes the "bottom nature" of men and women in *The Making of Americans* (1906–11), undertakes a quasi-sociological examination that gradually stands Aristotelian classification on its head, or vice versa. For she seeks to specify the kinds of men and women, to determine the politics of their exchanges in family life, and is drawn irresistably to a radical substitution of criteria. The roles that fix men and women as husbands and wives, brothers and sisters, are not sexually determined. It is a question, rather, of how the will chooses to exert itself:

> Some women have it in them to love others because they need them, many of such ones subdue the ones they need for loving, they subdue them and they own them; some women have it in them to love only those who need them; some women have it in them only to have power when others need them; some women have it in them only to have power when others love them, others loving them gives to them strength in domination as their needing those who love them keeps them from subduing others before these others love them.[7]

These are in some sense the explanations Melanctha is unable to make in *Three Lives,* the explanations that would turn Jeff Campbell's wife-quest into a different kind of courtship. So it goes in this tireless, often tedious, "thousand page book." There are the "dependent independent" and the "independent dependent," categories that are endlessly refined and shaded. Some fight by resisting, others by attacking. So various are the difference and blend of aggression and passivity in men and women that at length the entire issue of masculine/feminine modification trembles. The concept of *A Man* or *A Woman* standing behind *he* and *she* (as Platonic mannikins) slowly erodes, and then finally *he/she* also disappears. In this cleared space the massive coda of *The Making of Americans* lovingly relishes the indefinite pronoun: any one, some one, each one, every one. "Some are doing the thing they are doing in a family living," she writes. "It is done and done by them. There are enough of them doing some such thing, and certainly not too many, certainly very many, certainly some and each one of them is some one by whom something is done and done" (*MA*, p. 921). Gertrude Stein had thoroughly neutered discourse, and in much of her later experimental portraiture she would use this ambiguous reference (this one, some one, very many) as if indeed it were (for anyone) superbly illustrative.

It is from this theoretical vantage-point that she criticizes Matisse's loss of aggressive independence in the *Autobiography:*

Matisse intimated that Gertrude Stein had lost interest in his work. She answered him, there is nothing within you that fights itself and hitherto you have had the instinct to produce antagonism in others which stimulated you to attack. But now they follow.

That was the end of the conversation but a beginning of an important part of The Making of Americans. Upon this idea Gertrude Stein based some of her most permanent distinctions in types of people (*ABT*, pp. 80–81).

And it is from this reference, this rich sense of her own achievement in portraiture, that Gertrude's Alice amusingly recounts the method of Felix Valloton's portrait-painting. "When he painted a portrait," Alice relates, "he made a crayon sketch and then began painting at the top of the canvas straight across. Gertrude Stein said it was like pulling down a curtain as slowly moving as one of his swiss glaciers. Slowly he pulled the curtain down and by the time he was at the bottom of the canvas, there you were. The whole operation took about two weeks and then he gave the canvas to you" (*ABT*, p. 62). To sit for such a portrait gives Gertrude Stein a "strange sensation." And there, in two weeks, you were. Behind the curtain of Valloton's paint. Picasso, on the other hand, has a hard time with her portrait. He begins using a "very small palette which was of a uniform brown grey colour, mixed with some more brown grey" (*ABT*, p. 57), and then proceeds to lose his way. This first of some ninety sittings is vividly recalled; so too is the beauty of several preliminary sketches, and yet, just as the manuscript of *Three Lives* is in the process of being typed, just as Gertrude Stein arrives at this symbolic moment filled with a strong sense of herself: "All of a sudden one day Picasso painted out the whole head. I can't see you any longer when I look, he said irritably. And so the picture was left like that" (*ABT*, pp. 64–65). A mock combat is herein joined between the distance and mystery of the painted and the skill of the painter. At some high and cerebral plane, this contest is also amorous. Gertrude Stein flees, is captured, then escapes again. Although the drama of this combat is completely told in Chapter 3, the section in which the "heroic age of cubism" is established, there is constant reference to it thereafter (the portrait mediates their friendship), and in the final chapter, as we shall see, it is briefly retold.

The question before Gertrude Stein in the *Autobiography* is that of identity. Like conventional portraiture, autobiography typically strives for the likeness, the lifelike, strives to identify. It pictures through an arrangement of incident the meaning of one's life. It specifies the self writing about the self. Yet cubist portraiture, and Gertrude Stein's own portraiture in prose, breaks the historical prop (memory) that holds autobiography in its form. Recollection, or memory, realizes the object in a fictive dimension. It intervenes, stalls the quick motion of perceiving consciousness, and restrictively imposes the perspective of serial duration on the writer. Such is narrative: a beginning, a middle, and an ending. In the terms of her own writing, then, and in what she had seen in Picasso's painting, autobiographical narrative, if straight, is merely a form of journalism, as thoroughly true as the stories in a newspaper. It tells us too much, it tells us too little. "Really most of the time one sees only a feature of a person with whom one is, the other features are covered by a hat, by the light, by clothes for sport and everybody is accustomed to complete the whole entirely from their knowledge," she writes in *Picasso*, "but Picasso when he saw an eye, the other one did not exist for him and only the one he saw did exist for him . . ." (*P*, p. 15). Yet this is the text, this anecdotal narrative, that makes Gertrude Stein publicly visible for the first time in her career, makes a Gertrude Stein visible. Who, then, is the Gertrude Stein figured in Picasso's portrait, in Alice's portrait, in her own? It is a pronominal being in each case: a she, a he, and the concealed one who writes. Picasso decapitates the painted Gertrude Stein and for a year she remains headless in the portrait. In the meanwhile she takes her own head to Italy, Picasso goes to Spain. She begins *The Making of Americans*, that long questioning of sexual identity, the kinds of men and women, and then returns to Paris "under the spell of the thing she was doing" only to find (again the coincidence is apt) the portrait finished. "The day he returned from Spain Picasso sat down and out of his head painted the head in without having seen Gertrude Stein again. And when she saw it he and she were content. It is very strange but neither can remember at all what the head looked like when he painted it out" (*ABT*, p. 70). There she is then, Picasso's she, the celebrated Gertrude Stein.

But the *Autobiography* immediately jumps forward in time, almost to the present of its writing, and here Gertrude's Alice juxtaposes her own Gertrude Stein, the Gertrude Stein who first struck her, in Alice's own words, as a "golden brown presence, burned by the Tuscan sun," as a "Roman Emperor."[8] Again Picasso looks and does not see his Gertrude Stein. She has cut the braided queen's crown of hair that adorns her in the portrait, cropped her hair short, like a man, and now stands apart (in her own imperial splendor) from his identification. He has painted a woman, she has become a man. The *Autobiography* is stretched between these two points of reference: Picasso's she, Alice's he. And it is the writer, that latter-day Defoe, who comprehends both, who is neither.

> Only a few years ago when Gertrude Stein had had her hair cut short, she had always up to that time worn it as a crown on top of her head as Picasso has painted it, when she had had her hair cut, a day or so later she happened to come into a room and Picasso was several rooms away. She had a hat on but he caught sight of her through two doorways and approaching her quickly called out, Gertrude, what is it, what is it. What is what, Pablo, she said. Let me see, he said. She let him see. And my portrait, said he sternly. Then his face softening he added, mais, quand meme tout y est, all the same it is all there.
>
> (*ABT*, p. 70)

Picasso scrutinizes the cropped hair, takes in the difference. "And my portrait, said he sternly." The joke is slight, and yet in it Picasso speaks a judgment: *this is who you are.* She is not. Like Walt Whitman's "Song of Myself," the story of Gertrude Stein's escape in the *Autobiography* is the story of an escape into the namelessness of androgyny. "Failing to fetch me at first keep encouraged," Whitman advises us at the close of his song. If I am not here, if I am not there, "I stop some where waiting for you."[9] Gertrude Stein had similarly tutored herself in *The Making of Americans;* she had reached certainly the knowledge of Whitman's "Calamus," understood how difficult it was to express discursively the nature of desire, to sort it out in kind. That apprehension is clearly stated in a contemporaneous work, *A Long Gay Book* (1906–11). Here the writer slowly turns from self-contemplation to regard the fundamental natures of those who have confidently sorted the specific kind of their desire.

> Always all the men and women all around have in them some one of the many kinds of men and women that have each one of them many millions made like them, always all the men and women all around have it in them to have one fundamental nature in them and other kinds of nature are mixed up in them with this kind of nature in them so it takes all the knowing one can learn with all the living to ever know it about any one around them the fundamental nature of them and how everything is mixed up in them.[10]

Notice of her own mixed fundamental nature in the *Autobiography* is chastely handed to Louis Bromfield as an unpublished manuscript, *Things As They Are;* – and to the educated reader as the message: *I know you know.* Inadvertently, while looking for the manuscript of *The Making of Americans,* Gertrude Stein comes upon *Things As They Are.* "She was very bashful and hesitant about it, did not really want to read it. Louis Bromfield was at the house that evening and she handed him the manuscript and said to him, you read it" (*ABT,* p. 104). What Bromfield thought is not recorded in the *Autobiography,* but Hemingway, who fares poorly in the text, has recorded his thoughts about things as they were at 27 rue de Fleurus. His criticism of Gertrude Stein in *A Moveable Feast* begins by demeaning "truly ambitious women writers," moves through a brutal account of a quarrel between Gertrude and Alice ("please, pussy, please"), and then comes at last, unerringly, to the juxtaposition that figures so importantly in the *Autobiography:* "She got to look like a Roman emperor and that was fine if you like your women to look like Roman emperors. But Picasso had painted her, and I could remember her when she looked like a woman from Friuli."[11] The shot is cheap, but cheaper still is Hemingway's sparse mention of a single text, *The Making of Americans.* In the thickness of his thought, she is at her worst a woman writer, at her best the "woman from Friuli" who sits captured in Picasso's portrait.

The chapters that follow the recognition scene in Chapter 3 ("Let me see, he said. She let him see."), the moment of her escape, and this cryptic conclusion to Chapter 4, busily describe Gertrude Stein's double life: her existence as a historical figure, the connoisseur and critic, and her arduous struggle to be read, the loneliness of her life as a writer. At the same time Alice's uxorial voice throws upon that double life the tone of still another duplicity. For the Gertrude Stein who expands in her writing, who expounds, who chats companionably with Carl Van Vechten and Sherwood Anderson, assumes invariably a masculine stance. By the end of the narrative these two sets of duplicity are joined, remarkably fused by the Crusoe myth. We begin with the apotheosis, which is rendered in a suitably "noble" setting. Gertrude Stein has struck up a friendship with the Duchess of Clermont-Tonnerre, and the two women decide to cut their unfashionably long hair. "Cut it off she said and I did." For two days Alice cuts Gertrude Stein's hair until only a "cap of hair" remains. On seeing it, Sherwood Anderson remarks: "it makes her look like a monk." Briefly the *she* of the painting is recalled. "As I have said, Picasso seeing it, was for a moment angry and said, and my portrait, but very soon added, after all it is all there" (*ABT*, p. 304). The remark now hangs with the proper ironic ambivalence. The *Autobiography* then sweeps to its close. She can not write her autobiography, Alice protests, because "I am a pretty good housekeeper and a pretty good gardener and a pretty good needle-woman and a pretty good secretary and a pretty good editor and a pretty good vet for dogs and I have to do them all at once and I found it difficult to add being a pretty good author" (*ABT*, pp. 309–310). Capably, referring to Defoe, Gertrude Stein then makes her appearance as the writer, as the *I* who has done this voided portrait, and the *Autobiography* concludes. On the opposing page is a facsimile of the first page of the manuscript. The handwriting returns us abruptly to the dark figure of the unknown writer who sits, pen poised, at the desk in the frontispiece.

Friday's story is necessarily Crusoe's. It is Crusoe who gives him life and language, and such is the legend that informs this narrative. *We two alone on an island.* Here is a chronicle crowded with social occasions, spilling over with litanies of illustrious names, and it is about life on a deserted island. The affairs of the famous are duly noted, but the tale told is Crusoe's, a tale of primordial loneliness, of the agony of not being known. It is a mistake, Alice continually stresses, this refusal to know the discursive Gertrude Stein, to read her writing, to take her seriously. "Gertrude Stein was in those days a little bitter," she writes of the period 1919–1932, "all her unpublished manuscripts, and no hope of publication or serious recognition" (*ABT*, p. 241). And yet Alice's designation as Friday also distances us from the immediate travail of the writer. "The geniuses came and talked to Gertrude Stein," she observes, "and the wives sat with me" (*ABT*, p. 105). The important and prolific period of Gertrude Stein's early portraiture, the phase in which she forges her style, is telescoped into a few pages, set forth as a catalogue. We see in reference, dimly, Gertrude Stein alone, stranded and bereft, the solitary writer who writes before God for no one an unreadable "thousand page book," who writes so that she will not go mad, who writes to preserve and describe herself. Although Alice is a loving and helpful amanuensis, an audience, she never joins Crusoe in the vigil he keeps in discourse, in writing. She knows Crusoe, but not what Crusoe knows. A lover's joke, a writer's joke. Neither Picasso's portrait nor Alice's in the *Autobiography* constitutes Gertrude Stein. She is not that she, not this he, but the *I* who writes. Alice's Fridayness is in fact Gertrude Stein's ironic commentary on the competence of her narration. Like the painter Felix Valloton, the autobiographer begins at the top, at the beginning, and then sequentially strokes in the events, the dates, places, people, and then there you are. But the self revealed is always an other. If you are Alice, you write about Gertrude. If you are Gertrude, you write about Alice's Gertrude. Even if the autobiography is sophisticated, if it concedes its bias, understands the repressive acts of memory, it still contracts to identify, to represent and name a self. The best a sophisticated and earnest autobiography can do is to be as true as Rousseau's *Confessions*. If it is sophisticated, and not sincere, then it is *The Autobiography of Alice B. Toklas*. Autobiography is thus doomed to bad faith. It always describes a surface, illustrates the external, throws light on the familiar. It is what Friday sees.

But if the human being is not "paintable," if autobiography begins and ends with the statement, *I am not here*, what does this tell us about Gertrude Stein's writing? The vindictive treacheries stroked into this text at once declare her freedom from definition, seduce the reader, and subvert the form. Autobiography, the story of one's self, is narrative in the raw, narrative in its most perilous genre. We need to tell our story. We want to know about the lives of others. We want to know about this life, but not as it is, as it was. We desire effectively the alienation, the fiction, of an imposed order, a framed significance, and so we look for perspective in the security of the past tense and receive a fictive assurance of the real. The *Autobiography* provides this bogus materiality. It gives us an anecdotal narrative told by a scrupulous woman who is "very fond of needlework" (*ABT*, p. 159), and then takes it all back, recants. "And therefore," Gertrude Stein writes in *The Geographical History of America* (1936), "there are no witnesses to the autobiography of any one that has a human mind."[12] In this insouciant philosophical treatise, written between *The Autobiography of Alice B. Toklas* and *Everybody's Autobiography*, she methodically disjoins mind and nature, turns her poodle, "a little dog," into an empirical knower, and with great charm thoroughly addles Bishop Berkeley and William James. "No one knowing me knows me," she asserts, "And I am I I" (*GHA*, p. 113). Looking at us. Like Crusoe on his island, the Crusoe who has no audience, no witnesses, the "human mind is." What emerges from this radical distinction, however, is not the anguish of solipsism, but a cubist *jou*, I I, the play of a liberated subjectivity at large in itself, at large in the field of language. The *Geographical History* breaks its thoughts into a disordering sequence of chapters, parts, acts, scenes, numbers, plays, examples, pages and volumes, and then numbers them capriciously at random. "So once more to renounce because and become" (GHA, p. 192), Gertrude Stein declares in a section entitled "autobiography number one." And in this self-admonition we see the rigor of her experimental style. For she cuts from narrative the idea of origin and end, deprives such discourse of its teleological assumption, and attacks the alibis that give the writer protective distance. Without *because*, without *become*, he is left only the "continuous present" of his writing. There he is absolutely present, always the responsible *I*. His writing is the activity of consciousness purely expressed.

The enterprise of Gertrude Stein's discourse is a reaction to this moment, the instant of generation. Here the writer confronts language, his competence, its competence, and here grammar imposes its edifying force on him. The drama of utterance is always the thing seen in her writing. In *The Making of Americans*, for example, she stubbornly rethinks the conceptual structure of a chosen sentence and then rearranges its phase structure. Sentences are not repeated, they are regenerated, and at each juncture, each branch, she figures the difference. So her thoughts march gradually through all their permutations into other thoughts and she accumulates, without swerving, a vast redundant prose. Her project, it would seem, is more a grammarian's than a historian's: "To go on now giving all of the description of how repeating comes to have meaning, how it forms itself, how one must distinguish the different meanings in repeating" (MA, p. 294). Indeed the individual Herslands and Dehnings, whose characterizing repetition is Gertrude Stein's ostensible subject, disappear from the text for long stretches of time, and what is before us is the writer's repetition, a new subject: the work of making sentences that will do the work of referring, of representing, of being about something or someone. What is the meaning found in repeating? It discloses consciousness in its aboriginal motion, reaching to speak. Thus Gertrude Stein writes about writing by parsing thought as it passes into written language. She begins, that is, not from the point of view of Samuel Beckett or John Barth, but with utterance itself, in that tight space where the internal becomes external, is voiced, long before the question of form or mode or intention can be asked. Here she interrogates the act of speech. How does it occur? Why this version of a sentence, or this one and this one? Thought measures itself syntactically in *The Making of Americans*. With a boldness that is often truly stupefying, she risks all the priorities of a text. For who has the stamina to confront the massive articulation of consciousness as it seeks to determine a "bottom nature," to capture the being of a person, as it decides that nature in language? What we want in a text is the consequence of writing, the formed result. We want the finished portrait of thought.

In brief Gertrude Stein discovers in this exploded novel the metalinguistic stance that enables her to compose *Tender Buttons* (1914), the slender book that decisively places her as a writer beside the artists then fashioning the analytic phase of cubism. The great difference in these two texts signifies the drastic shift in her attention from the sentence to lexical choice, for here the setting is small, circumscribed, domestic. It is not the past, that widespread space, but the immediate field of one's experience. Within it, still painstaking, she strives to peel from the humble objects in her perception (carafes, cushions, cooking) their determining labels and see them apart from their obvious designation. To do so, she disrupts the predication of the sentence. Writing emerges now as poetic conflict, as a struggle *with* language *against* language. In effect she moves signification back to the *Ursprache,* the mythical instant when each Adam in his Garden, empowered with naming, regards this strange nameless creature, this strange unspecified thing, and the whole world so alive with diverse being is a "blind glass." A reflection. Which is where *Tender Buttons* begins, posing a carafe.

In the thirties Gertrude Stein undertakes a protracted seminar on this particular approach to writing: *How To Write* (1931), *Lectures in America* (1934), *Narration* (1935), but these texts, while often trenchant and witty, are not finally the commentaries that elucidate her style. They are instead works of art in their own right, lyrical extensions of the style. It is rather in the compromised autobiographical writing that we find, paradoxically, the clearest introduction to her experimental discourse. For the Crusoe myth encoded in the *Autobiography* constantly renews the question of identity and recalls the motivation of that discourse, Gertrude Stein's awakening, her early preoccupation "with finding out what was inside myself to make me what I was."[13] What was she? The *Autobiography* teases us with that question. "Let me see, he said. She let him see" (*ABT*, p. 70). It is a revenge that falls not only upon Picasso's proprietary sense of her womanhood, his sense of her subjection in the painting, but equally upon language itself. What he sees, what we see, is the I I of the *Geographical History.* "As I say a noun is a name of a thing," she writes in "Poetry and Grammar," "and therefore slowly if you feel what is inside that thing you do not call it by the name by which it is known."[14] For Whitman, whose "language experiment" so actively prefigures Gertrude Stein's, the right names, the right nouns, are always there to be used. We do not lack words, only the courage to use them. Gertrude Stein's criticism moves along the same angle of assumption, but is far more comprehensive. Language itself is politicized, an instruction. Long before the question of diction arises, there are the parts of speech, the rules of grammar, syntactical laws. The way we say precedes what we say. The sentence has already organized the world we wish to speak as we see it. What does it say of discourse, she asks variously, when discourse can not determine "what I was," when it can only interpose between *he* and *she* the reification of *it*? Autobiography extends the imprisoning form of the sentence, connects subject to object, organizes the life of an individual, and distorts it. In *Everybody's Autobiography* Gertrude Stein writes as Gertrude Stein, but her distrust of the form, of its connections, of the value of identity, remains constant. "That is really the trouble with an autobiography," she writes, "you do not of course you do not really believe yourself why should you, you know so well so very well that it is not yourself, it could not be yourself because you cannot remember right and if you do remember right it does not sound right and of course it does not sound right because it is not right." Yet here she is once more in the form, and this time without a deflective persona. Although Bridgman considers the book "one of her major successes," a text in which she "took up the most desperate problems she was then suffering from and managed to convey them without diminishing their complexity,"[15] *Everybody's Autobiography* is so perversely dependent on the context of the Toklas narrative that it is, properly speaking, an epilogue (or response) to the first book.

An introduction hinges the two narratives: "Alice B. Toklas did hers and now everybody will do theirs" (*EA*, p. 3). Gertrude Stein then reports a series of conversations with David Edstrom, Dashiell Hammett and Mary Pickford. In her talk with Hammett she complains that women writers in the nineteenth century "never could invent women they always made the women be themselves seen splendidly or sadly or heroically or beautifully or despairingly or gently, and they never could make any other kind of woman" (*EA*, p. 5). She is in Hollywood. Mary Pickford, who played these glamorous roles on the screen, regards Gertrude Stein suspiciously as a rival star and decides to keep her distance. Hammett patiently explains the narcissism of male writers. "It is nice being a celebrity," Gertrude Stein observes, "a real celebrity who can decide who they want to meet and say so and they come or do not come as you want them" (*EA*, pp. 3–4). People approach her on the street. Her books are in the shop windows. Her photograph appears regularly in the newspapers and magazines. Mary Pickford might well look upon her with jaundice. But what other kind of woman is Gertrude Stein? Having escaped the significance of Picasso's portrait in the *Autobiography*, she had set another image in its place, the esoteric celebrity, and the problem in this autobiography is once again to assert her difference, her human mind against her human nature, and disappear like Whitman, like Huckleberry Finn. But the success of the first autobiography mesmerizes her. Suddenly she is rich, everybody knows her, she has a public. It leaves her speechless, so she writes in *Everybody's Autobiography*, unable to write. This crisis, her sudden confusion of the external and the internal, plays throughout the text. "It is all a question of the outside being outside," she asserts, "and the inside being inside. As long as the outside does not put a value on you it remains outside but when it does put a value on you then it gets inside or rather if the outside puts a value on you then all your inside gets to be outside" (*EA*, p. 47). The destruction of her Crusoe life, her changed position as a writer, had radically altered her stance as an autobiographer.

To return to the form, then, Gertrude Stein had first to justify doing it. She could say legitimately, and did, that it was now her turn, Alice having told her story, but what then was she to write about, and from which point of view? She could write about her American tour, life in Bilignin, her work, her past, visiting notables, but in so doing she inescapably wrote the referential discourse her first autobiography had so wickedly emptied of relevance. That revenge falls at last upon the writer of *Everybody's Autobiography*. "Anything is an autobiography," she declares in the introduction, prefacing her talk with Hammett, "but this was a conversation" (*EA*, p. 5). Given her own sportive approach to literary form, this sanction is sufficient, but in fact the magisterial *I* that finally seizes Alice's story, that plays whimsically with philosophical discourse in the *Geographical History*, is troubled and uncertain in this wavering narrative. What are the resources of her inside now that so much of it is outside? The astonishment of her American tour and the impending strife in Europe (war in Spain, unrest in France) are compressive forces that obviously confuse her perspective, but as well it is the telling of her own past, her writing *about* herself, that also vexes the sureness of her solitude. How did she come to be called Gertrude Stein? The question emerges when someone asks "what skin the peau de chagrin was made of?" The word is looked up. Peau de chagrin "was made of anything mule calf or horse and I said how did it happen to be called peau de chagrin and Madame Giraud said and how did you happen to be called Gertrude Stein." The arbitrariness of the sign is once again affirmed, names are nouns that tell us nothing, but then she fixes on this haphazard name, Stein, her name, and at once stoically accepts and defiantly refuses it. It is impossible to judge her tone in this instance.

> Steins were called Steins in the time of Napoleon before that any name was a name but in the time of Napoleon in any country he went through the name of any one had to be written and so they took the name they gave them and Stein was an easy one. Then when any of us were named we were named after some one who is already dead, after all if they are living the name belongs to them so any one can be named after a dead one, so there was a grandmother she was dead and her name not an easy one began with G so my mother preferred it should be an easy one so they named me Gertrude Stein. All right that is my name.

The passage occurs in the midst of a meditation on death. She takes up ambivalently the burden of her name. Gertrude Stein, this peau de chagrin. "Identity always worries me," she concludes, "and memory and eternity" (*EA*, p. 115). It is as though she suddenly perceives the *a priori* of classical autobiography: that it is a summation, the presentation of a self about to die, a prelude to biography. The noun names. It identifies. It is the skin of a dead thing that has nothing to do with what the dead thing was. Names are taken from those already dead. We wear our names as we wear the skins of dead animals. In

Everybody's Autobiography Gertrude Stein's long attack on the coherence and stability of the noun takes a desperate turn. Here she is, then, wearing her dead grandmother's G: Gertrude Stein.

An escaped slave writes *The Autobiography of Alice B. Toklas*, doubling and redoubling his inversion of the mode. The first act of the fugitive is to change his name. *I am not here.* Gertrude Stein's appropriation of the Crusoe myth at once politicizes the text and invests it with erotic energy. Friday's point of view is also Crusoe's: this master has been a slave, and he knows what she knows. That cubism begins with a male deconstruction of the female form as it pre-exists in the eye of Picasso and Matisse. She, too, begins a deconstruction of how women are known, but that work is overlooked. Here we have only her portrait of their portrait-making, portraits of Picasso and Matisse conceiving and contemplating women, living with women: Matisse as the self-centered husband, Picasso as the charming rogue. With Friday's knowing look, Gertrude Stein regards these two typical sides of the master's face. It is Picasso who dominates the world set forth in the *Autobiography*, who loves Fernande and leaves her, who leads Georges Braque, André Derain and Apollinaire about like a "bullfighter" his retinue, who is "every inch a chief." It is Picasso who places her in the portrait and tells those who question the resemblance not to worry, she will become what she is in the portrait. "Let me see, he said. She let him see." Picasso's masculine authority is a congenial Spanish translation of Leo Stein's inflexible paternalism, the mastery of the brother to whom the world belongs, and it is in this book a pervasive force, the negative charge that gives Gertrude Stein the positive work of escape.

In *Everybody's Autobiography* Picasso appears briefly as a fool. He has left painting to write poetry, an exchange Gertrude Stein regards with anxious disdain. "Well as I say when I first heard he was writing I had a funny feeling," she admits, "one does you know. Things belong to you and writing belonged to me, there is no doubt about it writing belonged to me" (*EA*, p. 15). When Picasso at length reads his poetry, she is relieved: "I drew a long breath and I said it is very interesting" (*EA*, p. 17). In the room at the time is Thornton Wilder. As Picasso lapses from Gertrude Stein's life, his replacements (as the vigorous and productive male friend, the negative charge) grow less substantial: Hemingway, Juan Gris, Francis Picabia, Francis Rose, Thornton Wilder. She would go on in *Picasso* to round out her view of his artistry, but here his effective participation in her imaginative life is over. They meet again, once more in a gallery, as if in a novel by Henry James, and their roles are reversed. Here it is Picasso who is apprehensive, uncertain, and Gertrude Stein who authoritatively defines him, whose maternal admonition becomes an aggressive embrace. For his part, Picasso submissively yields like Molly Bloom.

> ah I said catching him by the lapels of his coat and shaking him, you are extraordinary within your limits but your limits are extraordinarily there

and I said shaking him hard, you know it, you know it as well as I do, it is all right you are doing this to get rid of everything that has been too much for you all right all right go on doing it but don't go on trying to make me tell you it is poetry and I shook him again, well he said supposing I do know it, what will I do, what will you do said I and I kissed him, you will go on until you are more cheerful or less dismal and then you will, yes he said, and then you will paint a very beautiful picture and then more of them, and I kissed him again, yes said he. (*EA*, p. 37)

The absence of Picasso as a symbolic factor, the Nietzschean rival, is conspicuous in *Everybody's Autobiography*. When Gertrude Stein now contemplates the hierarchical domain of the patriarchy, and all its intimidation, her view is not that of an escaped slave, malicious, alert, deceptive, but rather the long resigned view of the historian and autobiographer who wears in her name the dead grandmother's G: "Everybody nowadays is a father, there is father Mussolini and father Hitler and father Roosevelt and father Stein and father Lewis and father Blum and father Franco is just commencing now and there are ever so many more ready to be one" (*EA*, p. 133). Those periods of history where fathers loom and fill up everything, she observes, are always the "most dismal ones." The oppressive presence of her own father is recalled, and the importance of her brothers, especially Michael and Leo, and these familial politics are then framed by the larger issue of the patriarchy itself, the world ruled by fathers. "Sometimes barons and dukes are fathers," she writes, "and then kings come to be fathers and churchmen come to be fathers and then comes a period like the eighteenth century a nice period when everybody has had enough of anybody being a father to them ... just now everybody has a father, perhaps the twenty-first century like the eighteenth century will be a nice time when everybody forgets to be a father or to have been one" (*EA*, p. 142). The struggle of *The Autobiography of Alice B. Toklas* becomes a dream in *Everybody's Autobiography*, the dream of parricide, king-killing, the "nice period" of revolt when the very principle of identification (the father's business) is shattered.

Keys to Gertrude Stein's experimental mode are strewn throughout her venture into autobiographical narration. But it is in the disguised *mythos* of the first book, her shattering of the portrait as the sign, that we discern the struggle and presumption of her discourse. And more: not just her place in the "heroic age of cubism" or her role in the construction of modernism, but where Gertrude Stein stands in American literature. In the first writing of the *Autobiography*, Alice signs off in the fashion of Huckleberry Finn. A consideration that complicates and explains Gertrude Stein's subsequent use of the Crusoe myth. Life on the raft at 27 rue de Fleurus becomes life on a deserted island and the ontological dimension of the text is altered. Yet Friday speaks in Huck's plain style. And as Huck, the Huck who flees a brutal father who will not tolerate his reading of the world, Alice writes the story of Gertrude

Stein's life. But if the spirit of Mark Twain is alive in this text, it is the "language experiment" of *Leaves of Grass* that clarifies Gertrude Stein's discourse. Copyrighted by a Walter Whitman, the anonymous 1855 *Leaves of Grass* begins in its preface with the symbolic removal of a paternal carcass, the dead weight of the past. Whitman takes up the Jeffersonian precept that the earth belongs to the living and dramatically extends it to the "well-shaped heir" who has come to sing the "new life of the new forms" (*LG*, p. 5). Which is precisely where *The Making of Americans* begins: "Once an angry man dragged his father along the ground through his own orchard" (*MA*, p. 3). And it is where Donald Barthelme begins in his recent novel, *The Dead Father* (1975), ironically exploiting this recurrent theme by dragging for the length of his novel an immense Learlike Gulliver who speaks in the imperious person of the Superego, *We*. But Gertrude Stein does not get her dragged father from Whitman; she lifts him from the *Nicomachean Ethics*. The anecdote occurs in Chapter Six of Book Seven, just after an Aristotelian discussion of sexual perversion, and it illustrates the "commoner frailty" of anger. It is as though, at the start of her revolutionary book, she perceives the Definitive Father who thinks proairetically the harmonium of behavior she must undo.

It is not against the male writers of her period that Gertrude Stein measures herself, but the artists. T.S. Eliot, James Joyce and Ezra Pound do not figure importantly in the *Autobiography*. Nor, for that matter, does she figure largely in their writing. Her isolation in the history of modernism curiously aligns her with Whitman, the Whitman with whom Pound has such reluctant and distasteful commerce. Indeed the masculine Gertrude Stein, like the feminine Whitman, has had a hard time with her critics and readers. Both elude in their amiable formlessness, their repetition, and tenacious materiality, the tenor and mood of modernism. They create in their work a different movement, a homegrown modernity that regards tradition with lyrical impudence, refuses like Huck to put any stock in dead people, and restores the Edenic vision to writing. They begin at the beginning, always present in the *I*. "What a history is folded," Whitman marvels in *An American Primer*, "folded inward and inward again, in the single word I."[16] Emile Benveniste's essay on the nature of pronouns illuminates this first movement in their experiment with discourse. "What then is the reality to which *I* or *you* refers?" he asks. "It is solely a 'reality of discourse,' and this is a very strange thing. *I* cannot be defined except in terms of 'locution,' not in terms of objects as a nominal sign is. *I* signifies 'the person who is uttering the present instance of the discourse containing *I*.' This instance is unique by definition and has validity only in its uniqueness."[17] In the *Geographical History* Gertrude Stein reiterates the song of the ahistorical self in writing: "I am I I," and argues prescriptively that this is how the human mind must write—always in the captivating mystery of being at once hidden and apparent at the same time. How does Whitman come upon this remarkable discovery, this unique present by present moment of discourse, the *I* instance that enables him to break free of poetic form? By descending, as Gertrude Stein would, into the sublogic of the sentence and meeting in the parts of speech an awful namelessness, a silence. "Double yourself and receive me darkness" (*LG*, p. 108), he writes in "The Sleepers," that striking poem where desire eludes the reach of definition, where *he* and *she* merge in the baffled *I* who dreams and then writes. Whitman is frightened by what happens to language in this poem as he recalls the dream, and he imposes an operatic coda on the poem that brings him back into the stable world of the daytime. For in "The Sleepers" Whitman slips easily into what now looks like the incoherent privacy of Steinian discourse: "The cloth laps a first sweet eating and drinking, / Laps life-swelling yolks . . . . laps ear of rose-corn, milky and just ripened: / The white teeth stay, and the boss-tooth advances in darkness, / And liquor is spilled on lips and bosoms by touching glasses, and the best liquor afterward" (*LG*, p. 108). And at the nadir of the dream, just before the redemption of morning, he encounters himself as the "vast dusk bulk" of the submerged whale, his version of Melvillean whiteness.

Who then speaks in the dream, who writes the dream? Whitman finds the primordial function of language, naming, "folded inward and inward again, in the single word I." In *The Making of Americans* and *Tender Buttons* this confrontation with language, this silence, is always before us; we do not face the "vast dusk bulk" and then turn from the linguistic knowledge of the dreamer. What is a carafe, that blind glass? "A kind in glass and a cousin, a spectacle and nothing strange a single hurt color and an arrangement in a system to pointing" (*WL*, p. 161). Along the way in *The Making of Americans* Gertrude Stein does meet Aristotle, the History of Western Thought, Discourse that divides its world into the True and the False, and in *Tender Buttons* she gracefully soars beyond him/it.

The Autobiography of Alice B. Toklas and *Everybody's Autobiography*, to a lesser extent, point us to that system where "nothing is aiming," and discourse, the blind glass, enchants us by being so wrong. At the University of Chicago in 1935, Gertrude Stein joins Robert Hutchins in his seminar and promptly stirs all his students into passionate discussion. Hutchins is astonished. Even his silent students dispute and remark. She explains: "and then I said you see why they talk to me is that I am like them I do not know the answer, you say you do not know but you do if you did not know the answer you could not spend your life in teaching but I I really do not know, I really do not, I do not even know whether there is a question let alone having an answer for the question" (*EA*, p. 213). Such is the liberating hilarity of "a rose is a rose is a rose," the wise ignorance Gertrude Stein brings back from her encounter with Aristotle in *The Making of Americans* to this seminar on the Great Books, his shrine in Chicago. Teachers have questions. Fathers have answers. Hutchins is firmly placed on this professorial hook. What is the question? These are in fact Gertrude Stein's last words.

Notes

1. *The Autobiography of Alice B. Toklas* (New York: Harcourt & Brace, 1933), p. 310. Subsequent references will be indicated *ABT* in the text. Unfortunately the only available paper back edition of the *Autobiography* (Vintage) places Gertrude Stein's photograph on the cover and her name above the title, exposing the ruse that complicates the text. It also deletes the sixteen photographs that appeared in the first edition, the first and last of which are intrinsically related to the text. For a vigorous interpretation of the textuality of all the photographs, see Paul K. Alkon's "Visual Rhetoric in *The Autobiography of Alice B. Toklas,*" *Critical Inquiry,* I (June, 1975), pp. 849–881.

2. *Picasso* (Boston: Beacon Press, 1959), p. 8. Subsequent references will be indicated *P* in the text. In "Au Tombeau de Charles Fourier," *The Georgia Review* (Winter, 1975), Guy Davenport suggests that Picasso's painting of Gertrude Stein alludes to Degas's portrait of the American artist, Mary Cassatt. Both women sit casually with their "American elbows" on their knees.

3. Edmund Wilson, *The Shores of Light* (New York: Farrar, Straus & Young, 1952), p. 579.

4. L. T. Fitz, "Gertrude Stein and Picasso: The Language of Surfaces," *American Literature,* 45 (May, 1973), p. 231.

5. Richard Bridgman, *The Colloquial Style in America* (New York: Oxford University Press, 1966), p. 175.

6. James R. Mellow, *Charmed Circle, Gertrude Stein & Company* (New York: Avon, 1974), p. 124.

7. *The Making of Americans* (New York: Something Else Press, 1966), p. 163. Subsequent references will be indicated *MA* in the text.

8. Alice B. Toklas, *What Is Remembered* (New York: Holt, Rinehart & Winston, 1963), p. 23.

9. Walt Whitman, *Leaves of Grass, The First (1855) Edition* (New York: Viking Press, 1961), p. 86. Subsequent references will be indicated *LG* in the text.

10. *Matisse Picasso Gertrude Stein, With Two Shorter Pieces* (Barton, Berlin, Millerton: Something Else Press, 1972), p. 16.

11. Ernest Hemingway, *A Moveable Feast* (New York: Bantam Books, 1970), p. 117.

12. *The Geographical History of America* (Neww York: Vintage, 1973), p. 90. Subsequent references will be indicated *GHA* in the text.

13. *Writings and Lectures, 1909–1945,* ed. Patricia Meyerowitz (New York: Penguin, 1967), p. 85. Subsequent references will be indicated *WL* in the text.

14. *Everybody's Autobiography* (New York: Coopers Square Publishers, 1971), p. 68. Subsequent references will be indicated *EA* in the text.

15. Bridgman, *Gertrude Stein in Pieces* (New York: Oxford University Press, 1970), p. 284.

16. Whitman, *An American Primer* (San Francisco: City Lights, 1970), p. 4.

17. Emile Benveniste, *Problems in General Linguistics* (Coral Gables, Florida: University of Miami Press, 1971), p. 218.

How the World Is Written

Marc Dachy

Readers of Gertrude Stein and even some of her critics, such as Richard Kostelanetz,[1] have been of the opinion that the works which followed the *Autobiography of Alice B. Toklas* (1933), a bestseller written as such, were weaker than those from the earlier experimental stage.

As an attempt to equal the success which greeted the *Autobiography*, *Everybody's Autobiography* (1937) was a disappointment, as were *Paris-France* (1940), *Wars I Have Seen* (1945) and *Brewsie and Willie* (1946, the year of her death). *Picasso* (1938), the only one of her books written directly in French for a series of monographs is far removed from the portraits of her grand period ("Picasso" and "If I Told Him, A Completed Portrait of Picasso").[2]

By continuing to write in an autobiographical vein, the writer supposedly had given up more demanding work. But Gertrude Stein herself was ironic about achieving a success that may suddenly render obsolete a work up until then rejected for its audacity. The writer, in short, is never read in real time. It is always too early, then too late.

Furthermore, the intellectual regression that characterized the period preceding the Second World War did not prevent Gertrude Stein from producing at least two outstanding works, *The World Is Round* (1939)[3] and *Ida* (1941); they are closely related, as one was written immediately after the other. The themes of twin pairs, and identity, ubiquitous in Stein's writing, particularly bind these two books together.

Ida is Rose, the little girl of *The World Is Round*, grown up. In *Ida*, some readers of Gertrude Stein immediately recognized one of her great works, even if it did not meet in France with the hoped-for success, for reasons no doubt tied to problems of translation. Indeed, *Ida* is a trap for inexperienced translators of Gertrude Stein's innovative work.[4] Under cover of a prose that is in appearance banal and cursory, the author accumulates all the while attenuating effects developed throughout her writing career; it is the very fact that these effects become progressively more hidden that renders them invisible to the ill-informed translator.

This particular aspect of Gertrude Stein's last style, in evidence throughout the *Autobiography* as well, has not always been properly understood in France, notably in the case of the full translation of *Ida*. The defects in Bernard Faÿ's translation of the *Autobiography of Alice B. Toklas* which quickly appeared in France in 1934, one year after its publication in America, are now well-known.[5] These were less prejudicial to the *Autobiography* than to the prose of *Ida*. It was, however, to her translator and friend, Bernard Faÿ (a member of the College de France, the honorary society of French university professors), that Gertrude Stein, who was of Jewish-Austrian origin (via San Francisco), owed her protection during the war.

Written in 1938, *The World Is Round* appeared in English in 1939. The manuscript, the corrected typescripts and the proofs are preserved at Yale University. While this text for children is not mentioned in the best known biographies of Gertrude Stein, those by James Mellow,[6] Janet Hobhouse[7] or John Malcolm Brinnin,[8] it is nonetheless familiar to Steinians of France, notably Jean Marcet and Florence Delay.[9]

To her friend Sammy, Gertrude offered to read out loud a passage from *The World Is Round*, of which she had just received a few copies. Years later, in his preface to an edition of letters received from her, Sammy described his emotions and the conversation which had followed the reading. In one of these letters (February 1940), she discussed the text's being made into a film, an agent having inquired about such a possibility.

Donald Sutherland, author of the first book on Gertrude Stein, has devoted three eloquent pages to the subject: "Her particular narrative for children and philosophers is *The World Is Round*. It is the story, in a mixture of prose and poetry, of a little girl named Rose who climbs up a nameless mountain with a hard blue garden chair in which she will not sit until she has reached the summit. After a number of natural adventures and terrors and temptations on the way, she reaches the summit and sits and sings, but she is all alone and as night begins to fall she gets frightened, in particular because while she knows she is there where she wanted to be she cannot tell where THERE is. Suddenly the place is illuminated by the beams of a revolving searchlight run by her cousin Willie who is on another farther hill, so she is comforted and cries. That is the end, except that they turn out not to be cousins and get married and live happily ever after."[10]

The story of Rose is dedicated by its author to a little girl of the age of nine, Rose D'Aiguy,[11] in a circular typographic dedication reproducing the famous "Rose is a Rose is a Rose is a Rose." It is in fact in this text that the sentence "Rose is a Rose is a Rose is a Rose" appeared after its premiere in "Sacred Emily" (1913). As to the circular motif, it had already appeared on the original cover of the autobiography attributed to her "double," Alice B. Toklas, which suggests the extent to which Gertrude Stein identified with Rose. This identification is more obvious in a text of 1937 ("The Autobiography of Rose"), a preliminary sketch for *The World Is Round* (or for at least a passage of the book) that concludes with a dedication to Rose by "her friend Gertrude Stein." The style of *The World Is Round* comes across as all the more inventive when enriched by the childlike logic developed in the book.

In a statement reported by David Gascoyne, Gertrude Stein clarified: "I have written a story for children, a little girl discovers that everything is round because the world is round."[12] If the idea of Gertrude Stein suggests, on an abstract level, a "spherical world" (Sutherland), the children, and in particular little Rose, are brought to a discovery rich with meaning because, concretely, the world is round as the stars, the moon, the mouth and the wheels are round throughout the text.

So the world is round. And it turns, *Eppur,' si muove!* Gertrude Stein affirms for children one of the decisive moments of the evolution of knowledge (*Useful Knowledge*), the roundness of the world, and its rotation, the Copernican revolution (condemned for the last time in 1616 by Pope Paul V as contrary to Scripture).

As Stein's book is addressed to children, Donald Sutherland compares it to a French geography book of the period which began in this way: "La terre est ronde comme une boule. La terre tourne sur elle-même. La terre ne repose sur rien."[10]

Other circumstances also explain how this text came into being. *The World Is Round* was written in Bilignin (one recognizes the landscape, lake – Bart or Bourget – and mountains and Lucey Church in Gertrude Stein's novel, *Lucy Church Amiably*) in the Ain region. One of Gertrude Stein's friends there was the Baroness Lucy Pierlot (Lucy Guilland, the Countess Lucy d'Aiguy by a first marriage), who was the grandmother of little Rose, to whom the book was dedicated. In 1928 she had written in French and published in English a children's book, *Liline and Her Dumb Friends*, that may have originally motivated Gertrude Stein's decision to write a book for children. Upon reading the French manuscript (entitled *Fraîcheur* and never published) given to us by Rose d'Aiguy herself, one is struck by certain similarities between the Baroness Pierlot's manuscript and the book by Gertrude Stein: first of all, the structure of the manuscript (several short texts, two of which have the same title), then certain themes, such as that of the double. But the resemblance comes to an end where Gertrude Stein's writing and her reflections on roundness, a subject of both enchantment and fear for the child, begin, Rose d'Aiguy, the last of her name in her Béon castle, belongs to a family of musicians, painters and writers.

The story revolves around the idea of childhood. Circular in itself, but not in the manner of James Joyce's *Finnegans Wake*, which appeared in the same year (1939), the story is presented as a succession (one is tempted to write rotation) of thirty-four texts printed in blue (the color of little boys) on pink paper (the color of little girls), punctuated by the drawings of a well-known artist for children, Clement Hurd (for the American edition). The English edition was illustrated by Gertrude Stein's friend, Francis Rose.

In the French edition (3), the corresponding drawings are those of Elie Dayan who, upon a public reading of a few pages of *The World Is Round* and of *La Terre est ronde*, responded with a quadrangular representation of time, "Time Square."[13]

In a final interview, the so-called "Transatlantic Interview," Gertrude Stein explains her position on poetry and on childhood: "Somehow or other in war time the only thing that is spontaneously poetic is children. Children themselves are poetry. The poetry of adults in wartime is too intentional. It is too much mixed up with everything else. My poetry was children's poetry, and most of it is very good, and some of it as good as anything I have ever done. *The World Is Round* is going to be included in a new American anthology."[14]

The play on colors evokes, in addition to the dialogue between pink and blue, a painter's palette and the art of composition ("as explanation"): "grass and trees and rocks are green not blue there no blue was there but blue was her favorite color all through" (p. 33), "a lot too white to be blue, too red to be wed" (p. 38) "they call it an alpine glow" (p. 42), "close your eyes and count one two open your eyes and count one two and then green would not be blue" (p. 60), "of course her eyes were blue although her name was Rose" (p. 60). Finally her cousin Will, on another hill, made the light turn and "made the ground green not black and made the sky white not black and Rose oh Rose just felt warm right through her back" (p. 66).

"Since the world is round, how can you play square?" wrote Fernand Léger in 1950.[15] From James Joyce (via Vico) to Abel Gance (*The Wheel*) by way of Marcel Duchamp's "rotoreliefs" (*Anemic Cinema*) and *Cercle et carré* (Michel Seuphor's review and group), the avant-garde interested itself in the spherical. "The World Is Round" is for that matter the title of Picabia's last painting.

In 1920, Gertrude Stein wrote an astounding text entitled "A Circular Play, a Play in Circles" in which the circles and rings cross, mingle and are undone like the magic rings of the conjuror. A series of paragraphs succeed one another, their titles all variations on the word "circle" or on the theme of circularity.

Readers of Gertrude Stein will remember the sentence of the ring which follows the moon in the opera put to music by Virgil Thomson, *A Saint in Seven* (1922):

> [And when do they sleep again.] A ring around the moon is seen to follow the moon and the moon is in the center of the ring and the ring follows the moon.

This sentence was once characterized as "one of the most beautifully balanced sentences he had ever heard" by an Oxford dean at a conference given for Gertrude Stein.[16]

In *The World Is Round*, the roundness—which so disquieted the mariners of Christopher Columbus—worries the little girl as well. This roundness, an endless one in the concrete realm of things, takes on a dreamlike abstract form, itself disquieting, in the sleep of Rose's cousin, Willie:

SILENCE

Willie was asleep
And everything began to creep around
Willie turned in his sleep and murmured
Round drowned.

(The World Is Round, p. 8)

This passage, heavy with the loss of any cosmic reference, with the depth of the night of time, may also recall, by its circular form, the fall into sleep of the narrator at the beginning of *A la recherche du temps perdu* (*Remembrance of Things Past*, Marcel Proust) and his "swirling and confused impressions":

Un homme qui dort tient en cercle autour de lui le fil des heures, l'ordre des années et des mondes. Il les consulte d'instinct en s'éveillant et y lit en une seconde le point de la terre qu'il occupe, le temps qui s'est écoulé jusqu'à son réveil; mais leurs rangs peuvent se meler, se rompre.

In order to escape rotundity (and perhaps also a constantly challenged Euclidian geometry, questioned in the manner of children in the text), to free herself from the enchanted though infernal circle that is finite and infinite form, Rose undertakes the ascension of the mountain. This individual claim against the cosmic order is accomplished with the assistance of a blue chair, the sole comforting presence available to Rose during her reckless expedition.

Like most of the texts by Gertrude Stein, *The World Is Round* dovetails into the totality of her work by means of a recurrence of themes, images and a play on signifiers. Thus the theme of the drowning of Willie and another little boy, caught in water-lilies (*The World Is Round*, p. 14) and saved in extremis by a third, older boy, had already appeared in "They must. Be Wedded. To their Wife" (1931) seven years before. In this brief line can be found the narrative developments which were later to come in one passage of the book:

Act I

Three brothers. Of which. One. Saved. The two. One. By one. From drowning.

In *The Mother of Us All* (1946), written by Gertrude Stein in the year of her death and put to music by Virgil Thomson, Susan B. Anthony takes up the questions of little Rose on name and identity:

Susan B. Anthony is my name, a name can only be a name my name can only be my name, I have a name, Susan B. Anthony is my name, to choose a name is feeble.

This formulation was also used in *The World is Round* to treat the subject of night:

Well it was night and night well night can be all right that is just what a night can be it can be all night. (p. 65)

While the planet follows the invariable cycles of the revolution imposed upon it by the law of gravity, Rose climbs her mountain and the Steinian sentence sets into motion wheels, drums, round words in singing mouths, stars and "lakes [which] when they are round have bottoms to them." In this lake Willie and one of his friends, their feet entangled in the water-lilies, just missed being drowned.

Language also makes its revolution. The first name of the little cousin of Rose, Willie, is composed or rather demultiplied and in particular engenders his "poetic double," the lion-twin Billie, who disappears on the other side of the mirror by a magic stroke of the pen in three lines:

And Billie was back, was Billie a lion when he was back, No said Willie, Billie was not a lion when he was back, was he a kitten when Billie was back, no said Willie Billie was not a kitten when he was back, was he a rat when he was back, no said Willie he was not a rat, Well what said Willie what was Billie when he was back, he was a twin said Willie that is what Billie was when he got back.
(. . .)
So that was all there was about Billie the lion and he was never there any more anywhere neither here nor there neither there nor here, Billie the lion never was anywhere. The end of Billie the lion. (p. 30)

From William derive, in the course of the story, Willie, Billie, Will I am, will, hill, will he, Bill he. . . .[17]

Thus in the narration of Gertrude Stein the novel devolves from the words themselves, with the American language itself constituting the very subject of the work. The temptation to use anagrams (for example, name and mane) at times produces meaning:

. . . if the lion has a name as well as a mane and that name is Billie. (p. 27)

She did not have any ink she had nothing pink. . . (p. 53)

In his *Autobiography*, the writer William Carlos Williams declared his debt to Gertrude Stein at the time he was developing the objectivist poem: "I am convinced that it is Gertrude Stein who, by insisting on the literal, structuralist quality of words, has so strongly influenced us."

Translated into English by the author with the assistance of Laura Green.

Notes

1. Richard Kostelanetz, *The Yale Gertrude Stein*, Yale University Press, 1980.

2. "Deux soeurs qui (ne) sont pas soeurs" was also written directly in French. This brief text has been reproduced in *Luna-Park 4 Gertrude Stein*, Paris, Transédition, 1978.

3. Gertrude Stein, *La Terre est ronde*, trans. by Marc Dachy, illustrated by Elie M. Dayan, Paris, Transédition, 1984.

4. Except in a translation by Françoise Collin, in *Luna-Park 4*, op. cit., of the first two chapters of *Ida*.

5. Gertrude Stein, *Autobiographie d'Alice Toklas*, trans. by Bernard Faÿ, Paris, NRF, 1934. (The "B" was dropped in the French version of Toklas' name, the use of the middle initial being practically non-existent in France, where it is considered moreover a typically American way of writing one's name.)

6. *Charmed Circle: Gertrude Stein and Company*, New York and Washington, Praeger, 1974.

7. *Everybody Who Was Anybody*, New York, G.P. Putnam's Sons, 1974.

8. *The Third Rose: Gertrude Stein and Her World*, Boston, Little Brown, 1959.

9. Jean Marcet: "Le cercle enchanté de Gertrude Stein," Delta 10, May 1980, Université Paul Valéry, Montpellier; Florence Delay: "Dogs and husbands in *Ida*," colloque Stein, Cerisy, summer of 1980.

10. Donald Sutherland, *Gertrude Stein: A Biography of Her Work*, Yale University Press, 1951, p. 169. The letters of Gertrude Stein and Alice B. Toklas have been edited with a memoir by Samuel M. Steward ("Sammy"): *Dear Sammy*, Boston, Houghton Mifflin Company, 1977. The volume contains numerous little-known photographs, notably of the meeting of Gertrude Stein and André Breton in Bilignin (1939).

11. Rose (Lucie Renée Anne) d'Aiguy, daughter of the Baroness d'Aiguy, who translated Gertrude Stein.

12. David Gascoyne, 23.1.39 in *Paris Journal 1937–1939*, The Enitharmon Press, 1978.

13. Limited edition in nine copies presented at the library-gallery "Village Voice," Paris, on the occasion of a reading of *The World Is Round*, February 1985.

14. Gertrude Stein, *Transatlantic Interview* in *A Primer for the gradual understanding of Gertrude Stein*, edited by Robert Bartlett Haas, Black Sparrow Press, Los Angeles, 1971, p. 23.

15. *Fonctions de la peinture*, Médiations, Denoël, p. 152.

16. *The Autobiography of Alice B. Toklas*, 1933, p. 288.

17. In "Shakespeare in Progress" (reproduced in *Fragments du choeur*, Paris, Denoël, coll. L'Infini, 1984), Marcelin Pleynet analyzes the function of the "will" in the *Sonnets* of William Shakespeare, which Gertrude Stein is known to have read very closely.

The Impartial Essence

Kenneth Burke

The repetitions and blithe blunderings that Gertrude Stein has somehow managed to work into a style make her *Lectures in America* hard for a critic to discuss. Though they have as their subject a theory of writing, they are expressed so girlishly that we are tempted not to ask how the various parts fit together.

The keystone of Gertrude Stein's literary theories seems to be her doctrine of "essence." She would get at the "essence" of the thing she is describing. She thus tends to consider literature primarily as *portraits*. She makes portraits, not only of people, but of landscapes; plays are to her little other than group portraits; and eventually people and landscapes become so interchangeable that a play can describe a landscape by assembling portraits of people. Hence let us, instead of attempting to follow the order of exposition in Miss Stein's book itself, build up her literary schema in our own way with "essence" as the starting point:

The essence of a thing would not be revealed in something that it does. It would be something that a thing is. The search for essence is the attempt "to express this thing each one being that one." A thing's essence is something that makes it distinct from other things; it is, as she says at another point, a thing's "melody." Since it is something that the thing *is*, action would tend to obscure it rather than reveal it. Hence:

> In my portraits I had tried to tell what each one is without telling stories and now in my early plays I tried to tell what happened without telling stories so that the essence of what happened would be like the essence of the portraits, what made what happened be what it was.

Suppose, now, that you held to such a doctrine of essence, and wanted in your writing to get down the absolute essence of each thing you wrote about. Consider the sort of problems, in both theory and methods, that might arise. In the first place, you would have to worry about resemblance. In putting down

Reprinted from the public domain (*New Republic*, March 7, 1935).

the essence of Mr. A, you would have to guard against any tendency to think of him in terms of somebody he resembled—Mr. AI. Again, since essence is something that a thing now is, you would have to guard against the tendency to think of your subject in terms of memories (an exaction which might explain in part her tendency to feel that stories or acts obscure the perception of essence). And you would now have brought yourself to the paradoxical position wherein your knowledge of your subject's past or of people like him amounts to "confusion" (a sad state of affairs upon which Miss Stein dwells at some length).

At this point you might rebel; but if you go on, as Miss Stein did at her leisure, you will find attendant considerations arising. You will talk much about getting "inside" things (perhaps thus being led to note as the primary fact about English literature the stimulus it derived from insularity). And since you, as an *outsider*, are busied with the literary task of describing things until you get *inside* them, there will necessarily hover about your theories some hint of mystic communion. In time your doctrine of essence brings you to the metaphysical problem of the One and the Many, for if you start by trying to find wherein each one is that one, you begin to find a general intermingling; and particularly as you make that outside you to be inside you, you come, through the medium of yourself, upon a kind of universal essence:

> And so I say and I saw that a complete description of every kind of human being that ever could or would be living is not such a very extensive thing because after all it can be all contained inside in any one and finally it can be done.

How does this work out in practice? You start to write about something, to describe it, to make its portrait. You have a personal style, a set of mannerisms that suit your particular essence, and as you write you gradually get into the swing of them. When you get going, you are "excited." And since your excitement arises during your description of a thing, you may call this excitement the melody or essence of the thing. You may feel that each subject has its particular essence because you have used a particular combination of words in writing about it. But you feel the "unity" of all subjects because the quality of your excitement is the same in all cases (the way you feel when you get going), and you call this melody of yours the melody of the thing.

If the essence of external things is thus identified with the qualities of your style, you may tend to think of writing (description) primarily as a monologue act, done with little direct concern for an audience. And since this stylistic circulation about an object obliges you to consider the strategy of expression, you may arrive at the thoughts on the nature of naming that Miss Stein verbalizes as a shifty distinction between prose and poetry ("that is poetry really loving the name of anything and that is not prose").

However, you are now on the verge of a change. For the strategy of expression leads into considerations of the audience. From this point, you begin to suspect the suggestive values of narrative, since narrative unquestionably has a significant appeal to audiences. But at this point, if you are Miss Stein, you simply state that you have changed your opinion—and stop. As a kind of compromise between your initial notion of essence as non-dramatic and the fully revised notion that essence might best show itself in action, you may be grateful for her halfway metaphor: the essence is something like the engine in a car—a going without a destination.

It seems to me, however, that Miss Stein should have continued her revisionary process, until all the initial visionary assertions had been similarly modified. She might have considered, for instance, the ways in which remembrance and resemblance are inevitable; the ways in which the primary fact of English literature might be called its transcendence of insularity, etc. And then, and only then, should she have begun her book. As it stands, I maintain that it is (a) the first draft of a critical credo, (b) complicated by the co-presence of its revision, (c) further vitiated by the fact that the revisionary process was not applied to all its parts. Above all, I believe a complete revision would require her to stress (at least in this "imperfect world" of history) the *dramatic*, the *active*, the *partisan*, in direct contrast with the feature of *passivity* that is now infused through her doctrine of portrait and essence.

La Véritable Stein
(Excerpts 1938)

Wendell Wilcox

Now Miss Stein has attempted almost every form in the abstract manner. There are plays, novels and poetry and even travel. There are often just descriptions such as you get in *Tender Buttons*. In these she often tells you what the object is she is describing and then proceeds to evoke the object in her own mind by the use of disconnected words, words I mean not usually connected with the object. This can of course be called impressionism but it is not quite that. And it is not all together abstraction. In Miss Stein's mind there is always the concrete image or the concrete idea. When the word *thing* is used there is almost always in Miss Stein's mind the definite knowledge of what that thing is. She often tells you all about that thing without ever saying what the thing is. That is part of her personal paraphernalia which she feels it is unnecessary to tell the reader about. It is the writing about a thing that is important. Just as in reading *Bovary* you do not know from what corner of Flaubert's personal experience a particular sensation is drawn which is used to describe a sensation of Emma's, just as you do not really live Emma's experience because you have not had Flaubert's and do not know where he had his, so too the object behind the thing in Miss Stein is not revealed, but it is there and the writing and the words are clear and lucid and will (if they do) arouse in you a correspondence. You see a book anyhow is not life. It is an imitation of life, not the thing itself. It is a selection, not possibly real. If Emma were real there would be countless things that happened to her, countless people she knew and met everyday in the street during the very course of the narrative, eliminated necessarily from the story. There is not room for everything. A book is a condensation and a selection, obviously a fiction despite its very moving, very lively quality, and so the forms of literature are imitations of life and just so many of Stein's things are imitations. These long explanatory passages which explain a thing – the word that, strange to say, comes closer than any other word in the language to being nothing – liberates the passage from being an explaination of anything. In her mind yes, often, the real object is there. But the result is an explaination. The terms, the manner of phrasing, the sound, the way the whole passage runs, is explaination pure and simple. And if you like to read explainations of things, what difference does it make what is explained. It's a matter of taste there. Do you or don't you like explaination. Some people do. They will read an explaination of anything simply because they enjoy having things explained so why not read an explaination by Miss Stein where you will get . . . well, explaination, just that. Yet of course, you are human and you do feel there must be a reason for it. That is a human need. A reason. Reason. I do know that. And yet if you are an explaination reader you do read that sort of thing because it satisfies you. So for a while you might very much enjoy a Stein explaination. But wanting human reason the abstraction will pall. You can't go on with it forever. I will kill two birds with one stone and quote from *How To Write*, an obviously explanatory book, in which as often as not she is not so much telling how to write as actually giving you an example of writing. Here is a passage that contains both explaination and example simultaneously.

> This is a sentence that has no necessity they are agreeable and to be willing to be maintained that they are first at first without their clouding their allowance that they are to be threatened with their examples. . . .

Well, that is enough. You can see how perfectly there is the tone of explaining. You can see from the first words that it is an example of a kind of sentence just as you would get in a grammar book. You can see from the next phrase, "that has no necessity," that she is telling you that a sentence can exist as an explaination without having a reason. There necessity connects itself in her mind with the idea of actually trying to convey a meaning. They are agreeable. All that is necessary is that the sentence should be agreeable and willing to be maintained, but at this point the thing begins to slip away from understanding. You aren't quite sure she is still in her own mind even talking about a sentence or sentences when she says *they* yet you are fairly sure and you are sure from the tone of the whole that it is explaination. Words like the word *necessity* getting connected in her mind with *sentence* that have the necessity of conveying a meaning will be used again and again. They become part of a secret vocabulary into which the reader cannot hope to penetrate. The reader is purposely kept in the dark for the purpose of making the writing stand by itself, speak by itself, and be what it is by itself. In her own mind the meaning of the vocabulary is often perfectly clear. This is necessary because in order to convey the feeling of meaning without actually having it, her own energy must be working around the thing she does know.

Often, I am sure, in her own mind the word that has one meaning suddenly calls up a different association, and off Miss Stein will waltz into the new meaning. It is not a modulation in music but it is like one. The modulation here comes from memory and the look of the word itself. Frequently this leads to what she calls playing. One of the things the human mind loves to do is play.

In one place in *How to Write*, she actually tells you and shows you how it is done:

> If you think of grammar as a part.
> Can you reduce grammar to one.
> One two three all out but she.
> Now I am playing.
> Now I am yielding.
> To not attempting.

The word *one* is the word that brings on a modulation into play and off she goes. There is no need to explain the words *yielding* and *not attempting*. They are quite obvious. But you do see what a definite, what a horribly precise meaning the words take on as she uses them. *Attempting* is the struggle with the words to make them come out and connect as they should. *Yielding* is relaxing and not trying. They become so precisely connected with writing in her mind that they become nearly technical terms and part of the private vocabulary. So that their use in later passages will, if you have followed through, have even the same associations for you. Only let us be frank about it, they will not, because no one can follow through abstraction of this sort. The mind gets too tired. And so even in making a word convey definite meaning it does not convey it to the reader and she does not really intend it to. In doing this, in having this vocabulary, she does what any writer dealing with ideas inevitably does, she takes simple words, words that, as we have said a long way back, do not have too definite a meaning, whose meanings are slippery and cover a multitude of things, and uses them constantly in connections with certain things until their meaning does become clear and concise. That is the reason there is no need for semantics or for limiting the meaning of words. Every man has his idea, and if he is a good writer he chooses his words with extreme care and repeats them often enough in the proper context until at last they release the meaning he desires. Every writer puts his own limits on words and yet the words are still there for the next writer to take and use in the way he himself desires. This is not violation, it is merely craftsmanship.

Now Stein in her vocabulary has exactly this same kind of clarity. I have heard tell that she often worries about the extreme clarity of her work. This may sound nonsensical but it is not, since mostly it doesn't convey definite ideas to the reader. Her words as you read them do have the effect of tremendous clarity. They stand alone and they radiate this clarity. Just as her explainations explain so too her words are clear.

One must always remember that in this abstract writing Stein makes something that reads and sounds like the thing she wants—explaination, description, what not. The things stand pure and alone and are just what they are. And so the same is true of her words and her sentences. They are what sentences should be (whether or not they have meaning); they are perfectly, utterly and entirely readable. The words have a glowing pure clarity and the sentences read often as only the very finest and most lucid prose can read.

There is more confusion about what writing is than there is about any of the other arts. The only way anybody can ever come to understand what any of the arts are and do is first of all to come to some understanding about what the medium is, what the actual materials are with which the artist has to work. Music is almost the only art that never got confused. A note was a note and everybody has always understood that and no one has ever asked music to be anything but notes. True there have been times when music became descriptive, times when, by the processes of mood creation through sound, musicians have tried to present ideas. No one ever got very worried about it, however, because it was all still so obviously notes. Vocabulary is always a drawback. People can, by borrowing from philosophy, speak of musical ideas, but even so they usually understand that this idea consists of a brief melody which can be elaborated and expanded. They do not usually think that the musical idea says anything. Painting has its phases, but they are not confusing. Everyone knows that the materials are surface, paint and frame and that these three things are the fundamental conditions of all painting.

But writing is confusing. Obviously the material of writing is words. But words of course were first used as designations of objects, then used as a useful way of conveying wants and needs, and then even later as a way of conveying ideas. They have been connected with conversation and with communication. But eventually words also were connected with writing as an art. In this case the word is written. Writing as an art is concerned with the written word. Writing as literature is the arrangement of words, primarily that; but due to the fact that these same words have been so intimately connected with other functions confusion has arisen. There are so many theories about it, and about what writing is supposed to do. Well, there are poems and plays and novels and books about things. The latter are not necessarily art, but of course they may be. For a long time now it has been the general feeling that writing was concerned with the conveying of ideas. As I have already said, ideas though they do depend on words are not easily communicable unless the idea is already fairly well known to the reader. If you will stop to consider what has happened to the reader lately you will see what I mean. You know yourself that you very seldom read all of the words in any book. You read the ideas. A hasty glance over a page will give you the idea and feeling that you have the gist; you hurry on and you pay very little attention to the words themselves. Now obviously enough if you read in this fashion as most people, you read for ideas,

in ideas, and not for or in words. It is also equally obvious that if you can pick
the ideas thus rapidly from the page that you are not really receiving new ideas
but merely recognizing ideas you already know. You are not reading with
words at all. The words in their arrangement do not even need to be particularly exact. They are merely indications of an already well-known idea. And
on the whole, though it may be momentarily satisfactory it is not particularly
satisfactory. It would be if the ideas were new perhaps, but obviously if they
can be comprehended thus swiftly and without the actual reading of the words
they are not new ideas but merely old ones easily recognized. The pleasure is
really not the pleasure in observance of the actual world but the pleasure in
having old beliefs confirmed. Anyone can see that it is not reading at all.

Now Stein, in keeping the ideas private, by speaking in a private
vocabulary and in using words as an end in themselves, brings the reader back
once again to the words on the page. If you read her at all you must read the
words, each and every one. They are the important thing—their arrangement
and the pattern they make. Words are the medium of writing and the writer
is brought vividly back to them. In her use of words the meaning is never
distorted. The words mean exactly what they mean. They stand out for you
with clear and shining purity, a purity that makes them almost frightening,
especially so since they are combined in illogical ways. An adjective is placed
with a noun that is not accustomed to having such an adjective connected with
it, and the result is that both the adjective and the noun retain their separate
meaning with utter clarity.

> Tooth cake, teeth cake, tongue saliva and more joints and more
> joints all these make an earnest cooky.

Cookies are not earnest but now in this passage one is and this makes both
the feeling of *cooky* and *earnest* very lively and clear. The whole sentence makes
a pleasant and vivid description of eating.

The fact that all the words are arranged in an unusual way gives the effect
of isolating the words and anything that has been isolated and placed in an
unusual light begins to live freshly again, because the person observing it is
forced once more to look at it for the first time. That is the pleasure that sur-
realism gives. It is the isolation of terrifically clear objects in queer lights so that
the looker is forced to really look and see the object living alone and in itself.
In a thing like painting you do not so much question the painter's right to do
this. You look and you receive the pleasure of really witnessing the object.
Because it is so apparent that a certain amount of skill has been expended in
the doing and arranging you do not question the triviality of the experience.
The skill tells you there has been art and you can relax and receive the pleasure
without question.

But when it is done in words you are immediately dubious of the writer's
skill. You have used these words all your life and they are easy words. But this

particular treatment of words is not more trivial than that particular treatment of the object in painting. And it does for the word exactly what the painter does for the object.

If writing is ever again to be of any use either as an expression of human experience, an expression of ideas, or merely as an artistic expression, the writer must return to the word. The word must be given the lively quality it had before we became so used to it we could scorn it, and above all the reader must be forced to read the words. Miss Stein has done this. I am not certain that she has succeeded from a public viewpoint. The work in itself is perfectly successful, and it is successful for some readers. Her task in the tackling of abstract writing was the restoration of meaning and vividness to the words themselves, to the very fundamental materials of writing. She has explained a great deal of this in her lectures. She does not however explain herself. But she does explain words and their function. If one has the patience to listen to this very important and extremely fundamental discussion of words and what they have done and do, he will begin to see what Miss Stein has been trying to do.

* * *

Here I think we have come to the reason why abstraction is possible in painting but not in writing. When I say not possible in writing, I mean not for long. A painting is before the eye. You look at it for a few minutes and then you go on to something else. You get what it gives quickly and it is very satisfying. It would cease to be satisfying if you had to sit in front of it for several hours. You can return but you cannot stay. Well, writing is a long line that has to be followed for a length of time and the human mind just does reject going on abstractly in a long line. It does just get bored. But if it encounters abstraction briefly, for just a minute or two, it is refreshed.

Well, *Tender Buttons* is description, and description has its relation to painting. It doesn't go on forever, and so it is satisfying.

Now all this writing of Stein's being fundamentally abstract never does travel in a straight line as writing used to do and I sometimes think must do. She herself does not write for very long at one sitting. The result is that even in a lengthy work the writing is always fragmentary. Even when it is a book with a single idea like *The Geographical History of America* the writing is fragmentary. She is always starting and stopping again. She is always picking up any part of her idea. She is always picking up any idea. And it is made up of a hundred tiny pieces, instead of moving along in an organized way from idea to idea. Anything can be introduced at any time. In the course of this book she tells us that form is no longer important. That it is content that is important and not form.

Now everybody has always felt she didn't have form, but many people have felt she didn't have content. So the statement might come as a surprise to them. Her books always did have content. They were bags containing many many things all dropped down in a mess. The titles themselves would more or less tell you that was so—*Many Many Women, Useful Knowledge, Tender Buttons.*

And yet in a book where you are concerned with the lives of people, as in *Three Lives* and in a book where you are concerned with a central idea, as in *The Geographical History*, form, even when approached in this confusing way, is almost inevitable. The constant striking at the central idea gives the book at last a rather pleasing and discernible form. A book you write of a life will take the shape of the life, no matter what you do in the course of telling. I really think that in the beginning that is the way form is made. For me Lawrence's books have been masterpieces of form. They didn't have the form of the ordinary novel, but each separate book made its own form, a form that rises spontaneously from the content. Nevertheless the constant habit of rejecting the linear construction that writing seems almost compelled to take [suggests to some that, RK] Stein has lost the ability to organize her thought. I do not think this is anything to be held against her. Nobody ever did everything, and she herself has done a great deal. Why insist on everything? Her method is one that is opposed to the consideration of ultimate form, one in which each separate particle receives the utmost, the most brilliant and illuminating attention. But now I guess she worries about it. She has so much energy that she wants everything. Now, quite late, she has gone back to intelligibility and with that return she has the desire to return a little to form though in a way she does not think of it as just that. She thinks of it as something else. I really believe that the statement in *The Geographical History* is in a way a witness to this. It is in a way a sort of self-justification in the face of defeat—a little silly too, since, after all, hers was another battle and why should she fight this one. It wouldn't surprise me if she decided to be two generations instead of just one.

I have shown how the books grew naturally from the comprehensible to the incomprehensible. I think from what I have said it is easy enough to follow the various forces that moved it in that direction. One element was the obvious influence that abstract painting had upon her with the result that words were taken out of their natural positions for the sake of putting in a striking light, just as the painters had brought into juxtaposition unrelated objects, or else removed from their natural environment certain objects and put them in unusual lights. The influence of the distortion in painting led to distortion of the sentence in writing. That was the outside influence, the immediate and tangible one. I have shown too how this tendency came from within herself as well as from the outside and how the sentence began in the natural, moved toward distortion, then toward logical diagram and then broke down at last, permitting a perfectly arbitrary arrangement. I am not asserting that the so-called modern painting did or did not have a direct influence. People in any age move together motivated by a certain force, moved in certain directions by the same forces acting upon all. It was a time when all the arts were trying

to return to the pure conditions of their own medium. There is always inter-
action among activities of any age, and yet each activity is motivated separately
by what you may call if you like the spirit of the age. I have no intention of
telling what it was that created abstraction in the arts in general. Stein herself
has written to show how it grew out of the life that everyone lived and how
this life was by and large an American product. I recommend that the reader
go directly to her writing for this, as I have no desire to repeat Stein's own ideas,
but merely to try to give you some sort of approach to a kind of writing which
is more difficult to understand than any other kind. It is mostly habit that
stands in the reader's way.

There is only one idea of hers which I care to discuss and that not very
fully, this is the idea of the continuous present, an idea, like all others difficult
if not impossible to explain. It is best done by herself. I am not going to attempt
literal translation. I am only going to try to give in my own way what my own
idea of her idea of the continuous present is. It will explain something of her
nature as well and that is rather essential if you are going to try to approach
even the more lucid writing.

It would be difficult and I think a little dangerous to try saying anything
about why she returned to the intelligible after so many years of the unintelligible. She had at last to take into consideration the idea of an audience. In the
creation of the masterpiece she tells us that either you are your own audience
or else, perhaps, maybe, yes, perhaps there is no audience at all in this kind
of creation. Who could ever really create a pure and independent thing if he
were to consider in the act of writing every last reader. There are too many
readers, they have too many different viewpoints, and the result would be that
there could be no viewpoint in the writing at all if the audience, the so multiple
audience, were to be considered. A masterpiece is something that is written
in private, away from the world and whatever energy creates it flows down a
single arm and onto the paper. Two people cannot create a masterpiece, for
where there are two a struggle takes place that leads to one or the other
yielding and there is a rift in the work that stops it from being whole. That
is why ultimately the drama and the movies can never really be masterpieces,
for too many fingers are in the pie. The masterpiece requires the most intense
concentration of energy to achieve itself, and if more than one person is involved that concentration can not be achieved. Even the creator of the masterpiece must be a very single person, a person so all of one piece within himself
that he can achieve this supreme effort of concentration.

Well, at the moment of creation, one must be such a person, but once the
creation is over naturally anybody likes to have an audience. I think it is
natural enough that in the end Miss Stein should take a step toward the world,
moved perhaps by the desire of widening the circle of her audience. Anyhow
anybody likes to be a public person. It is fun. There was the pleasure of travel-
ing and the pleasure of presenting oneself. There was the pleasure of making

money. It was logical that eventually she should write the autobiography of her life in Paris in terms that would be easily grasped. The book was written and it did sell very well and naturally publishers like books that sell well and it was logical they should want another, it was logical she would enjoy making more money, it was logical she would enjoy talking to the public about herself some more. It was logical too that in lecturing she should choose a language that could be understood by an audience that was right in front of her. Much of the material used in these works was material she had already written out in her own way, much of it was material that came to her hand at the moment of writing. It had always been her habit to work as she went and to use the material of the day she had just been living. I do not believe that anyone ever did more thinking and meditating than Stein and her thoughts and meditations like those of any one else were aroused by happenings of the day she was living. In any of her works you will find references to the day on which she was writing. The shapelessness of her work, if you want to call it that, allowed for the intrusion of anything at any moment. Read *The Geographical History* and you will see how often her own day is mentioned in the course of this book which is a discussion of the relation of human mind to human nature, or vice versa. This process always lends to her work an extremely lively quality, keeping it constantly connected with the actual living of life. This is anyhow a very good book for any one to attempt. It was written after her first vital connection with audience, and it stands half way between the intelligible and the unintelligible. At all points the thing that I have spoken of as her private language is always more or less visible, and it is quite possible with an effort to make the whole of it almost clearly visible.

Well, to return to the idea of the continuous present. Reduce it to its simplest terms and it means little more than what anybody already knows, that the present is always here. You live in the present moment, just that and little more.

This idea has always been present in the minds of men and yet every age has brought to it its own interpretation in the lights of its own hopes and processes. But Miss Stein has been more sympathetic to it than perhaps any other person who ever lived. She is the last word in the first person present singular. And that is as far as realism and common sense can be carried.

It has been her way of life, it has been her philosophy and it has become one of the things on which her writing is based. It has led to so many thoughts and complications that it would be almost impossible to repeat them without simply rewriting a large part of her works. It is part of the unintelligibility, and it is also something that goes to make even her intelligible writing a little difficult to grasp. It is the thing that makes her adverse to political ideas and social ideas, and this aversion is part of the thing that makes her unpopular. It also creates her apparent insensitiveness to suffering. In the last autobiography she says she has never been unhappy, a statement that would be very likely to arouse intense anger in some people. The remark is even carried a little farther and there is vaguely the idea that nobody ever is really unhappy. And that God knows is not calculated to arouse much love in the hearts of anyone. But it is really a perfectly logical and sensible thing to say.

Let us go on to just a few of the implications of the idea that the present is continuous. It led her to say that there is no beginning and no ending, not really. There is only the middle. Something is always going on. Of course, too, though something is always going on, something else may be starting, something else stopping. Here is the justification of formlessness, based on the actual shape of life. It is quite logical enough. The old novel did not have a natural structure. It had a beginning and an end. Nothing in life has. So beginning and ending are the really difficult things because after all they are things that in reality are not. As a result, in writing she discards the idea that the beginning has to be at the beginning, and the end at the end. Something is always starting, something else stopping, something else going on. Her work does not have a beginning and an end and a middle. At any moment she is apt to stop what she is doing and to start doing something else. All through any book, there are beginnings. It led to her putting those queer chapter numbers or part numbers just anywhere in the book. In life any thing happens at any time. And so chapter four can come anywhere. She says simply now we will have chapter four and we have it.

I have already said that writing was an imitation of life, but not life, a purely artificial creation. I have already pointed out how much elimination has to take place, how any life has to be stripped of most of its incidents and most of its acquaintances. The old method of beginning at the birth and going on to the death of a man was about as logical a form as any book could take. Even so, it was not all together satisfactory since every life is dependent not only on its span of time but also on the lives of the people that went before, the ancestors. Naturally it is impossible to tell it all. Stein prefers the destruction of time and the consideration of the continuous present—a constant starting, a constant stopping, a constant going on. That too is an imitation of life. It is not as may appear at first blush either confusion or formlessness. It is merely another way in which literature, pressed constantly by the necessity for imitating reality, has again tried to come closer to life. Every age grows tired of the way in which it has been approaching life. The process at first natural becomes intellectual, and gradually, as the contact with the actual sources, fire water and soil disappear, dullness sets in. Then again the writer looks at life and sees again its form, and starts again with the new approach that is to refresh his generation. To my way of thinking the masterpieces, the works that really live, are the ones whose authors have really perpetrated this new contact with nature. Those who have gone back in themselves to the sources and returned to give to men fresh new power. After the masterpiece come many works in repetition, many of them extremely excellent, but always in great or lesser degree a repetition of the author before, until at last the magic wears out, and the return is made again. It is the genius and only the genius who can make this return within himself, those who can effect the real act of creation.

This mind that creates the masterpiece is the thing which Stein calls the human mind. In the human mind she says there is no memory, for the human mind lives in the present tense, it is in the process of actually experiencing the source. If it pauses to remember the others who have gone to the source, then it is not the human mind. It is human nature remembering and repeating. Everybody has human nature, but the genius has human mind, the mind that actually makes the present contact. Now people have been very rebellious to this idea. Psychology tells us that of course there is memory and that even a genius is a human being and remembers. Well, I suppose so. But even so in the process of actual creation there is not any remembering, there is only the actual present moment of creation.

It is perfectly true. It can't really be explained much farther than that. If you can see it you can and if you can't you can't. Yet, if I may be allowed to, I would like to say that in the act of creation that takes place in the lives of most men and women there is very little memory. In the actual act of human coupling the memory goes, or sleeps. If it does not sleep the act is not successful in itself. The more nearly the mind goes, the more successful is that act. You do know that. The more you remember, the less actual pleasure or benefit you receive from it. It is the only analogy I can think of. And yet I do not think it is a forced analogy. There is some reason for words. And it is not without reason that both writing and coupling have been acts of creation. On certain levels certainly. And yet.

For Stein human beings fall into two classifications, ordinary mortals and geniuses. Ordinary mortals are possessed of human nature, geniuses of human mind. Up to and through *The Making of Americans* her mind had been busily preoccupied with considering the actions of men, but during the course of *The Making of Americans,* in which she set out purely and simply to tell the story of her own family, seeing the similarity of people, seeing how they were arranged in patterns and combinations of other people – the pattern always being similar and yet varying slightly – a slight addition here, a slight addition there – she set to work all at once to describe not just her own family but everybody, everybody who ever had been, was, or ever would be. It is at this point that the thing I have called the diagrammatic sentence begins to appear. She saw or began to see how it was quite possible in this way to describe anyone and everybody and for many pages she goes on working out these quite dull diagrams of people. In the end she herself grew tired of it and *The Making of Americans* came one fine morning to an end. She simply got tired of it. Once the possibility of performing this task was clear she saw well enough that there was no necessity to do it. Like Freud's approaching human beings from the analytical rather than the descriptive side, she grew weary of it. Out of this I think grew the seeming contempt for psychology and preoccupation with human beings in general.

Later in *The Geographical History* we have the constant reiteration of the fact that human nature is not interesting, that only human mind is so. Human nature might be occupying, as she calls it, it might be amusing, it might be something you loved, but after all it was not interesting. Only the human mind, the one thing which escaped diagrammatics was interesting.

The human mind was purely and simply the genius, the creator of ideas and of literature. The ordinary man remembered. He learned. He lived by what he learned. He repeated. But only the human mind created. The human mind created the thought, created probably, though creating the thought, even the action of the rest of the world. Since human beings lived on memory and repetition it seemed obvious that genius never remembered and never repeated; it only created, and in the act of creation there is no time, there is only the present moment, the moment of creation. The genius then is a man who lives without time. The past does not exist. The future does not exist. But only the moment of creation. Either the future or the past would act as a distraction to the concentration of energy [that] goes into the creation itself.

We have just recently all of us gone through a rather heavy siege with the psychologists. We have by now become fairly familiar with the workings of the minds of the mind men. Suddenly confronted with a concept of mind that apparently discards the memory all together and time through which memory travels we are unable to make the proper disassociations which will enable us to face this new concept with any amount of clarity. We are not all of us geniuses. We are merely the receptacles of human nature and as such we cling to the known patterns, repeating what we have learned. And yet every step in the widening of the mind's circle is made only through this process of direct contemplation of facts and forgetfulness of the old knowledge. Though Freud himself has occasionally tackled the problem of genius, he himself admits that he has never solved it and it seems to be fairly reasonable to say that it is impossible of solution in terms purely psychological. By breaking with familiar terminology and beginning with her own, Stein makes a start. By using her own language and her own approach she makes a picture for us of the masterpiece and of genius. Unless a thing can be described in terms of an art or science they have already mastered, most men think, the thing either does not exist or else there is no truth in the description. But please do try to imagine a man in the reign of Justinian, say, faced suddenly with a Freudian explaination. Remember too that by every age and by every artist the world has been taken apart and reassembled and that each of these various arrangements have been true in their time and place and that each has added in its time to the sum total of man's understanding.

Stein's ideas are for the most part connected with writing. And they must be considered in that context; otherwise, they are not comprehensible.

Anything removed from its context becomes either silly or incomprehensible. Of the rest of her ideas I intend to speak not at all. They are perfectly clear if the reader will approach them with an open and unbiased mind. If he persists in insisting that they are incomprehensible merely because a certain portion of the woman's work has been in the vein of what for lack of a better word we have to call the unintelligible, he can not expect to get much from them. And not even the unintelligible writing should be considered incomprehensible. I have done what I can in this essay to tell in what that incomprehensibility consists. Her work is too often regarded as some kind of foreign language which can be translated once the reader has been given the grammar. It cannot be. It is not intended to be. It is all of it written in a language that might be called the language of as if. Take for the loveliest of examples the advertisement in the front of *Lucy Church Amiably:*

ADVERTISEMENT

Lucy Church Amiably.   There is a church and it is in Lucey and it has a steeple and the steeple is a pagoda and there is no reason for it and it looks like something else.   Beside this there is amiably and this comes from the paragraph.

Select your song she said and it was done and then she said and it was done with a nod and then she bent her head in the direction of the falling water.   Amiably.

This altogether makes a return to romantic nature that is it makes a landscape look like an engraving in which there are some people, after all if they are to be seen there they feel as pretty as they look and this makes it have a river a gorge an inundation and a remarkable meadowed mass which is whatever they use not to feed but to bed cows.   Lucy Church Amiably is a novel of romantic beauty and nature and of Lucy Church and John Mary and Simon Therese.

And there you have this rather but not really incomprehensible description of what you will find in the novel, a description written as if it described. And yet if you listen it does describe. The whole delightful pastoral feeling of this book is described. Direct translation is impossible but take the single phrase "a remarkable meadowed mass which is whatever they use not to feed but to bed cows" and you will see clearly the idea of as if appearing. Carefully considered the whole advertisement tells you exactly how any of the writing of Miss Stein is to be approached. There is no reason for it and it looks like something else and besides that there is amiably.

It has often bothered me how little difference there is between the unintelligible writing and the intelligible. If you remove your mind from the matter the sentence is the same, the sound is the same, the whole effect the same. So why should the unintelligible not be comprehensible. By the same token why should not the incomprehensible be intelligible. Well there is no reason for it. It is as it is. And either way it is always a pleasure.

Something More
about Gertrude Stein

Ellsworth Snyder

Gertrude Stein liked theories. Indeed a great deal of her writing consists of theories of one sort or another, but none of it as important as that which contains theories concerning the creative act. Among these, the essay *What are Masterpieces and Why are There so Few of Them* is one of the most significant. The reasons are simple: the statement is straightforward and clear, and the theory is a philosophical stance for one of the 20th century's most far-reaching contributions to the fine arts, hermeticism. The following quotations will illustrate:

> It is very difficult so difficult that it always has been difficult but even more difficult now to know what is the relation of human nature to the human mind because one has to know what is the relation of the act of creation to the subject the creator uses to create that thing.[1]

> At any moment when you are you you are you without the memory of yourself because if you remember yourself while you are you you are not for purposes of creating you.[2]

> . . . . . it has to do with the human mind and the entity that is with a thing in itself and not in relation.[3]

> It is very interesting that letter writing has the same difficulty, the letter writes what the other person is to hear and so entity does not exist there are two present instead of one and so once again creation breaks down.[4]

> . . . . . knowing that there is no identity and producing while identity is not.[5]

> Think about how you create if you do create you do not remember yourself as you do create. And yet time and identity is what you tell about as you create only while you create they do not exist.[6]

These statements tie Stein into the history of other ideas, ideas that when taken with hers are philosophically very revealing concerning hermeticism.

For instance, though there is no direct evidence that Stein ever studied Zen, viewing the above ideas through Hui-Neng's doctrine of No Mind is most illuminating.[7]

According to Hui-Neng, when the mind is devoid of all its possible contents except itself, then the mind can see itself as reflected in itself, thus becoming a void of inexhaustible contents. That is, then (as Stein suggests), the moment most propitious for the creative act. The most useful in the sense of the Mind because it is pure experience. The now-moment (Stein's continuous present) when you are creating you. It is what Gertrude called entity suspended in time. It is self-identity but not identity. In identity there are two entities (identity, the knower, and identification of the identity, the known). In self-identity there is only one entity, identity is transformed into itself. As Allegra Stewart in her very admirable book *Gertrude Stein and the Present* points out this is a spiritual orientation:

> The groundless act of presence—an act by which a man may realize at one stroke his own "human mind" and the beauty or meaning of some aspect of the cosmos.[8]

The composer John Cage has said that one way to prepare for this is to perceive a similar spiritual essence in the world external to oneself. In the fine arts this would mean getting into the spirit of the material, which the creative mind has chosen. When the spirit is understood the form creates itself. It is necessary to become one with this material. The discipline consists in studying the material inwardly with the mind thoroughly purified of its subjective, self-centered contents. It is essential to keep the mind in unison with the emptiness, thus the one whose attention and devotion are centered in the material ceases to be the one outside that material. Both those engaged in the creative act, and those coming in contact with the result of that act, are then enveloped in the famous Zen concept that some/thing must correspond to no/thing.

Words were, of course, Stein's primary interest and it is provocative to tie her concept of the creative act using the material of words with the ideas of the 20th century's great language philosopher, Ludwig Wittgenstein.[9] By comparing Stein's theory as viewed through the Zen doctrine of No Mind with Wittgenstein's approach to how we use language we are able to make a powerful statement about hermeticism, namely, that if there is a word or sign, it does not hold that there must be a corresponding thing or essence.

In his book *Wittgenstein and Buddhism* Chris Gudmunsen quotes from Wittgenstein and Nāgārjuna:

> The mistake we are liable to make could be expressed thus: We are looking for the use of a sign, but we look for it as though it were an object *co-existing* with the sign. (One of the reasons for this mistake is again that we are looking for a "thing corresponding to a substantive.")

Nāgārjuna pointed out the same mistake:

> These stanzas [of Nāgārjuna's] refute the contention that since the
> Dharma talks about the passions (kleśas) and misconceptions
> (viparyāsas), these must be existent. This contention is a typical example
> of the "doctrine of names" ..., the belief that words must mean
> something and thus that if there is a word, there must be a thing as its
> counterpart. Nāgārjuna denies this.[10]

A few paragraphs later Gudmunsen writes:

> It isn't just that we can divide up the objects in the world in any way
> we choose. We divide up the world *into* "objects." Once we have made
> the distinctions, the distinctions are real enough, but nothing new has
> been brought into existence, the world has changed in no way except the
> way in which we use words. Even here we must be careful not to slip back
> into the assumption of "essences." It is not that when a distinction has
> been made we can *then* (at last!) compare the word with the objects we
> have made it represent. There *are no* essences for the words to repre-
> sent.[11]

This concept is quite extendable to all the fine arts, not just that which uses
words. The configurations and colors in abstract painting,[12] for instance, or the
sounds and their horizontal and vertical movement in music. Hence, the philosophical stance for hermeticism in all the arts gains a more solid footing.

If we now apply these ideas to a hermetic work such as Stein's own *Tender
Buttons* we will be in a vastly better position to cope with it. Let us take the
following for example:

A CARAFE, THAT IS A BLIND GLASS

> A kind in glass and a cousin, a spectacle and nothing strange a single
> hurt color and an arrangement in a system to pointing. All this and not
> ordinary, not unordered in not resembling. The difference is spreading.[13]

Norman Weinstein in his excellent book *Gertrude Stein and the Literature of the
Modern Consciousness* is quite right that ingenious representational interpretation, or consideration as automatic writing will not suffice as an explanation
of this example. It might even be suggested that his own use of the "linguistic
moment" as the means of explanation is not adequate.[14]

It is more appropriate to consider such works as *Tender Buttons*, and this
example in particular, as examples of true 20th century hermeticism. The point
being that there is no known object co-existing along with the use of the word
carafe. Using Stein's concept of the creative art, some/thing has, through the
creative process of the No Mind, become no/thing. Or to relieve all those who

continually ask about anything hermetic, What is that supposed to be?, there is an answer: It is nothing which is something. A something the experience of which your own private mental events will give meaning. But this something will remain secure as a masterpiece only if the creative process has come from a quality of mind that allows, as Stein maintained, "entity suspended in time." Her attraction to theories, along with her keen intelligence and poetic impulse, can still hold our attention. Whether it was her intention or not, Gertrude Stein helped solidify a philosophical stance for 20th century hermeticism. There is still time to be grateful.

Notes

1. Gertrude Stein, *What are Masterpieces* (Los Angeles: The Conference Press, 1940), p. 85.

2. *Ibid.*, pp. 85–86.

3. *Ibid.*, p. 88.

4. *Ibid.*, p. 86.

5. *Ibid.*, p. 91.

6. *Ibid.*, p. 92.

7. This section is based on a reading of D. T. Suzuki, *The Zen Doctrine of No Mind* (New York: Samuel Weiser, Inc., 1973).

8. Allegra Stewart, *Gertrude Stein and the Present* (Cambridge: Harvard University Press, 1967), pp. 212–213.

9. Toklas has said Stein did not know the work of Wittgenstein. In a letter to Allegra Stewart Toklas wrote "Gertrude Stein didn't know Wittgenstein. She was a pupil of Santayana and towards the end of his life we went down to Rome to visit him, but he was no longer there. . . . She was under the influence of James and Whitehead of course, but not Bergson."

10. Chris Gudmunsen, *Wittgenstein and Buddhism* (London: MacMillan Education Ltd., 1977), p. 38.

11. *Ibid.*, p. 39.

12. Stein herself did not approve of abstract painting, indeed she deemed it an impossibility. In a letter (1947) to Louise Taylor, Alice Toklas wrote "Please don't encourage Red [Louise Taylor's husband] in any change that is a violent one in the direction of abstract painting. . . . It is that there really is no such thing as abstract painting as Red would find out probably quicker than most who have believed and been disillusioned. Gertrude was convinced it couldn't be done. She had reasons too long for a letter. It had bored me considerably for some months—eventually they are neither paintings nor decorations—not even illustrations." From Alice B. Toklas, *Staying on Alone, Letters of Alice B. Toklas* (New York: Liveright, 1973), p. 47.

13. Gertrude Stein, *Tender Buttons* (New York: Claire Marie, 1914), p. 9.

14. Norman Weinstein, *Gertrude Stein and the Literature of the Modern Consciousness* (New York): Frederick Ungar Publishing Co., 1970), pp. 59–62.

Some Questions about Modernism (An Excerpt)

David Antin

Of all the writers in English only Gertrude Stein seems to have had a thorough understanding of how profoundly Cubism opened up the possibilities of *representation* with this analysis. But then she was the writer in English with the deepest interest in language, the only one with an interest in language as language. I know almost everybody will object to this, but I've never understood why anybody thought Joyce, Eliot, Pound, Stevens or Williams were innovators in language. Essentially all of their interest was concentrated at the level of rhetoric. The image, for example, as Pound conceived it was a psychological ensemble, "that which presents an intellectual and emotional complex in an instant of time"; but as he employed it, it was a rhetorical element rather than a linguistic one, or what could better be described as a presentational strategy mounted on the perfectly conventional English sentence. It really is not very different from the rhetorical figure Quintilian calls an image and warns lawyers and orators to avoid, because its detail is distracting and therefore more suited to the stage ("Who is that winding up his face like an old man with his feet wound up in wool?"). Eliot and Pound were much more involved with presentational and narrational strategies, the manipulation of sequences of pieces of discourse and their arrangement. Joyce comes the closest to an interest in language in his fascination with punning, which is an interest in arbitrary and often cross-linguistic homonymy. But Stein of all of them had a philosophical commitment to the problematic double system of language – the self ordering system and the pointing system – and from the beginning of her serious work she had encountered the peculiar conflict between the two, even in her early stories. She also had a thorough awareness – shared by Joyce more than any other of her English language contemporaries – of another fundamental structural ambiguity of language: that utterance is play before it is address or discourse or representation. And sometimes this mad jingling play can throw light on something in the world ("Sometimes Melanctha was so blue that she didn't know what she was going

Reprinted, abridged, from *Occident* (Spring, 1974), by permission of the author. Copyright © 1976 by David Antin.

208

to do")—and sometimes swamp it in a grammatical or phonological ocean. But she was a writer with a profound representational commitment in all of its problematicalness, and she probed the subtlest distinctions of grammar for the most refined distinctions of meaning. There is probably nothing in the English language to compare with the seemingly infinite series of meaningful distinctions about living and aging and dying that Stein draws phrase by phrase for nearly twenty-one pages out of minute shifts in the aspect of the English verb in the litany that closes *The Making of Americans*. Coming with this refined grasp of the language as medium—and of language as medium—she was well prepared to understand the work of Picasso and Braque, who were embarked on a similar project in another medium and had in some ways made more progress than she had. It didn't take her long to close the gap, and she was the only writer who did. *Tender Buttons*, which was written by 1913, is not derivative from painting, but it is the only language work that lives in the same time as Picasso's Cubism. But Stein's work was never adequately understood until fairly recently.

I'm not really sure why, though I think it was at least partly because of the genre problem, the question of what it was she was writing. You have to remember that at that time most of the American poetry avant-garde made a big thing of the distinction between "poetry" and "prose" and that Stein started out as a writer of narrative fiction, or at least she presented her early work in the context of the "story" and the "novel," which were generally considered "prose" forms. But by 1908 and 1909 she had embarked on a career that could not be defined in terms of "fiction." *Three Lives* may superficially resemble the story genre, and she evokes a deliberate comparison with Flaubert; but her three "stories" are much less stories than the pieces in *Dubliners* and much more language constructions. And if this is at all true for *Three Lives*, it became more and more true for *The Making of Americans*, and was quite clear in the portraits like *Ada* or "Miss Furr and Miss Skeene" that what you had were language constructions not stories. Yet they were presented in a "prose" format—with capital letters beginning what look like sentences, periods closing them and periodic paragraphing. I've said it before, but I think it's worth saying again: prose is a kind of concrete poetry with justified margins. It is essentially characterized by the conventions of printing and the images of grammar and logic and order to which they give rise. But whatever it looks like, a characteristic passage from "Miss Furr and Miss Skeene" is poetry in any intelligent sense of the word:

> There were some dark and heavy men there then. There were some who were not so heavy and some who were not so dark. Helen Furr and Georgine Skeene sat regularly with them. They sat regularly with the ones who were dark and heavy. They sat regularly with the ones who were not so dark. They sat regularly with the ones that were not so

heavy. They sat with them regularly, sat with some of them. They went
with them regularly, went with them. They were regular then, they were
gay then, they were where they wanted to be then where it was gay to
be then, they were regularly gay then. . . .

This is a traditional phrase poetry in spite of the illusion of punctuation, with
its seemingly orthodox commas and periods, that at times seem almost appropriate, but then become as irrelevant as flyspecks randomly distributed
over a musical score. Stein's language is as difficult to contain within the page
punctuation conventions of "prose" as *Beowulf* or the *Iliad*, which were mad-
deningly punctuated even in scholarly editions. But these same scholarly editions are quite careful to present the line breaks that will assure you you are
looking at "verse," which is not the same thing as "poetry" but almost the same
thing for most people. Still there's no reason why Stein's prose punctuation
should fool a poet, even though the prose costume probably contributed to the
mistaken expectations for a certain type of narrative presentation that were
from then on usually disappointed. This disappointment may have led to occasional mockery by people like Sinclair Lewis of what otherwise seems like
straightforward poetry, with its measured out and chained phrases, locked
together by shared recurring words that are systematically placed and dis-
placed in the slightly varying pitch curves of the different length phrases and
sentences. In a profoundly traditional sense, this is a very elegant prosody; but
is a prosody immanent in English intonation, not the arbitrary conventions
of meter. Still, the poetry of the portraits resembled sufficiently a poetry of
incantations and litanies that, for a poet with as sensitive an ear and as
generous sensibilities as Pound, was not really a problem. After all he recognized at least three different kinds of melopoeia, including the litany, and was
willing to assume others as yet unknown to him (". . . and with the subject
never really out of my mind I don't yet know half there is to know about
melopoeia"). Pound may have been provincial, but he wasn't really an
academic; or if he was an academic, he was academic in the only sense that
ever gave a positive meaning to the word. I don't think the novelty of her work
gave Williams any problems either but that's where the sympathy for her work
ended—with the Pound-Williams modernists. But even there the interest of
her work was narrowly conceived, partly because these poets were surprisingly
involved in the poetry/prose distinction, as most American poets seem to have
been for the next fifty years. While the problem seems relatively trivial now
with the 60s in back of us, it's easy to see that the meaning of poetry itself
seemed to be at stake in the question thrown at all modernist poetry: "what
separates it from prose?" Generally the poets who got into the argument took
one of two tacks. They either made problematic distinction between "poetry"
and "prose," like Pound, or else, like Eliot, they made an apparently banal
distinction between "verse" and "prose" and as far as possible declined the

gambit of what "poetry" was. But Eliot, who was assuming what looked like an antimodernist position in his criticism, could afford to do this more easily than Pound or Williams, self-declared modernists, who had an obligation to define the scope of operations and the unique medium of "poetry," a term they were unwilling to surrender. The problem is an old one and the issues develop in the West along torturous lines filled with traps, sacrifices, tempo shifts and recoveries, all precipitated by the opening, which when handled by players of great skill on both sides of the question leads to no significant outcome because the insolubility of the problem is built into the opening. The basic idea out of which the question opens is what seems like a commonsense observation: that poetry as usually practiced is different from ordinary discourse; the next two moves are to identify all ordinary language use as ordinary discourse and then to identify ordinary discourse as "prose"; from there on the game is predetermined except for blunders. The point is that it's worthwhile to question every single one of these assumptions. Even the first assumption, what is it? That poetry is different because it has a funny sound, a funny way of talking, and a funny way of thinking. Which is to say, it is distinguished by an arbitrary, conventional, overstructured phonological arrangement (if you like Jacobsonian formalism); and by eccentricities of syntax and eccentricities of semantic structure or mode of representation (figures of speech and figures of thought, if you like classical rhetorical notions). But "distinguished" from what? ordinary talk? It's possible to attack the whole notion of "ordinary talk" and watch it crumble, and that's my way, to assault the whole gambit; but Pound and Eliot as well, when he talks of poetry, take variants of the "Sublime Continuation," articulated in slightly different ways by John Dennis, Vico, Bishop Lowth and finally Wordsworth: poetry is emotional speech (what Dennis called "a pathetickal and numerous Discourse"). Pound tracks both the musicality and the mode of representation to the emotional origins of poetry ("The Serious Artist," 1913).

If I may say so, I think the emotion source is the most disastrous element of the Sublime theory, and it haunts most early 20th century modernism, but not quite as much as it haunts the whole of 20th century academicism. The reason for this is simply that the theory proposes to explain what is well known by what is less well known—the phonological and conceptual resources of language by the mysteries of physiology intersected by current events. The result is a pseudotheory rather than a theory. Probably Wordsworth was the experimental poet with the most refined mind and the most profound way of dealing with the problem. In the preface to the 1802 edition of the *Lyrical Ballads* he appears to decline formally the Prose/Poetry gambit: ". . .much confusion has been introduced into criticism by this contradistinction of Poetry and Prose, instead of the more philosophical one of Poetry and Matter of Fact, or Science." What he actually does is respond to a more fundamental sense of the word prose, which you could call its etymological sense ("prose" from *prose oratio, prosa* from *prorsus* shortened from *proversus* —straightforward, therefore "prose" as "straightforward talk," which is opposed by means of a deft folk etymology to *versos,* supposed from the Latin *Vertere* —"to turn" and therefore "verse" as "turned talk" = as or "twisted talk" or "roundabout talk"). But the difference for Wordsworth between the domain of poetry and the domain of science is rather more subtle than a distinction between the language of the emotions and the language of fact.

> The objects of the Poet's thoughts are everywhere, though the eyes and sense of man are, it is true, his favorite guides, yet he will follow *wheresoever he can find an atmosphere of sensation in which to move his wings.* . . . If the labors of men of Science should ever create any material revolution, direct or indirect, *in our condition and in the impressions we habitually receive,* the Poet . . . will be ready to follow the steps of the man of Science, not only in those general indirect effects, but he will be at his side, *carrying sensation into the midst of the objects of Science itself.* The remotest discoveries of the Chemist, the Botanist, or Mineralogist will be as proper objects of the Poet's art, as any upon which it can be employed, if the time should ever come *when these things shall be familiar to us,* and *the relations under which they are contemplated by the followers material to us as enjoying and suffering beings.* If the time should ever come when what is now called Science, thus familiarized to men, *shall be ready to put on, as it were a form of flesh and blood,* the Poet will lend his divine spirit to aid the transfiguration, and will welcome the Being thus produced, as a dear and genuine inmate of the household of man. (Preface of 1802)

So that Wordsworth claims for poetry the phenomenological domain of all human experience, and if he had followed this claim back into his consideration of language he could have avoided the commitment to a language arising from "emotion" for a commitment to a language appropriate to illuminate the whole domain of human experience, whatever that happened to turn out to be. So it might have turned out for Wordsworth, the modernist, that even in theory matter of fact and matter of poetry, like language of fact and language of poetry had a very great overlap. But Wordsworth was less driven by melomania than Pound, and he certainly was capable of much more "matter of fact" poetry than Pound, if that commonsense term means very much once it is really pushed. But a theory of poetry is worth very little if it can't deal with Wordsworth's "flatness" or Lawrence's, or Stein's, when it appears. And any poetics that can't throw light on Williams' wheelbarrow poem or The White Hunter in *Tender Buttons* isn't worth the name.

The White Hunter

A white hunter is nearly crazy

Aristotle to Gertrude Stein: the Arts of Poetry (An Excerpt)

Frank O. Copley

In all the literature of criticism, there is probably no question more frequently asked and left more vexedly unanswered than, "What is poetry?" We
all read poetry, and we are all sure when we read what we have been told is
a poem that it is in fact a poem—a good poem, perhaps, or a bad poem, but
nonetheless a poem. As to why it is, or what makes it so, how it is different
from prose, what poets do when they write a poem, and above all why they
do it as they do: all these questions have remained inadequately answered. From
time to time attempts have been made to answer at least some of them. People
have asserted that poetry is form, specifically a form not imposed on prose (for
example, the sonnet), that it is language written according to certain prescribed
sound-patterns, e.g. rhyme, and following certain laws of rhythm, i.e. metre.
Others have claimed that the difference between poetry and prose, the thing
that makes a poem a poem, is its use of metaphor or of "poetic" language, but
apart from periods when a wide use of archaisms (the so-called grave style)
clearly marked poetic language off from prose, it is very hard to say what
"poetic" words are, and our contemporary poets definitely eschew anything
that smacks of what they call "literary" language, to say nothing of "poetic."
As for rhyme and metre, in an older day these were fairly rigidly prescribed,
but for a long time free verse has been very much in vogue, and when poets
now turn to fixed schemes of metre and rhyme it is almost in a spirit of irony.

What then are we to look for? Is the definition of poetry a matter of guess-
work? Is there no objective way in which we can distinguish poetry from prose?
Is a poem only a poem because somebody supposedly in authority has said that
it is? Or is the whole thing a gigantic fraud? Emily Dickinson once attacked
this problem:

> If I read a book and it makes my whole body so cold no fire can ever warm
> me, I know that is poetry. If I feel physically as if the top of my head were
> taken off, I know that is poetry. These are the only ways I know it. Is
> there any other way?[1]

Reprinted, abridged, from *Mosaic*, V/4 (Summer 1972) by permission of the author and the
publisher. Copyright © 1972 by *Mosaic*.

Her definition has distinct limitations. It proclaims that poetry is to be recognized by its physical, emotional effect upon the hearer or reader. This is all very well, but what of the fact that the identical piece of literature will affect one hearer as Emily says poetry does, but will leave another equally intelligent, equally sensitive, equally experienced reader quite unimpressed? I doubt if there is any poem—not even Homer's *Iliad* or Keats's *Ode on a Grecian Urn*— that could be counted on to produce the "Emily-syndrome" in everyone who read or heard it. In point of fact, her statement is a good definition of what poetry *does* or at any rate *may* do; as a statement of what poetry *is*, it is no more helpful than any other.

* * *

Let us try another approach. The late Gertrude Stein may have been an odd individual, subjected to much undeserved ridicule because of her famous "Rose is a rose is a rose." She was nevertheless a profoundly thoughtful woman with a sensitive and penetrating intellect, who had great influence on the course of American and English poetry in the early part of the twentieth century. In her collection of lectures, *Narration*, she says, ". . . prose is dependent upon the sentence and then upon the paragraph and poetry upon the calling upon names."[2] Prose, in other words, is a matter of explicitly organized structure, dependent for its understanding upon a relatively simple mathematics, whereby the elements of the work are laid out one after another in logical fashion, and then carefully appended to a central proposition in such a way as to show their relation both to that proposition and to each other. Out of this architecture of verbally formulated ideas arises a prose work, whether it be exposition or narrative. Prose, in other words, is not a matter of a type of material or the creation of an effect, but rather a matter of how material is put together. To put it in another way, prose is language subjected to explicit logical structure.

To turn now to the second part of her definition, "poetry," she says, "[is dependent] upon the calling upon names." She does not say that poetry is a matter of the use of certain "names" for things; she does not say "naming things," but rather *"calling upon names."* In what sense do we "call upon" names? We do this when we put names to service, categorize, classify, set things in their proper niches, draw them in such a way that we see their essential nature and can at once compare and contrast them with other elements in the poem. Poetry, in other words, is language not subservient to logic, but conveying ideas by a succession of images. Take for example these lines by Emily Dickinson:

And this brief drama in the flesh
is shifted like a sand.[3]

To use Gertrude Stein's terminology, Emily here has "called upon" three "names," drama, flesh, and sand; in order to categorize the activities and vicissitudes of human life, she has "called upon" the "name" of drama (obviously an ancient and well-tested metaphor). Now we know in which category she wishes us first to place these activities and vicissitudes. We are to think of them in terms of the action upon a stage, in which each of us is required to perform a set of actions and to say prescribed words but, by giving them a character derived from our own peculiar manner of performing the actions and of saying the words, to leave our audience with the impression that it is we and not some other individual who is speaking. This entire complex of situation, action, speech and personality is laid before us by a simple "calling upon a name," "drama."

But the concept must be still further defined, and this Emily accomplishes by "calling upon" another "name": "flesh." The drama to which she refers is not just a stage-play, furthermore, it is not a set of actions and speeches that goes on indefinitely, or may be carried out by any living creature under any circumstances and at any time; rather, it is specifically drama in the *flesh*, that is to say, a phenomenon of human life which lasts only so long as the flesh lasts, and can be performed only by those who have human identity. All of this is conveyed to us by "calling upon" the "name" of "flesh." It should be noted that we have not proceeded logically from one "name" to the next as a prose passage might have done, but have, so to speak, moved without interruption from one "name" to the other, have superimposed one category upon the other, or one picture upon the other, and by this superimposition and juxtaposition, have categorized and defined a specific concept of human life, the one that the poet asks us to keep before us in this particular poem.

Notice now what Emily does in the next line: "is shifted like a sand." To move, as Emily does, from the stage to a sand dune in the course of half a dozen words would be virtually intolerable in prose. A prose writer is nearly bound to explain the logic in his shift of metaphor, to say that the "drama in the flesh" is of such and such character and that this justifies his describing the changes in human life as like those that occur on a sand dune when the wind blows across it. But the poet does no such thing. She simply moves from one "name" to another, and by "calling upon names" in this way both categorizes the elements that go to make up her poetic statement, and creates out of them the complex of ideas she wishes to present to us. For the "drama in the flesh" of which she speaks moves not in the fashion of a play on the stage, in which director and actor together work out a predetermined series of speeches and moves, but is subject to capricious change dictated by an uncontrollable element: we never know what shape the moving sand will take, nor do we know in which direction or with what force the wind that shifts it will blow. In the poem there is no logical explanation, no moving "from sentence to paragraph," simply a "calling upon names," a synthesis or piling up of images which point to certain categories of thought and require us to put them together without intervening directives.

Prose and poetry, then, according to Gertrude Stein, are to be differentiated not by subject-matter, not by vocabulary, not by degree of emotional intensity, not even by form, but by their differing techniques or methods. Prose directs us to proceed in more or less explicit logical steps from one idea to the next. Poetry, by contrast, presents us with a series of images, pictures, ideological categories—"names"—: as each of these appears before us, we are expected to envisage the thing or idea the "name" implies, and to supply for ourselves the progression of thought, other than the merely syntactical, by which each name is connected to the name that precedes it.

Poetry, then, need not be written in verse or in any prescribed form, nor need it employ any predetermined or peculiar vocabulary, nor confine itself to any particular sphere of thought or activity. In every instance, when the writer devotes himself to "the sentence and then to the paragraph," he is writing prose; when he "calls upon names," he is writing poetry. Herein, to Gertrude Stein, lies the difference between the two categories, and her statement, together with its implications, does not differ in any fundamental way from the principles we sifted out of Housman, Scaliger, Horace, and Aristotle. Her contribution—and it is of the utmost importance—is to point out with unmistakable clarity where lies the truly strategic difference between poetry and prose. For the first time, the definitions of the two do not overlap.

* * *

What then is a poem? What *is* poetry? Let me venture a definition. Poetry is patterned speech, and its pattern has two aspects, a mode of procedure (Gertrude Stein's "calling upon names"), and a characteristic structure (Scaliger's *methodos*). It is based on the poet's function as creator (Aristotle's *poietes*), and demands intellectual discipline (Horace's "prescriptive art"). Its range of interest and of subject-matter is limited only by the poet's interests and imaginative capabilities (Housman). It is characterized by a flow of images, pictures, and symbols, more than by explicit logical discourse, and has a tightly-knit structure, consisting of repetitive elements, strategically placed and balanced one against the other, with a balance that is usually not precise, but is somewhat skewed and out of balance—this in order to create the movement that E. E. Cummings saw was essential to poetry.[4] The preferred pattern is the pyramidal, with the poem rising from point A to point B and then receding again to point A. By preference, the two sides of the pyramid are of unequal length or weight, and the chief variation on this form is provided by the ever-differing contrasts in length and weight of the two sides, and by the interlocking and counter-balancing of different sets of paired items. This structure is repeated so often as to be almost a constant; other structures do occur—such as, for example, the linear or narrative-type—but they are relatively rare, and never quite as satisfactory, from the structural and strictly poetic point of view, as the pyramidal. This, it seems to me, is what a poem *is*—an artifact made up of words, an artistic creation sprung from the mind of its creator, the poet, clothed in pictures, images, symbols—"names"—and put together under the laws that govern all artistic creation: symmetry, design, movement, and color, carefully shaped and precisely molded in the hope of creating an esthetically pleasing artifact and an harmonious whole.

Notes

1. *Letters of Emily Dickinson* (Harvard, 1965), #342a.
2. Gertrude Stein, *Narration* (Chicago, 1969), p. 26.
3. Emily Dickinson, *Complete Poems*, ed. T. H. Johnson (Boston, 1960), #664.
4. E. E. Cummings, *is 5*, Foreword, *Collected Poems*, 1923–1954 (New York, 1954), p. 163.

Bibliography of Criticism
Focusing upon the Other Stein

Bloom, Harold, ed. *Gertrude Stein*. New York: Chelsea House, 1986.

Burke, Kenneth. "Engineering with Words," *Dial*, 74 (April 1923).

Burns, Edward, ed. "Gertrude Stein Issue," *Twentieth Century Literature*, XXIV/1 (Spring 1978), with contributions by Leon Katz, Clive Bush, Bruce Bassoff, Thornton Wilder, Pamela Hadas, Cynthia Secor, Kate Davy, et al.

Chessman, Harriet S. "Representation and the Female: Gertrude Stein's "Lifting Belly" and *Tender Buttons*," in Polly Young-Eisendrath and James A. Hall, eds., *The Book of the Self: Person, Pretext, and Process*. New York: New York University Press, 1987.

Copeland, Carolyn Faunce. *Language and Time and Gertrude Stein*. Iowa City: University of Iowa Press, 1975.

Davidson, Michael; Eigner, Larry; Perelman, Bob; McCaffery, Steve; Seaton, Peter; Mac Low, Jackson; Grenier, Robert. "Reading Stein," in Bruce Andrews & Charles Bernstein, eds., *The L=A=N=G=U=A=G=E Book*. Carbondale: Southern Illinois University Press, 1984.

DeKoven, Marianne. *A Different Language*. Madison: University of Wisconsin Press, 1983.

————. "Gertrude Stein and Modern Painting: Beyond Literary Cubism," *Contemporary Literature*, XXII (1981).

Dubnick, Randa K. *The Structure of Obscurity: Gertrude Stein, Language, and Cubism*. Urbana: University of Illinois, 1984.

Dydo, Ulla E. "How To Read Gertrude Stein: The Manuscript of 'Stanzas in Meditation,'" *Text: Transactions for the Society for Textual Scholarship*, I (1981).

————. "Landscape Is Not Grammar: Gertrude Stein in 1928," *Raritan*, VII/1 (Summer 1987).

Fifer, Elizabeth. "Guardians and Witnesses: Narrative Technique in Gertrude Stein's *Useful Knowledge*," *Journal of Narrative Technique*, 10 (Spring 1980).

————. "Is Flesh Advisable? The Interior Theater of Gertrude Stein," *Signs*, 4 (Spring 1979).

Gass, William H. "Gertrude Stein: Her Escape from Protective Language," *Fictions and the Figures of Life*. New York: Vintage, 1972.

————. "Introduction," to Gertrude Stein, *The Geographical History of America*. New York: Vintage, 1973.

George, Jonathan C. "Stein's 'A Box,'" *Explicator*, 31 (February 1973).

Hejinian, Lyn. "Two Stein Talks," *Temblor*, 3 (1986).

Hoffman, Michael J. *The Development of Abstractionism in the Writings of Gertrude Stein*. Philadelphia: University of Pennsylvania Press, 1965.

————. *Gertrude Stein*. Boston: Twayne, 1976.

————, ed. *Critical Essays on Gertrude Stein*. Boston: G. K. Hall, 1986. With previously published contributions by Edith Sitwell, B.F. Skinner, Edmund Wilson, Mabel Dodge, Carl Van Vechten, Wyndham Lewis, Michael Gold, W. H. Auden, Leon Katz, et al. and new contributions from Elyse Blankley, Jane Bowers, Lisa Ruddick, Laura Riding Jackson.

Kawin, Bruce. *Telling It Again and Again*. Ithaca, N.Y.: Cornell University Press, 1972.

Kostelanetz, Richard. "Gertrude Stein (1975), *The Old Fictions and the New*. Jefferson, N.C.: McFarland, 1987.

_____. "Gertrude Stein," in Richard Kostelanetz, ed., *American Writing Today*. Troy, N.Y.: Whitson, 1990.

_____. "The Reinventor of English," *Margins*, 17 (2/1975).

Lodge, David. "Gertrude Stein," *The Modes of Modernist Fiction*. London: Edward Arnold, 1977.

Loy, Mina. "Gertrude Stein," *The Last Lunar Baedeker*. Highlands, N.C.: The Jargon Society, 1982.

Major, Clarence. "*Three Lives* and Gertrude Stein," *Par Rapport*, II/1 (Winter 1978).

McCaffrey, Steve. "Prefatory Notes on Stein and the Language of Hygene Programme," *White Pelican*, 3 (Autumn 1973).

_____. "Tenderizing Buttons," *Open Letter*, Second series, 6 (Fall 1973).

Mellow, James R. *Charmed Circle*. New York: Praeger, 1973.

_____. Foreword to Gertrude Stein, *Operas & Plays*. Barrytown, N.Y.: Station Hill, 1987.

Moore, Marianne. "The Spare American Emotion," *Dial*, 80 (February 1926), reprinted in Patricia C. Willis, ed., *The Complete Prose of Marianne Moore*. N.Y.: Penguin, 1986.

Neuman, Shirley C. *Gertrude Stein: Autobiography and the Problem of Narration*. Victoria, B.C.: University of Victoria Press, 1979.

_____ & Ira B. Nadel, eds. *Gertrude Stein and the Making of Literature*. London: Macmillan; Boston: Northeastern University Press, 1988. With contributions by Charles Caramello, DeKoven, Dydo, Alan Knight, Perloff, Schmitz, Stephen Scobie, Robert Martin, Alan Knight, Susan Hawkins, Henry M. Sayre, et al.

Nichol, bp. "some beginnings on GERTRUDE STEIN'S THEORIES OF PERSONALITY," *Open Letter*, Second series, 2 (Summer 1972).

_____. "When the Time Came," *Line*, 1 (Spring 1983).

Perloff, Marjorie. "Poetry as Word-System," *The Poetics of Indeterminacy*. Princeton, N.J.: Princeton University Press, 1981.

Porte, Joel. "Gertrude Stein and the Rhythms of Life," *New Boston Review*, 1 (June 1975).

Rule, Janice. "Gertrude Stein," *Lesbian Images*. New York: Pocket, 1976.

Ryan, Betsy Alayne. *Gertrude Stein's Theatre of the Absolute*. Ann Arbor, Mich.: UMI Research Press, 1984.

Schmitz, Neil. "Gertrude Stein as Post-Modernist: The Rhetoric of *Tender Buttons*," *Journal of Modern Literature*, 3 (July 1974).

_____. *Of Huck and Alice*. Minneapolis: University of Minnesota Press, 1983.

Secor, Cynthia. "Gertrude Stein: The Complex Force of Her Femininity," in Kenneth Wheeler & Virginia Lee Lussier, eds. *Women, The Arts, and the 1920s in Paris and New York*. New Brunswick, N.J.: Transaction Books, 1982.

Sitwell, Edith. *Aspects of Modern Poetry*. London: Duckworth, 1934.

Snyder, Ellsworth. "Gertrude Stein and John Cage: Three Fragments," *Open Letter*, Third series, 7 (Summer 1977).

Steiner, Wendy. *Exact Resemblance to Exact Resemblance*. New Haven, Conn.: Yale University Press, 1978.

Stimpson, Catherine R. "The Mind, the Body and Gertrude Stein," *Critical Inquiry* (1977).

_____. "The Somagrams of Gertrude Stein," *Poetics Today*, VI/1–2 (1985).

Sutherland, Donald. *Gertrude Stein*. New Haven, Conn.: Yale University Press, 1951.

_____. "Preface: The Turning Point," *Stanzas in Meditation and Other Poems*. New Haven, Conn.: Yale University Press, 1956.

Tanner, Tony. "Gertrude Stein and the Complete Actual Present," *The Reign of Wonder*. Cambridge, England: Cambridge University Press, 1965.

Waldrop, Keith. "Gertrude Stein's Tears," *Novel*, XII/3 (Spring 1979).

Walker, Jayne L. *The Making of a Modernist: Gertrude Stein*. Amherst: University of Massachusetts Press, 1984.

Wasserstrom, William. "The Sursymamericubealism of Gertrude Stein," *Twentieth Century Literature*, 21 (February 1975).

Watson, Sheila. "Gertrude Stein: The Style Is the Machine," *White Pelican* (Autumn 1973).

Weinstein, Norman. *Gertrude Stein and the Literature of Modern Consciousness*. New York: Ungar, 1970.

About the Contributors

Sherwood Anderson (1876–1941) was a novelist and essayist whose pioneering 1922 appreciation of Stein represents the zenith of his critical career.

David Antin is Professor of Visual Art at the University of California in San Diego. His recent books include collections of his "talk poems."

John Ashbery is a prolific poet and critic of both art and literature.

Charles Bernstein (1950–) is a poet and critic. His essays were collected as *Content's Dream* (1986).

Leonard Bernstein (1917–) is internationally renowned as a composer and conductor, as well as a writer and lecturer on music.

Kenneth Burke (1897–) is a distinguished American person-of-letters long residing in Andover, NJ.

Frank O. Copley is Professor Emeritus of Latin, The University of Michigan. He presently lives in Rogers City, MI.

Marc Dachy (1952–) is a Belgian-born critic and editor currently living in Paris and completing a comprehensive book on Dada.

Randa K. Dubnick teaches English at the University of Kansas. She authored *The Structure of Obscurity: Gertrude Stein, Language and Cubism* (1984).

Ulla E. Dydo teaches English at Bronx Community College, CUNY. She is currently completing a book about Stein's "writing from 1923, when Stein, with 'An Elucidation' began systematically to examine her own writing, to 1932, when her work split into *Stanzas in Meditation* and *The Autobiography of Alice B. Toklas*."

Harry R. Garvin is Professor of English at Bucknell and sometime editor of the *Bucknell Review*. He did his doctoral thesis on Stein's *Four Saints in Three Acts*.

Allen Ginsberg is an internationally known poet and now a professor of English at Brooklyn College, CUNY.

Dick Higgins has published books of poetry, criticism and plays, in addition to doing visual art. As the publisher of the Something Else Press, he reprinted many of the more radical Stein texts.

223

Richard Howard (1929–) is a prolific poet, critic and translator, especially from the French. *No Traveler* (1989) is his most recent collection of poetry.

Jo-Anna Isaak teaches at Hobart and William Smith colleges. Her recent research focuses upon avant-garde Russian art. She lives mostly in New York.

Lawrence Kornfeld is Professor of Directing at SUNY-Purchase. Co-founder of both the Judson Poets Theater and the Theater for a New City, he has received many awards for his productions.

Richard Kostelanetz (1940–) has authored and edited many books of and about contemporary literature and art.

David Lodge is Honorary Professor of Modern English Literature at the University of Birmingham and author of several books of fiction and literary criticism.

Jackson Mac Low has published several books of poetry and experimental texts.

Robert Marx presently administers The Performing Arts Research Center in New York. Previously editor of *Yale/Theater*, he has contributed criticism to *The New Republic, The New York Times* and *American Scholar*.

Neil E. Schmitz is a Professor of English at SUNY-Buffalo. His books include *Of Huck and Alice* (1983).

Ellsworth Snyder is a musician, living in Madison, WI, who is devoted to both John Cage and Gertrude Stein.

Donald Sutherland (1911–1978) was professor of Classics at the University of Colorado. His *Gertrude Stein* (1951), the initial critical book on her work, remains a seminal guide to her radical achievement.

Jayne L. Walker is a literary agent and consultant. She authored *The Making of a Modernist* (1984), which focuses upon Stein's work from *Three Lives* to *Tender Buttons*.

Wendell Wilcox (1906–1981), who first met Stein in 1934, published fiction and criticism. Gertrude Stein's letters to him were published in the 100th *Paris Review* (Summer–Fall 1986).

William Carlos Williams (1883–1963) was a major American author of criticism, drama, and fiction, as well as poetry.